Shopping for God

Shopping for God

A Sceptic's Search for Value in Britain's Spiritual Marketplace

Roland Howard

HarperCollins*Publishers*

HarperCollins*Publishers*
77– 85 Fulham Palace Road, London w6 8jb
www.**fire**and**water**.com

First published in Great Britain in 2001
by HarperCollinsPublishers

1 3 5 7 9 10 8 6 4 2

A catalogue record for this book
is available from the British Library

ISBN 0 00 628173 7

Printed and bound in Great Britain by
Creative Print and Design (Wales), Ebbw Vale

For Mum and Dad
And for Keelin and Jake,
Sam, Jesse and Calum

Acknowledgements

Thanks to Gill Merritt and Matt Stevens for proofreading. Thanks also to devotees, disciples and members of contemporary spiritual or religious movements for hospitality and openness to questions.

Contents

1

🛒

Lost in the Supermarket

It is hard to say exactly when it started. There was no set moment, just an accumulation of incidents that started to pull me in a rather unusual direction. They are hard to articulate – but not because they are shocking, intense, complex or excruciatingly painful. On the contrary, the problem is that to spell them out is a bit like wearing a T-shirt with the legend, 'I'm dull, anaemic, mediocre: you **don't** want to know me,' printed on the front. On the back (where the exotic tour dates should be) it would read, 'And I take myself far too seriously.'

I am loath to explain the gritty little details that forced me onto the road of what Americans might call 'spiritual questing', because they are so banal. Describing these spurs is akin to exposing myself in a personal ad: 'Boring, neurotic 37-year-old male, NSOH, WLTM *Meaning of Life* for fun and spiritual fulfilment. Non-smokers only. No time-wasters.'

It started about a year ago, after I bought some running shoes in an attempt to get fit. Strange things happen when you go jogging. It is probably something to do with the rhythm, but your mind certainly starts to wander. This afternoon, for instance, I set off up the hill in the August sunshine for my humble mile and a half, and I started thinking that I would like to have a go at a half-marathon (13 miles). Then I thought of this leggy blonde bombshell I vaguely know, who is actively training for one. *Training with her would be all right*, was my next thought. Nearly up the hill, running towards the cornfield, I was reminded of an obscure verse in the Bible

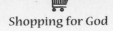
which says something like: 'If you are tempted by a beautiful woman, run from her.' I imagined some ancient scribe copying out the Bible and accidentally changing 'run from' to 'run after'. *In one slip of the pen*, I thought, whizzing down through the corn to a dried-up spring in a clump of trees called Purtle Springs, *the history of Christianity could have been transformed. Empty churches? Empty football stadiums, more like. Pubs going out of business...*

Jogging locks you into a rhythm. You can't speak, you can't interact or do anything but jog; your body is under pressure. You can look around (my route is scenic), but you can't fully appreciate what you see. You can think, but you can't formulate complex thoughts, or sometimes even concentrate. Perhaps it is the creative right side of the brain which opens up to allow such ramblings. I know that the 'jogging muse' visits me quite regularly. I get my best journalistic ideas when pounding up the hill and through the fields. I can also get a clear overview of a situation and see connections that had not been apparent earlier. Occasionally, however, something else happens.

Sometimes I start to have what teenagers would call 'deep thoughts' – asking the kind of questions that perhaps we don't talk about because there are no easy answers, but also because such questions embarrass us. These inklings are best described as 'spiritual' because they stretch us past the mundane and material, towards ethics and a larger purpose, something beyond. They reveal us to be ultimately vulnerable, even silly. Thoughts such as: *Is my need for purpose merely a distant echo of pathological egoism?* Or, perhaps more reasonably: *Why is it that nature resonates so deeply?* Or even: *If there is no 'other', no creative force, why this sense of right and wrong, this ideal of integrity that we seek? Does it really come from our gene pool?* Other deep thoughts that have cropped up *en route* to Purtle Springs are these: *Do we have such a thing as a soul or spirit, or is the idea just narcissism? Are we simply food for worms, next century's compost? Why is community good and isolation bad? Do these spiritual thoughts, these cosmic inklings, point to a universal energy or being, or are they hard-wired into us by some quirk of evolution?*

I want to be clear that these thoughts percolated up in my mind over a period of some months. The path to Purtle Springs was no Road to Damascus. Even so, the questions worried me – or, to be more accurate, *having* the questions worried me. I had to concede that I was a tad overburdened with the types of question that plague the sort of people who reside in secure accommodation and call themselves John the Baptist, the Virgin Mary or Merlin. I could also see that these preoccupations might be a sign of mid-life crisis. At 37, with the beginnings of middle-age spread, a receding hairline (or an increasing forehead, whichever you prefer), 10 years in the same job and nearly 14 in the same house, I had to admit the possibility. There were two problems with this explanation. Firstly, it seemed to me that your average man's 'mid-life crisis' was merely an elaborate excuse for 'debriefing' the secretary. I had no secretary. Secondly, whatever a person's age, the questions have some pertinence. It would be dishonest to ignore them.

Things all came to a head in a god-forsaken place: the Milton Keynes shopping centre. I was taking my three eldest sons to see a mountain-biking display in the central mall. The complex is a disorientating grid-plan of indoor walkways, like graph paper except for the fact that, at any intersection or point on a line, one's senses are assaulted by a bewildering array of 'unmissable', 'unbeatable', unbearable offers. It is hard to know exactly which intersection one is at. It may be a linear grid-plan, but it seems like a labyrinth to me, and one shop is indistinguishable from any other.

After the display, Sam (aged 13) dragged me into a sports shop for some football boots. There ensued a 20-minute dispute concerning the deeply nuanced, esoteric significance of various tiny stripes, lines and curves and their effects on the desirability (and price) of the boots. A compromise was reached and we asked for the boots. They were out of stock. A few yards away, Jesse (aged 11) had found a sweatshirt. An identical discussion followed concerning magical hieroglyphs (or logos) and we left the shop with nothing except two sulky

tempers. We walked on, past crowds of shoppers, and Jake (aged 15) rushed into a music shop to get a poster. Jesse, meanwhile, was telling me that he was hungry and trying to drag me to a McDonald's.

I had almost no idea how to get out into the open air. I knew everything would feel better outside. I sat down on a marble wall, home to an artificial palm tree, real compost and bark chippings. I bought the boys ice creams to quieten them down, irritated with their pestering. I felt trapped. Ridiculous as it sounds, being lost in a sprawling, marble and plastic mall felt like inhabiting the velvet-lined intestines of a bloated monster. *Surely I can't be the only person who harbours a secret desire to set fire to these places*, I thought to myself. People continued to walk by, however, festooned with bulging carrier bags and apparently not sharing my misgivings.

These thoughts are hardly original, but I found myself interpreting the accelerated, sugary blandness of 'mall culture' in terms of religious symbols. The mall was a Temple of Mammon; the offers and enticements were a Tower of Babel; Choice was the deity, robbing us of dignity, genuine freedom and cash, belittling and enslaving us. It was in this histrionic state that I realized I had to do something about it. If my children were fashion victims, then it was partly because I could not provide them with good enough reasons to dig deeper, to see a bigger picture. I decided that I was going to shop for God, actively seek out a form of spirituality robust enough to challenge mindless consumerism and, perhaps, even answer some of the questions that had been starting to corrode the smoothness of my slide into middle age.

I had not intended to include a visit to the local Church of England establishment in my search. It seemed too quaint, too peripheral, too *nice* – a bit like asking Derek Nimmo to explain my place in the cosmos. The Anglican Church seemed too much like a forgotten corner of the British heritage industry. It resonated a stuffy respectability from a bygone age. Was I really likely to obtain any answers from a lumbering organization that had nearly split over allowing women to be priests and was currently rent in two over whether they were to allow homosexuals to have the same rights as everybody else?

Nonetheless, while I was jogging over the top of a hill known as 'the Moon' one evening, I noticed the church spire breaking the horizon. After that, every time I jogged across the Moon the spire nagged at me like a splinter. It reminded me that, while I was planning to worship with druids, get in touch with my shamanic energies, meditate myself onto a different plane and speak in tongues, I was ignoring sleepy, unpretentious St Mary's. Eventually, full of preconceptions and very self-conscious, I went to Evensong.

I approached the church in the same way that some men approach the top shelf at the newsagents. There was much aimless shuffling around, looking with exaggerated interest in other directions (the St Mary's Playschool notice board) and then, with a quick glance to either side, a sudden rush through the door. If I could have entered the nave in a brown paper bag, I would have done so.

I knew that the Church of England was in a bad way, but I did not expect to have difficulty finding the service once I was inside the church. I passed a wooden table displaying parish magazines, missionary leaflets and velvet offering purses, in search of people. The nave was brightly lit but empty. Then, in a side chapel, I spied a desultory collection of Laura Ashley dresses. They were singing.

I crept over to the back pew, beneath the faded British Legion flags, and picked up a hymn book. The old lady next to me eyed me up suspiciously. I am under 60, after all. Her gimlet eyes swivelled round to my jacket and zoomed in on my Nottingham Forest badge with muted horror. She steeled herself, smiled and stabbed her finger at the hymn number in her book. I fumbled through my own book to find the right page.

I tried to relax, to absorb the atmosphere. There were seven elderly women and two men. The man in front had a voice like toothache. Someone in a blue and white vestment was punching at a piano. A candle burned, prayer cushions hung from the backs of pews, the hymn and prayer books looked old but strangely precious. The hymn finished and everyone sat down. Then I noticed the curate: early forties, white vestment, ecclesiastical purple shirt, friendly, serious and honest demeanour – and a woman!

She started reading the liturgy and I was surprised on two counts: the beauty and resonance of the language and the emphasis on shame. Personally, I do not have a problem with self-loathing. In the right mood, I can quite enjoy it. I can say, 'I am not worthy, Lord,' with as much gusto as the next 'man'. It's true, whether I believe in the Lord or not. I only started to trip over the liturgy when the congregants' response read, 'O Lord, save the Queen.' However hard I try, I really cannot convince myself that I care about the Queen. She seems to get on just fine without my prayers. The prayers for peace in Kosovo and East Timor seemed more relevant – although the line about 'turn all their hearts to you and your perfect ways' stuck in my gullet like a sickly sweet.

The curate's sermon was interesting, but it might as well have been a signpost instructing us all to leave the building. Taken from the book of Ezekiel, what she said had the ring of truth. She explained that Ezekiel was a prophet who spent years urging the people of Israel to give up, to stop pretending. He told them to accept that Jerusalem was occupied by the Babylonians and that the monarchy and temple were redundant as institutions. They should repent and hold onto God in the hopelessness. Ezekiel was effectively telling people to question how they should live in the heathen world of the Babylonians.

The curate was even brave enough to draw the obvious parallels. We were fooling ourselves, she told us, if we still thought that Britain was a Christian nation. We must struggle to make sense of faith in the hopelessness of modern society. She reminded us of Ezekiel's prophecy of dry bones dancing which, she said, spoke of rebirth. What was left unsaid, however, seemed to be another obvious parallel: that we should give up on institutionalized religion, just as Ezekiel had urged the Israelites to give up on the temple. The idea of my own dry bones dancing seemed about as likely as rats joining a sinking ship. This particular rat was not going to. After a polite nod to one or two demurely animated Laura Ashley prints and a brief chat with the curate, I sidled out.

Clearly it was time to get on the road – but where to? The more I looked into groups exploring spirituality, the more choices I discovered. The UK is home to an amazing number of new religious movements. They are legion and vastly different. There are levitating meditators, Christian funda-mentalists, witches, personal transformation groups, druids, sound healers, chanting monks, seekers of the 'cosmic orgasm', and people all too keen to give my chakras a spring-clean and my aura a polish. My experience at St Mary's confirmed my predilection for avoiding the mainstream and pushed me towards fringe religionists – the exotic or radical groups that promised transformation and a challenging per-spective on modern life. I had not written off Christianity, but I was not in search of bland mediocrity or boredom. I wanted my pilgrimage to be vibrant, offbeat and varied. Seeking out the extremes of the spiritual fringe had another advantage: I would not have to spend time decoding the nuances of faith; the heart of it would be there in madcap, earnest, sometimes jackbooted technicolour.

My intention was to visit, to listen, to participate. I wanted to be as open as possible, to throw off my prejudices and see first-hand what was going on. Some groups would be consid-ered cults or sects, some mad, bad or dangerous, others deeply tedious. I did not expect to answer all of my questions. To find a tentative foothold in the cosmos would be enough. If I was lucky, I might find a form of spirituality to which I could commit myself. So, in search of a spirituality to take me into middle age with purpose and integrity, I set off. My only tools were a questioning mind, a low bullshit threshold and some running shoes.

2

🛒

Chasing Rainbows

Sweeping round bends in my new, metallic dark green motor, I imagine myself as the subject of one of those slick, stylish adverts in which the car roars seductively round curves in the road, leaning smoothly into the corners. As I head along the A40 towards Cheltenham, I notice dark grey clouds piling up, hanging precariously in the charged, greenish light. Within minutes rain is intermittently spattering the windscreen. Soon it is coming down in sheets and I envisage slow-motion water drops arcing gracefully up from my new Firestone tyres. Cars and lorries start to pull over and I feel like some short-cropped, besuited Italian, thrusting ahead of the pack.

I stop at a red light and excuse my uncharacteristic fantasy (in my mind, cars normally feature in the file labelled 'Prosaic', alongside washing machines, toothpaste and cork tiles) as the product of owning my first ever new car. I look up through the frantic windscreen wipers and see a chink of sunshine coming through the clouds. *A rainbow would be perfect*, I think. The clouds close, however, and I pull away, realizing that it would be hard to have less auspicious August weather for my stay at a tents-only healing camp in the middle of a field in Worcestershire. I am tempted to turn round.

I arrive at the Rainbow Circle Healing Camp, discreetly signposted (with a small rainbow) off a nondescript B road above the River Severn. The camp is three sodden fields on a gentle slope, with four large marquee-style tents, a dozen

tepees, various other small tents and a couple of hundred people. To tell the truth, I am not quite sure what to expect. I am searching for a neo-pagan group called the Rainbow Tribe, but I am also curious and keen to experience any 'spiritual healing' that the camp offers. Among the rugs and reed mats, upturned crates and incense of the welcome tent, I pay for my pitch (£10 per day, less for the unwaged) and ask the half-dozen hippies what's on. They explain that the programme is decided each evening for the day ahead and written on a blackboard in the café tent. I am told to pitch my tent and go and enjoy. Although I am given a site plan, no one quite tells me *what* I am to enjoy.

I wander around the tepees and tents trying to find out. Nothing much seems to be happening. The people, a mixture of card-carrying crusty traveller types and bright, anoraked characters on an away-day from suburbia, are talking in clusters round campfires or drinking coffee at the café tent. Some tepees have signs ('Carl's Lodge' and 'Wellbeing'), but there is nothing in particular to *enjoy*. On the contrary, I notice distressingly open-plan latrines which seem deliberately designed to humiliate. Without seats (just a hole in the plywood and an uncomfortably short drop) and doors (you simply walk up and, if someone is already squatting, you keep going), they are painted in the most lurid, eye-catching colours possible. Gaudy murals cover the side and waist-high back panels, as if to announce to the campsite, 'Look at me, I'm squatting on a latrine!'

Feeling slightly out of place, I find a quiet corner to pitch my tent, a few feet above a pond and a safe distance from the latrines. This done, I look up and notice that the sun has broken through the clouds. Then my jaw hits the mud. About 15 metres away from me is a group of naked women, stretching themselves out in the watery sun. From a small, steaming dome tent behind them, a naked man walks out and sits cross-legged in their midst. He is apparently meditating, beaming serenely into the middle distance, oblivious to his surroundings.

I unzip my tent and hide, thinking to myself: *That meditation is potent stuff!* Yet I am also struck by how completely unselfconscious and unsexual the women are. They appear to be doing what comes naturally, naturally. Later I am told that the steam tent is for spiritual and bodily purification, so perhaps that explains their uninhibited innocence. I am a fool for setting myself challenges, but I start to ponder whether or not I will be pure enough to take my clothes off and go into the steam tent before I leave the camp.

That evening, as it starts to drizzle, I go to a seminar led by an eco-warrior astrologer called Steve. The title is 'Accelerated Evolution and Crop Circles'. About 60 people sit around the edge of the candle-lit 'big top' tent, listening to what Steve has to say. With short-cropped hair and dreadlocks at the back, Steve is a striking, animated, earnest speaker. He explains that 30,000 years ago, buried deep in prehistory, there lived an intelligent, technologically advanced people who used the holistic, creative, right-hand side of their brains. They lived for tens of thousands of years in harmony with each other and nature, building the pyramids, the temple at Angkor Wat, the Mayan temples and Stonehenge, before the ice age which wiped them out. Indeed, such was their high-tech harmony with nature, the creators of Stonehenge may well have been the 12 choirs of ancient legend ('fairly accepted legend', we are assured) who levitated the stones with their 'kinetic sound patterns'.

Since then, nasty, mechanistic, rapacious, left-brained people have taken over and ruined the planet. Religion, science and academia have tried to suppress this fact, so that the pillage could continue – until the crisis that we now confront. 'History has been deleted. Ninety-five per cent of history is lies,' Steve explains (which would explain why he dates the pyramids and Mayan temples a mere 10,000 years earlier than the archaeologists do). A key moment, however, came in 1969. When people saw the famous picture of the earth taken from the moon, a resurgence of holistic, right-brain energies occurred: the Age of Aquarius was dawning. Crop circles are signs from Gaia, the Earth Goddess, designed to open up the right side of the brain and encourage 'lobal sharing'. People

attuned to Gaia are making an 'evolutionary leap' and operate on a rarefied level that means they need much less food.

As thunder starts to shake the tent around us, Steve's seminar becomes increasingly apocalyptic. The choice is ours: we can die, rotting in our consumerist filth, or we can make an 'evolutionary leap' and join the 'new humanity', the 'lobal sharers'. Steve probably does not help his cause by announcing, 'I believe that I'm an interstellar being, almost a demigod. I soak up negativity and transform it into light and energy.' The media, the Church and the government, he says, are all purveyors of negativity, only out to manipulate and distract us. 'This is your last best chance,' he concludes, more in accusation than pleading. 'Let go of the shit or die out.'

Now, I have a theory about conspiracy theories: *they're out to get you*; it's a conspiracy! Back in the 1930s, a sinister, high-powered elite of boffins and top civil servants got together in a secret bunker beneath a crashed UFO and devised a thought system which was designed to encourage people studiously to avoid global, economic and political reality and disappear up their own backsides. Codenamed 'Project Conspiracy Theory', its real nature was hidden in Carthaginian hieroglyphs which translated 'Hull City 4, West Bromwich Albion 2'. My other theory is that conspiracy theories are needed by those promulgating blatantly stupid ideas, to explain why no one else accepts those blatantly stupid ideas – ideas such as crop circles being Gaia's inspirational doodles, choirs carrying rocks by sound patterns, or the lovely Steve being an interstellar being or demi-god. The only way to convince people of such ideas is to chuck history, science and common sense into the bin marked 'Conspiracy Theory'. This paranoid nonsense is not for me.

The next day I decide that it is time I got some healing, so I head up to the large rectangular marquee where people queue up for 'treatments' . A book contains a list of what is on offer: shiatsu massage, reiki, reflexology, crystal-bowl healing. I have only a rudimentary notion of what these treatments might involve, but a massage sounds like a good idea. I am approached by a young practitioner called Philippa. She does not do shiatsu, but reiki is quite similar, she tells me. She also works with crystals and flower essences, and does a bit of 'star-channelling' on the side – a sort of New Age massage with extras.

Philippa takes me to a trestle table draped with blankets and asks me to take my shoes off and lie on my back. She speaks with a soft, Northumberland accent and holds her hands above my body before gently applying a slight pressure, starting from the top of my head and gradually working down to my feet. Within minutes I find myself floating serenely on some higher plane, best described as 'enjoying being pampered'. The massage is perhaps a bit too gentle, but it is deeply relaxing. After 35 minutes I am brought round by a foot massage.

I open my eyes and Philippa tells me that I have a blockage in my solar plexus. 'Your energy is trapped. It's not getting down. Are you angry about something?' she asks.

'Not really,' I reply.

'It could be completely wrong,' she says, 'or it could be left over from another life.' She continues with a startling revelation: 'You've a very strong bond with a female, possibly your mother.'

She gets out two vials (essence of comfrey and passion flower) and rubs them into my forehead, advising me to get some 'bodywork' while I am at the camp and to drink lots of water to flush out the energy blockage. I need grounding, she says as I sit up to leave.

I decide to attend the morning meeting in the marquee to see if it helps with my grounding. The camp organizers, known as the 'council', explain the itinerary for the day and invite facilitators to describe their workshops. It is refreshingly democratic: all are free to speak. They explain who is the troubleshooter (council members take it in turn to be troubleshooter for any arguments or problems on site). A leader of the children's workshop has a problem: 'Parents are too busy healing themselves to look after their children. The teenagers are running wild. We're so pissed off with them that we're stopping the workshops.' A heated but orderly discussion follows. A community decision is taken to find the responsible parents, and some facilities for the kids are to continue.

By coincidence, that afternoon there is a 'talking stick' session in the tepee called Carl's Lodge to discuss parenting. At a talking stick session, people sit in a circle and a stick is passed round. On receiving the stick, the person says 'Ho!' and the rest of the circle replies 'Ho!' Then the person says what they want to say, while the others sit in silence. The stick is then passed to the next person in the circle (or the next person who wants to speak), who commences with another 'Ho!' This ritual may sound as if it comes from a very *camp* camp of Red Indians in a spaghetti western, but I am informed that it has bona fide Native American credentials. Unfortunately, as I listen in, there is little of the much-touted Native American wisdom.

'Ho!' says one man.

'Ho!' the rest echo.

'Some of those kids are total b*****ds. Where are their parents?' the man says.

'Ho!' says a young mum, taking the stick.

'Ho!'

'We're here to talk about our own parenting experiences, not to diss what's happened. That's being dealt with.'

Three or four 'ho's later, I give up. All those 'ho's remind me of a particularly distasteful brand of rap song and I am tempted to respond, 'Who you calling a ho, mother?' The 'ho, ho's also draw a smile, but ultimately it is all too slow.

I wander off in search of a workshop on Mayan dreamspells. Entering an adjoining tepee, I find a dozen or so people round the embers of a fire, all daubed with bright blue paint. Geoff and his partner Kirani are explaining the Mayan system of divination and the blue paint apparently opens up our receptivity to the truth of the words. We all give our dates of birth and Kirani looks each one up in a book, rotates a disk onto the Mayan calendar and then tells us our 'dreamspell'. 'Get your galactic signature and play with it, get the phrase

and let it resonate,' she says. Kirani tells us that she is an 'electric monkey', and that resonates with her playfulness. Nobody asks how the Mayans knew about electricity.

As we go round the circle, people mull over their new 'signatures' and Kirani stresses that it does not work for everyone and, if it does not feel right, we should simply ignore it. Some people's dates are 'galactic activation portals' which, I gather, means that they are more open to the spirit world. I am told that my glyph (mystical symbol) is a wizard, and that my galactic signature is a 'white magnetic wizard'. My phrase is, 'I unify in order to enchant, attracting receptivity. I seal the output of vision with the lunar tone of challenge. I am guided by the power of accomplishment.' This means nothing to me, but there are two obvious problems with this sort of divination exercise. Clearly it is distinguished by its vagueness, but it is also likely that the more I think about it, the more I will interpret it, and the more links I will see. It is rather like our occasional surprise at spooky coincidences: we only register the coincidences, not the endless events which are not coincidental. We could measure out our lives in spooky coincidences, but it would not be reality.

That evening there is a dance/music workshop in a large candle-lit tent. It is supposed to be therapeutic. The chief musician, Gandharva, dressed in saffron robes with his long blond hair trussed up behind his head, explains that we will be following a traditional Indian dance sequence – from birth, through struggle and death, to transcendence. He is softly spoken and invites musicians onto a podium in the centre of the tent. The rest of us are encouraged to let ourselves go, to let the music take us over, to do exactly what we feel. I am expecting a terrible, unrehearsed cacophony, but most of the dozen musicians have already practised the improvisations and, as they open themselves to Gandharva's gentle leadership, the 'awakening' movement begins to take shape. The tabla and guitar rhythms grow in stature as guitar and clarinet harmonies canter off in different directions. We relax and move, sliding into unselfconsciousness.

Gandharva explains each movement in terms of its significance to the human journey, and then the musicians start.
Within minutes the whole tent is moving as one. It is during
the movement focusing on struggle and suffering that things
become difficult for me. The rhythm is sombre, the discord
unsettling, and two didgeridoos are wailing continuously. My
father died two months previously, and the pain of the music
is allowing me to explore my own feelings. I remember things
that we did together, things I wish I had said, my father's
sometimes difficult idiosyncrasies, his goodness and his
doggedness. The ponderous music pulsates on, and I find
tears streaming down my face. I have cried several times since
his death, but this allows me to explore and express my sorrow. The music and my dancing become a *physical* mourning
process. I can 'mime' my feelings towards my father in the
movements of the dance.

The freedom within the tent and the unhurried sections of
the dance are wonderful: almost a rite of passage. Certainly it
is the sort of thing that we English do not usually do very
well. Others are also deeply moved. I see a young woman
tearfully swaying through one movement. Another is curled
on the floor, sobbing. Others are happier, but are still pos-
sessed positively by the music. After nearly 90 minutes,
Gandharva draws it to a close and invites those who were affected by the music to talk to him if they wish. I tell him how
cathartic and helpful it has been. He hugs me and I realize
that, whatever reservations I have, two qualities I really like
about this camp are the unselfconsciousness and the warmth.

Later that evening there is a ceremony to welcome the first
full moon since the eclipse. Everyone mucks in to do something. I join 50 people (led by a friendly and energetic woman)
in singing the Chief Seattle Song Cycle. We are split into
groups to sing parts of Chief Seattle's speech to George
Washington. I am grouped with four other men and we are
told to sing, 'Every part of the earth is sacred to my people.' It
is an impressive speech (although its exact contents are much
debated and I have read a very different version) about

attitudes to the land. Once all the parts of the cycle are being sung with gusto, we march round the camp and lead people up to the 'magic circle' at the top of the hill, marked by several slender, painted tree poles with streamers.

In the centre of the circle is a fire. We are led round and round the circle by a benign-looking lady with a purple robe, a long staff, long blonde hair and a crooked nose. I think she is a council member, and I saw her earlier reading someone's stars in the nude. Once we are stationary, a man comes round and wafts us with a smoking twig to ward off evil spirits (this is known as 'switching'). We are then sprinkled with lavender water. There are pronouncements to the four points of the compass and then, as the moon rises, filling the whole estuary with light, we do a series of communal 'Om's. The deep, guttural sound resonates loudly around the camp. We are supposed to be raising energy to save the planet.

Next we are led over to a 'fire labyrinth', a sand and saw-dust maze resembling an intricate crop circle. In the darkness, a group of fire jugglers come up from the bottom of the hill, accompanied by a jazz trombonist, guitars and the samba rhythms of a dozen drummers. Flaming sticks and batons whirl exuberantly around their heads and up in the air. The jugglers surround the labyrinth and their leader, who has a helmet with a lit Bunsen burner sticking out of the top, touches the labyrinth with his flaming stick. Seconds later the labyrinth is alight, the flames dancing a foot into the air. Set against the fevered rhythms of the musicians, it is an awesome experience. The purple-robed lady leads us (carefully single file) into the narrow, blazing passageways.

Beside the labyrinth is the sacred garden, an area beneath an oak tree, surrounded by potted shrubs and a trellis made from arched willow branches. The tree is festooned with lanterns, prayer flags, web-like 'dream catchers' and wind chimes. The musicians lead us in a series of Hindu chants of the 'Hare, Hare, Hare Krishna' variety, before we are given some fruit to conclude the celebration. Chatting to the people beside me as we eat, I learn that the healing camp has been going for 15 years and that it is deliberately anarchic and non-profit-making, unlike some competitors.

I wander up to the fire in the magic circle and start to walk round it. 'Can you walk round the fire the other way?' a young man asks. 'We're trying to keep the energy in one direction.' He adds, 'We can't have cooking or litter burnt on this fire. It's sacred.' After a polite pause, I stroll down to the non-sacred fire outside the café tent.

I sit down next to a tall, grey-haired, bedraggled 50-something with a wise, humorous face. He introduces himself as Tom and says that he has recently arrived from a Rainbow Gathering in Hungary. I have asked several people about the neo-pagan Rainbow Tribe and the answers have been confusing or vague. I ask if Tom was with the Rainbow Tribe. He was, he says, but explains that it is not a group with a membership, but a consciousness. He lives in a tepee settlement in a valley in South Wales and the community there embraces what he calls 'rainbow values'. 'Our society's mistake was putting our doorpost at the foot of nuclear science. In Tepee Valley we have our doorpost at the foot of nature,' he says. Up to 100 people live in the valley, which was bought by some rich hippies in the 1970s. There are two settlements, he explains, called Fluffy and Spiky. Fluffy, based in the centre and on the sides of the valley, is where the tepee-dwellers live. Spiky, by a road at the top of the valley, mainly consists of travellers living in caravans and old coaches.

I ask for directions and he warns me that the community are wary of outsiders, although they keep a Community Lodge (also a tepee) where visitors can stay. 'The thing is,' he explains, 'we get visits from King Arthurs every other month, and people claiming to be Jesus come every fortnight.'

'I'd like to meet King Arthur,' I say, relishing the idea of meeting a twenty-first-century robed warrior-king.

Tom laughs. 'And if it ain't nutters, it's the plods looking for marijuana.'

Tom gives me directions to Tepee Valley and tells me to

look up Ric the Vic, a vicar banished from the Church of England for smoking marijuana.

The next morning I decide to have a couple of treatments and fulfil my appointment with the steam tent before beating a hasty retreat to Tepee Valley. I find a crystal-bowl healer called John in the large treatment tent. He explains that, according to Tibetan thought, there are seven 'chakras' (spiritual energy points – crown, third eye, throat, heart, solar plexus, sacral and base) and, in order to allow divine earth energy to move down through us, we must keep these clear. The earth can also give us energy from below. When he rotates a stick around the crystal bowl, he tells me, the frequency of the sound massages individual cells which makes them shed their dross, hence allowing the free flow of energy through my body. The bowl, it seems, helps him to tune into clients' energy.

Asking me to lie down on another trestle table, he places a large, opaque crystal bowl between my stomach and chest. He taps the bowl twice, making light, tinkling rings, before he starts to rotate the stick around the inside. A deep, smooth sound reverberates through the tent (and surely far beyond), getting louder as he rotates faster. The sound vibrates through my chest. He stops, and the otherworldly resonance hangs in the air. Placing his hand on my heart, he tunes into my energy. He rings the bowl again, this time creating a loud, clear sound, a stillness that rises, levels out and slowly fades.

After 10 minutes he says, 'Phew! You've done a lot of work on your heart this week. It's very, very clear.' He pauses, then adds, 'You need some protection. Wear something around your neck; rose quartz or amethyst.' It is only when he tells me that I may be too emotional and that I wear my heart on the outside that I start to pity him.

My last therapy is a shiatsu massage in a tepee. Lynn, who works part-time at Gatwick airport, also uses shamanic energy. She asks if I have any ailments. 'Aching neck, psoriasis, a bit self-conscious,' I say, my rendezvous with the steam tent in mind. 'Not much, then,' she chuckles, recognizing a hypochondriac when she sees one. She lies me on my stomach before pressing, rubbing and holding me from top to toe. It is sumptuous and joyously slow. Strangely, the long pauses are almost as good as the touches. Then, at the end, *she thanks me*! Quietly, she says, 'I saw an eagle flying, looking down from a great height. You might try to look at the overview. Don't look at the nitty-gritty in such detail.' I thank her and make my way past the steam tent back to my own.

Immediately I start to psyche myself up for my journey back to innocence. I undress, preparing to sprint the 15 metres to the steam tent and rush in. The more I think about it, the more tense I become. I close my eyes in dread. I try to think of Lynn's advice about taking the overview. I open my eyes slowly and, after a brief overview of fast-shrivelling parts, I unzip the tent and dash past various naked and semi-naked bodies into the steam tent.

There are two benches in the cramped, steam-filled tent. I can't see a thing. It is literally boiling: sweat pours down my face and body. I greet the equally dripping bodies that I can dimly see, just inches away. The man beside me explains that, to be fully purified and cleansed, I need to have a cold shower in the unisex cubicle next to the tent and then come back in, before a final shower. *Well, OK, I've got this far*, I think. *Might as well do it right*. A woman opposite me is talking about the complicated relationships at the camp. Her ex-partner is on site with a new woman, she says, and it's awkward bumping into them, especially when her (and his) children are there. 'I treated him like dirt for years, and as soon as I started being decent to him, he was off,' she says ruefully. 'Ah well, treat 'em mean, keep 'em keen,' she laughs, leaning back, her splayed legs sticking out of the sweltering mist. I relax and enjoy the conversations until the heat gets the better of me. Then I rush out, and thankfully the shudderingly cold shower is empty.

Later, driving off site after my second session in the steam tent, I have to admit it: I feel purified. Every pore feels cleansed, every muscle refreshed. Heading deeper into Wales, I think about the seekers and healers at the camp. They are friendly, open (probably too open) and benign people. I half expected them to be po-faced and humourless, but am surprised at the amount of self-deprecating humour, even irony, that I found. I liked them. I was moved by their warmth and refreshed by their disregard for convention.

What about their spirituality, though? What makes people take such a diverse mish-mash of apparently silly beliefs seriously? The phrase 'pick and mix' is usually a pejorative term. This seems strange, when really it is simply a sign that we are becoming more discriminating, more willing to question. These people are questioning the authoritarian, institutional religions, possibly as a demonstration of their disillusionment with mainstream culture. They are more 'picky' about what they accept and appear to want to create an alternative society. Yet so much depends on the 'mixing'. Are their beliefs and practices coherent?

All the practitioners at the Rainbow Circle Healing Camp revere nature and, in some form or another, worship the energy or force behind it. They have good intentions towards each other and the planet. The rituals and symbols that they follow allow them to care for each other. They also provide a belief structure that gives them an alternative cultural and spiritual hinterland. Perhaps this explains why they are so suspicious of mainstream culture (science, the media, government, the Church, even clothes!) whilst being so credulous in relation to exotic, romantic beliefs, some of which seem to have a tenuous grip on reality.

I am also fairly sure that, despite all their individual commitment, these people are not about to save Mother Earth. Most are not activists – they are environmentally friendly consumers of alternative culture. As consumers in search of personal fulfilment, they mirror the culture that they reject. As I drive on, it seems quite likely that Tepee Valley will be more radical.

I arrive at Tepee Valley in the early evening, having got lost, driving down tiny wooded lanes and across deserted moors. A rough metalled track leads past a farm (owned by the community), where a man tells me to park my car beside the road, then walk into the valley. I'll see the tepees, he says. The valley floor is 50 yards across, with a river winding along one side, flanked by trees. The sides are covered in thick mixed woodland, leading up to moorland at the top. There are no discernible tepees. I was expecting a circle of lodges around a campfire, but there is just a pretty, unspoilt valley. After half a mile, I see some white canvas through the trees.

I cross a stream and find a deserted tepee by a path through the grass. A hundred yards further, I come out by some thatched, African-style huts with Perspex windows. In front of them is a tiny stream and a vegetable plot, but no one is there. I follow a tiny path and arrive at a tepee with voices and smoke rising from the top, but the people retreat into it and go silent as I approach. I notice the vegetation. It looks strange. Creepers hang between trees, wild flowers sprout in unusual places, trees fight for space in the dense woodland. It is mysterious and enchanting, presumably because it has not been farmed for nearly 30 years. There is a bewildering network of tiny streams, paths and stone steps between the tepees. Some tepees have carefully tended flower gardens (roses, hollyhocks, nasturtiums and marigolds) and prolific vegetable plots. Some are beside wells dug into the valley side, brimming full with clear water. One has two solar panels beside it, another has a tiny windmill generator.

I find two couples beside a round, Tibetan-style tent called a yurt. They are friendly enough and give me directions to the Big Lodge (or Community Lodge), but do not initiate any conversation. I am told to follow a sliver of a path through reeds and creepers until I reach the 'motorway', a grassy avenue of trees leading up the valley's side.

I find the Big Lodge and meet Geoff, a young man from Birmingham who arrived earlier in the day and hopes to get his own tepee (prices from £400) and live in the valley. His life, he tells me, was turned around following an accident which meant that he could not work in the building trade. Now he works as a security guard, but he wants to see the seasons pass by at close quarters by living in a tepee.

The Big Lodge is well equipped. The floor is covered in marram grass and sheepskins; there are saucepans, crockery, cutlery and a water container; there is a saw, an axe and some wood for a fire. The white canvas tepee could probably hold about 20 more people. Geoff and I light a fire and cook some tinned soup. We visit a couple of girls living in a tepee 50 yards up the hill, to buy a candle. They give us a candle, but do not invite us in or talk to us beyond the demands of politeness. We drink whisky and listen to distant owls hooting as we fall asleep.

The next morning we climb up onto the moor in search of more information. It may be that we both have short hair and bear a passing resemblance to policemen, but no one seems to want to talk to us. People exchange greetings and walk on. We pass the community library (a dampish shed full of dampish books), a stone circle made by Italian visitors and several tepees, wells and streams. It is only when we meet another visitor (a heating engineer from the Midlands) staying with a member of the community that we learn anything.

He explains that the inhabitants are wary because they are expecting a 'raid' from the police and because they receive regular undercover visits from the DHSS (most people are on benefits, although some run craft businesses) and journalists keen to stitch them up. They have dropped out and yet, perversely, sometimes feel that they are in a goldfish bowl, scrutinized by the (bemused) culture they have tried to leave. The original inhabitants have lived here for 26 years. Unwelcome visitors are told to leave (for stealing, disruption or violence) after a group decision is made. Some residents have been environmental activists; all live a sustainable lifestyle.

There is no clear form of spirituality, but sweat lodges (which happen each month) are thought of as spiritually beneficial. In the winter, the tepees move down to the valley floor where it is warmer and they form a more interdependent community. Inhabitants are jaundiced about outsiders' romantic notions of life in the valley. The reality is that they spend a lot of time walking to get water, food, firewood, the post or the DHSS cheque. They wear practical rather than tribal clothes, and it is tough in the winter.

I leave later in the day. It is clear that no one in the valley will speak to me for days – and who can blame them? Nonetheless, I am sad to leave and resolve to return. It is a refreshing, strangely magical place. I would like to show my older children such a vastly different lifestyle and set of values. I am sure that there are all sorts of anomalies and compromises involved in living in Tepee Valley, and I am equally sure that it must get very boring. Yet they are not greedy, untidy or violent; they simply get on with their lives, and they do so simply. Probably to be close to nature is enough. It really is a radical microcosm and, in August, seems an idyllic place to drop out.

I am dubious about rejecting outside culture so completely (despite receiving a dole cheque), but it is a strangely 'spiritual' experience. Without making a song and dance about it, this community is seeking to be radically close to nature while rejecting mainstream greed, consumerism and progress. Although the exchequer is underwriting their radicalism, I respect their resilience and their ideals. Their valley is beautiful, almost a public service. I would not choose such a lifestyle, but it does appeal to the romantic in me. At least for a weekend. I get into my plush new car and, with regrets, roar off homewards.

3

The Saviour's New Clothes

The ravaged wilderness of the Celtic fringe seems a long way away as I drive off in the late August sunshine in search of a very different sort of healing. Instead of the winding lanes leading to Tepee Valley, I am on the purposeful but character-less M25. Instead of the rather friendly but nebulous healing of the Rainbow Circle Healing Camp, I am expecting full-blown miracles. I am visiting a church of charismatic, Bible-believing, miracle-working Christians. The people I am visiting claim to be God's miracle-workers, healing people with serious disabilities and illnesses. People associated with their organization even claim to have raised the dead.

Leaving the M25 for the bland, slightly shabby streets of Brentwood, I note how efficiently signposted the 'All Churches Miracle Crusade' is. There seem to be signs at every corner. It is impossible to get lost, impossible not to arrive at the crusade. There are large billboard adverts featuring Martin Luther King, Mother Teresa, John Wesley and Florence Nightingale, with the legend, 'When you are inspired by Jesus Christ who knows what you can do?' These billboards have been placed around London, giving the impression that what-ever organization is behind the All Churches Miracle Crusade, it is altruistic, campaigning and concerned with civil rights and the underprivileged.

I follow the signs and arrive at Brizes Park, a large Georgian mansion with a yellow- and white-striped big top in the grounds, large enough to hold all the tepees and marquees at the Rainbow Circle camp put together. There are a dozen car-park attendants, who direct me across a field with white-marked 'roads' and several hundred carefully painted parking spaces, all in neat rows. I am waved into my allocated parking space. I cannot help but notice the multitude of shiny, new, muscular-looking BMWs, Mercedes, Vauxhall Carltons and luxury four-wheel drives parked all around me. At the Rainbow camp and Tepee Valley, I felt self-conscious because my new Fiat Punto was a thoroughbred among donkeys. Here it is a minnow among sharks.

Leaving the car, I am pointed in the direction of a fenced walkway which leads to the big top. Men in blazers, pastel shirts and ties with pressed cotton slacks, patent leather shoes and zip-up leather Bible cases walk beside me. They sound like city types: investment consultants, sales executives and merchant bankers. The women are wearing smart twin-sets or flowery frocks. The children (and there are quite a few) are smaller versions of their parents. They are shiny, happy people who belong in adverts for a breakfast cereal. I feel a little awkward in my jeans and Nottingham Forest bomber jacket as I realize that the 'smart-casual' clothes are what these people wear when they are trying to relax, to let their hair down.

At the end of the walkway, two ushers point me towards the big top's entrance, quite plainly visible without anyone's deferentially outstretched arm. Feeling a little claustrophobic, I follow a sign to the toilets, half expecting another sign telling me how to flush them. Minutes later, heading past the US-style hot dog stands, I notice a sign that makes me smile: 'First aid tent'. Shouldn't such things be superfluous at a miracle crusade? There is little chance of people leaping out of wheel-chairs if they can't cope with cuts, grazes and wasp stings, after all.

I decide to take the plunge and follow the beckoning ushers. At the big top entrance, a man smiles unctuously and directs me to *my* seat. *Perhaps this group have a strong belief in predestination,* I think. *Could it be that they think there is only one divinely appointed parking space and seat for me, that was decided billions of years ago before the heavens were formed? Is it their responsibility to make sure I sit in it?* More likely, they are trying to give an impression of efficiency and warm welcome. Instead it feels like a compulsive need for control, the sort of control-freakery more usually associated with a political party's communications office.

This impression is confirmed as I sit in my divinely allocated seat. Four portly men (two with dog collars and purple vestments, two with blazers and ties) sit on the stage, which is flanked by a blue velvet curtain and fringed by piles of gaudy flowers. I am surrounded by about 600 homogenously dressed people, all smart-casual and bland. They have the look of the remorselessly nice. They are watching a man with a big smile and an American accent, who is playing a cheesy jazz trumpet version of 'To Him Be The Glory'. He is a showman, sometimes playing two trumpets at the same time.

Next comes a purple-robed choir, whose powerful but syrupy singing is accompanied by a tinkly piano, footling around with some reverential minor chords. The whole effect is of people abasing themselves. Like a sickly love song, sentimentally crooning about a wonderful lover, this 'inoffensive', lachrymose music oozes with an awed, floodlit reverence. There are some great singers, but they show no *character*: once their solo is over, they merge facelessly into a cloud of purple robes. It is as if they are seeking to extinguish their personalities. Their finale is a jazzed-up version of Handel's 'Hallelujah Chorus', which is hideous and highly professional in equal measure.

After they have finished off with some choreographed 'jazzy clapping', the choir's director tells them to sit down. 'I haven't given you permission to sit,' quips one of the men in vestments on stage. It is Bishop Michael Reid, leader of Peniel Pentecostal Church, and as he laughs, I cannot help but think to myself that our jokes betray us. This is confirmed during the rest of the meeting when he says, with the unassuming arrogance of one who knows that he will be obeyed, 'Sit',

'Stand', or 'Raise your hands'. Yet his manner is easy-going and gracious as he ambles across the stage and introduces a ridiculous-looking man called T.L. Osborne, who is to speak.

Osborne is a short American with a formal black suit, pink shirt and an inadvisable tie. Perhaps because of his beard, wispy moustache and deeply unnatural-looking hair, he resembles a hybrid between one of America's founding fathers and a garden gnome. I suspect that the founding fathers did not go in for toupees or hair dye, but T.L. Osborne's healthy auburn-brown hair, perching a little too perfectly on his head, belies his 75 years. Yet there is something puritanical, even Old Testament, about his appearance. He is an energetic, terrier-like man on a mission from God. He receives news of a cheque from last night's congregation for his mission work with what looks like a pretence at boyish modesty. T.L. then tells us that he has been teaching in Bulgaria, Venezuela, Brazil, Madagascar, Nigeria and 10 French-speaking African countries. There is a bit of banter on stage before Bishop Reid sits down and T.L. starts his talk.

I am a great believer in avoiding unnecessary cruelty, so I shall be brief. T.L. speaks for well over two hours. He starts with another reminder of his preaching work all around the world, which in any other context would be seen as bragging. The theme of his talk, he says, is 'People, Peace, Power and Purpose'. Theme? THEME? Perhaps 'P' is the theme – or could that just be pointless alliteration? He starts by talking about poor self-worth, concluding, 'If Jesus thinks I'm wonderful, what right have I to deny that?' *Ah, I get it*, I think, *I'm worth something because ... er ... because He says so!* I am beginning to understand why these people seem hell-bent on extinguishing their personalities. He even says, 'Conventional religion will always make people crawl,' without seeing that, if the only reason for self-worth in his religion is dependent on another entity (God), then it is not self-worth at all: it is crawling subservience. Every so often, T.L. pauses to enthuse: 'Say, "God is good!"' or 'Say, "I like it!"' or 'Say,

"I'm a friend of God!" ' The congregation repeats his words parrot-fashion.

Then comes the forgiveness bit, and some rather implausible stories. T.L. describes his grandson's dark night of the soul: 'He was a dope addict, in stupid clothes, he wore greasy moccasins, he was drooling at the mouth and couldn't speak or spell his name. He was left to die by his dope friends when Satan tempted him to become a musician in Nashville. He yelled, "*No*! I believe in Jesus!" and was healed and saved.' T.L. goes on, fighting through his tears, telling us that his grandson was transformed and within two days converted 14 of his 'dope buddies'. Now *he* preaches in 40 countries.

Next come stories showing God's power. After a mission in Kampala, Uganda, when a quarter of a million people were trying to leave his open-air mission, T.L. saw an old cripple about to be run over by his chauffeured car. Naturally T.L. did the decent Christian thing: he stopped his car. Then he leapt out and started to help the man across the road, but the Lord said to him, 'Is that all you're going to do?' Papa Musoki (the crippled man) was miraculously healed and they walked out together, got him some decent clothes, and now the good man is a tremendous witness throughout all Kampala.

Then comes the challenge: 'The whole idea of Jesus is to help people, so you've got to do it. God has reserved for you some cities, houses, towns, supermarkets, some countries.' *And some seats and parking spaces*, I think. T.L. tells us that he is 'anointed of God' and wants us to give our lives to Jesus. Looking around, I am convinced that at least 95 per cent of the congregation are already Christians. Without some kind of religious dog leash, who would want to sit through T.L.'s lurid and tearful power-preaching? He prays and asks people to raise their hands. No one responds, so he offers a few helpful suggestions to ease them along. 'Religionists, backsliders who aren't walking with God, raise your hands,' he says. A few hands start to go up. 'Those with secret sins and habits, those habits will be broken,' he adds. Merchant bankers' hands creep guiltily into the air.

'Don't miss your chance,' T.L. whispers prayerfully. 'I don't want to pressurize you, but don't miss it.' He tells those with their hands raised to go to the front, and probably a couple of hundred go forward. 'Say, "I believe in Jesus Christ," ' he says. They do. They are then ushered into an adjoining tent to receive a free gift and to leave their addresses so that they can be directed to a spirit-filled church in their area. I am just beginning to feel slightly annoyed at the lack of miracles, when T.L. says he is going to pray for the sick.

It is quite simple: if we are sick, he will pray and we will touch ourselves where we are ill. I am wondering if he can heal my boredom and, tentatively, I touch my head. T.L. prays, and then he says that we must claim our healing. 'Now, if you're sick, *resist* your sickness. Decide not to be sick. Don't count yourself amongst the sick,' he says. *Hmm*, I think. *Not counting yourself amongst the sick is not quite the same as not being sick*. There is a woman in a wheelchair on my right. How does she feel, I wonder? I know how I would feel at such callous treatment. T.L. then claims that the deaf can now hear and the blind can see. Perhaps my cynicism has blinded me, but the floor is hardly littered with hearing aids and white sticks. Then I realize that I have been healed: miraculously, my boredom has been transformed into anger. As I walk out, Bishop Reid announces that the congregation have raised $27,000 for T.L.'s ministry.

Expecting miracles at a miracle crusade was probably naïve, because the miraculous thing about miracles is that they always happen somewhere else. Bishop Reid's late friend Benson Idahosa claimed to have raised several people from the dead (until he died himself). Where did this happen? In Africa. Did he ever provide firm evidence – death certificates, medical records? No. The other supernatural characteristic of miracles seems to be their ability to disappear into thin air on close inspection. Peniel Pentecostal Church claimed that Bishop Reid had prayed for a child called Sam and that he had been miraculously healed of a rare form of leukaemia. They sold videos highlighting his story. There were several problems with the claim that this was a miracle, but the main difficulty was that the child was dead. They claimed that he *had* been healed, but had then got cancer again and died. They continued to sell the video without actually mentioning that inconvenient fact: the child had died. To insist on a miracle when the child is dead seems to be taking control-freakery or 'perception management' to new limits. Nonetheless, the death of Sam apparently concentrated their minds. He had been mentioned months earlier, on my first visit to the church for a Sunday morning service.

Dressed in a black suit with dog collar and purple vestments, he had looked every inch the elderly Church of England minister. Yet, when Bishop Michael Reid strolled casually across the platform, radio microphone in hand, filmed by five cameras and projected onto monitors around the swish, powder-blue auditorium, he immediately started to resemble an American televangelist. When he referred to 'Baby Sam', his Teflon coating started to show. 'Baby Sam *was* healed,' he said, 'but that doesn't make him immortal.' Flanked by the 100-strong robed gospel choir and surrounded by 400 smartly turned-out churchgoers, he smiled and said, 'Hey, the most important thing in life is to live in victory.' Victory was theirs, he explained, unless they chose to be dominated by Satan.

Despite the Teflon coating, Bishop Reid's sermon cast him in a more alarming light than the manicured sincerity of the televangelists. It took a combative turn. Consumed with a burst of energy, he described 'effeminate Christians' as 'snivelling little wretches'. Christians who believe in evolution were told to 'get out and take your filth with you'. People who doubted Reid's miracles were described as 'little jellies' and 'worshippers of Satan'. The congregation were rapt. He laughed, they laughed. He ranted, they nodded.

Reid's purest bile, however, was saved for the Prime Minister Tony Blair. He was enraged at a poll in which Blair had been voted the moral and spiritual leader of Britain. 'Blair

– that goofball with a bunch of queers!' he railed. 'God deliver us. Not a pervert who surrounds himself with perverts. He can't even keep his cabinet ministers from Clapham Common. God deliver us from a pervert!' He went on to tell his congregation how to deal with Christians who held differing views: 'Ostracize them. Don't partake of their sins.' He added, 'You talk to people, they don't listen, they're in error.' People who disagreed with Reid were told to 'get out'.

Despite this, one person who disagreed with Bishop Reid and his methods of 'miraculous healing' claims she had some problems getting out. Anne Barker, 33, claims to have been held for several months against her will. She joined the community in 1988, seeking treatment for eating disorders after hearing stories of miraculous healings in the group. 'They were incredibly verbally abusive and controlling,' she says. 'I was allowed no contact with the outside world. Reid told me that I was at Peniel for good.' When she did receive a visitor, they were constantly chaperoned by a Peniel member. 'I repeatedly told them that I wanted to leave, and they refused to release me. Reid demolished me. He said that my disobedience meant I would burn in hell.' She claims that she was held in a house inside the Peniel compound, but eventually booked a taxi, scaled the compound fence in the middle of the night, and fled to her parents in Solihull.

Anne Brown, in charge of Peniel's public relations, stresses that Anne Barker's parents were desperate for Peniel to help their daughter. She says, 'Over a period of 24 years in the life of a church there will, of course, be one or two whom we are unable to help, or who do not want the help we can offer. She decided that Peniel wasn't for her and left. That's it. We've heard nothing from her since.'

Some ex-Peniel members allege that the group has some of the characteristics of a cult. Max Carter, who left the group after several years' involvement, claims that Reid often brought disharmony and discord into the lives of many people who knew him. 'I heard him say to people who disagreed with him that they would go to hell,' he recalls. Caroline Green, 31, who left with her children in the late 1990s, says, 'Bishop Reid appears to have total control over families within the group. His word is law and they are largely cut off from the outside world.'

Peniel strongly denies it is a cult. Anne Brown believes that Reid is a good leader, who leads from the front. His church, she says, is not a controlling organization. 'I have been a member for 15 years and Reid speaks the truth with compassion. Sometimes this is challenging, but there's always a gospel message and that's not always palatable for people,' she says. 'He's always got their eternal destiny at heart; that is the most important thing,' she adds.

Caroline Green alleges that the corporal punishment regime that Reid then advocated had a devastating effect on her children while they attended Peniel Academy, the church's private school. She also claims that Reid pressurized her family into giving money or buying policies from companies which he runs. 'We paid £400 a month to Peniel and we had over a dozen policies from Reid's companies,' she says. Reid now fronts a business empire in which one company alone controls funds of £41 million.

Anne Brown is clear that the Peniel Academy did formerly practise corporal punishment, but is unaware of it damaging Green's children. 'It was never mentioned when they were in the school,' she says. Brown believes that it is natural to buy insurance policies from within the community, but stresses that people are not allowed to promote their companies in church services. She feels that Peniel has been unfairly tried by the media because of former members' allegations. 'We've no axe to grind with these people. They come to the Bishop asking for help and when it doesn't work, they bite the hand that feeds them. It's absolutely sickening. It's not fair,' she says.

Bishop Reid's past is interesting. A former policeman and salesman in his late fifties, he became a Christian nearly 30 years ago and was expelled from two congregations for 'railing' against other church members. One minister who knew Reid in the 1970s describes him as 'verbally abusive, manipulative and appearing out of control'. He founded Peniel Church in the late 1970s and visited other churches to persuade members to leave and join Peniel. People have moved to Brentwood from all around the country to join the church. Pastor Adrian Vaughan says, 'He stole over half my church – over 50 people left Wales to follow him. He has an incredible hold on people's minds.'

Reid, who sometimes calls himself 'Doctor', is married with children and holds a number of honorary degrees from fundamentalist colleges in America. He has an MA in Practical Theology from the Oral Roberts University. He was ordained bishop by Benson Idahosa of the International Communion of Charismatic Churches, a little-known fundamentalist Pentecostal organization based in Washington DC. Pentecostals, who originated in working-class Los Angeles in 1906, are usually informal and 'low church' as a point of honour. Strangely, Peniel and ICCC, which is a Pentecostal offshoot, enjoy some of the trappings of 'high' religion, including bishop's mitres, crooks and colourful vestments.

My final visit to Peniel is to see a bishop invested. I have long since lost the possibility of gaining spiritually from Peniel, but I am fascinated by the dynamics, the control, and I have found out enough to want to see more. The meeting involves the usual high-octane choruses, homogenous congregation and purple-robed choir. I try asking a couple of people beside me what they gain from Peniel, but they appear too embarrassed to answer. One person, however, smiles meaningfully and simply says, 'Blessing'.

Bishop Reid is joined for the ceremony by Bishop Dr Margaret Idahosa, Bishop Silas Owite and Dr Francis Ole Wake, who is to be consecrated as bishop (although, strangely, he appears to have been a bishop for some time already, according to an ICCC leaflet). They are all wearing gowns and mitres, which they inexplicably replace with skullcaps at various points. Bishop Owite, from Kenya, speaks at length about the miracles he has done, jokes about the fact that his second wife is often mistaken for his daughter – moments before wiping away tears for his late wife, Fanny. He also tells us (twice) that Kenya's President (and human rights abuser) Daniel arap Moi is a 'personal friend'. He works the congregation with impassioned whoops and verbal pyrotechnics, yet the more he speaks, the more he resembles a graceless braggart. But for his skin colour (which surely would preclude him), he would fit in perfectly as a televangelist on an American Christian television channel. This is a very different sort of homogeneity from that of the congregation: the shepherds are very different from the sheep.

It is at this meeting that I learn that Peniel's Christian Academy has become affiliated with the college that awarded Reid his doctorate: Oral Roberts University, an American college founded by a notorious right-wing American televangelist with a gift for making money. Oral Roberts famously declared in a fundraising telethon that God told him he would 'call him home' unless he raised 9 million dollars. The donations did not dry up, but he never made the divinely ordained sum. Roberts' similarities with Bishop Reid are marked. They both believe in the 'prosperity gospel' – the idea that, if Christians are obedient, God will make them rich – and they both became involved in right-wing politics. Oral Roberts was involved in the Moral Majority and backed Republican Pat Robertson for President.

Bishop Reid's political involvement started after 119 members of his congregation marched into Brentwood and Ongar Conservative Association early in 1998. At the time Bishop Reid claimed that his congregation's simultaneous interest in Conservative Party politics was a coincidence. Some within the local party felt that it was a 'takeover'. Eric Pickles MP supported Reid and described Peniel members as 'wonderfully normal'. His constituency agent said, 'I am quite sure that there is no hidden agenda. There is nothing sinister about this.'

Since then, the objectors claim that they have been ousted.

'Peniel members were bussed in and took over all the key posts and expelled all those who had publicly asked questions about them,' says Tony Donnelly, an ex-member and former Tory councillor. He says that the number of Peniel members in the Conservative Association rose exponentially and their influence was such that 200 disgruntled Tories formed a breakaway Independent Conservative Party.

Michael Parrish, chairman of the Brentwood and Ongar Association, has a different perspective. 'The Association is free from *any* influence from *any* outside organization. We welcome anyone who fulfils those criteria, irrespective of their age, race, sex or religious belief.' He claims that the surge in Peniel members took place over some months, and points out that Conservative Central Office have investigated and rejected the allegations.

Donnelly claims that the investigation was cursory and estimates that Peniel members now make up the majority of members in the Association. He is also unhappy that William White, the outgoing party chairman, wrote to members of the Association urging them to vote against Donnelly's anti-Peniel candidature for the chairmanship. This was shortly before White bought Brizes Park, the £1.3 million property where the miracle crusade took place, which he sold on to Peniel on the day of purchase. 'In my view there was a clear conflict of interest,' Donnelly says.

Although both Peniel and the Conservative Party refute allegations of a takeover, it is undeniable that links between them continue. William Hague has personally invited Davina Maillard, a Peniel member and businesswoman, to join his Group 1000 think-tank. Bishop Reid and several senior Peniel members have joined the £1,000-per-head Quota Club and are alleged to have dined with John Major and Kenneth Clarke at party functions. Eric Pickles provided Peniel members with the House of Commons Dining Room for a function. Brentwood Conservative Association funds have rocketed from £2,000 to £70,000 since Peniel joined, and a sum of £8,000 has been lent to Conservative Central Office.

Some senior Conservatives have blamed Peniel for their decision to leave the party. County Councillor Alison Enkel claims she resigned from the Conservatives after threats from within the local party warning her that she must publicly praise Peniel or be deselected. Mrs Enkel, who was national chairwoman of Conquest, a network for young Conservative councillors, is now a Liberal Democrat councillor, tipping the balance of power away from the Tories. She explains, 'A senior member of the local party said that, unless I agreed to say something good about Peniel Church publicly, the party would make sure that I was not selected to stand for my county seat.'

Councillor Valerie Fletcher stood down and left the Conservative Party following what she saw as a conflict of interest. Fletcher, a former mayor of Brentwood, is a fundraiser for a local hospice and received a donation of £3,500 from Peniel. The chief executive of the council agreed that there was an interest to declare, but the Conservative's constituency agent disagreed and told her to rescind her declaration of interest. 'I felt that I had to be whiter than white, so I resigned,' she says. Fletcher had been a councillor for 20 years, but felt unhappy at the way Peniel members and others sympathetic to them started dictating to established party members how things should be done. 'The way the Conservative Party has handled the Peniel thing has been unhelpful to old members. The man in the street is asking, "What's going on between Peniel and the Conservatives?" and the party should be concerned by this,' she says.

The influence of Peniel in the Brentwood and Ongar Conservative Party has meant that one change is likely. It looks increasingly as if the Conservative Party may lose the constituency (and their sixth-safest seat) at the next election. Martin Bell MP (the white-jacketed sleaze-buster who famously stood against Neil Hamilton in Tatton following the cash-for-questions scandal) has decided to fight the seat as an independent. He is unhappy with the Conservative Central Office investigation into the affair. He cites an abuse of the democratic process as his reason, saying, 'If 119 people join a party in one day, there should be alarm bells ringing.'

As I leave Peniel Pentecostal Church after the bishop's investiture, I resolve not to return. Reid's far-right political attitudes are deeply unappealing. He is in favour of capital and corporal punishment, of women obeying men and, despite his work with Africans, some of his attitudes seem nationalistic. On his website (www.peniel.org) he explains his attitude to Europe under the headline 'Europe: Time to say *Nein*'. He writes, 'Opposition to greater European integration should not rest on the contentious issues of a single currency and sovereignty but upon the undeniable truth that Europe opposes Christian values. The very clarity of Christianity is alien to the European nature.'

I am unclear about exactly what Peniel's agenda is in local politics. It appears that Peniel have local influence in Brentwood. Perhaps it is an another example of the need for control? Yet too much religious and political control causes conflict. Conservative Party members have left the party in droves (while other droves have joined), headlines have been made and writs have flown. Reid's leadership style reminds me of Margaret Thatcher's. I am not about to be handbagged into repentance and frogmarched into faith, however. As a form of spirituality, it seems about as inspiring as John Major on a rainy day.

What I really dislike about Peniel are the characteristics it has in common with the extremist wing of the Conservative Party: the intolerance, the need for authoritarian control, the absolute distinction between leaders and followers, shepherds and sheep. The homogeneity of the separate groups seems oppressive. It reminds me of the relationship between television personalities and their audience. The leaders seem to possess television-sincerity and the followers seem about as charismatic as pillars of salt.

I decide that it is only fair to visit other Christian churches later on in my pilgrimage. They will not all be complicated by political intrigue and allegations of cult-like abuse. Christendom, I know, has more acceptable faces than the tongues-speaking, exorcizing, prophesying, miracle-working, charismatic type of church.

4

The Technology of the Soul

Once a year I do something that I tell myself is good for the soul. Each November a local friend invites us to his bonfire party and, normally, I leave my wife at home and take our four children 100 yards down the road in the drizzle. Then we eat undercooked, factory-made cheese-and-onion quiche, lukewarm, slightly tanned chicken drumsticks and triangular fish-paste sandwiches. We listen to Reet Petite, Boney M and The Shadows on a 1970s jukebox in the corner of the lounge. Then we stand around a bonfire, see the Guy collapse and watch some fireworks.

No, I don't think burning effigies of Catholics is good for the soul. The factor that turns Bonfire Night into an ascetic form of spiritual exercise is that my friend's guests are the most resolutely dull people it is possible to meet. Most of them (and I am not joking) collect old petrol pumps, which they then try to sell on to other collectors. The guests who are not united in their obsessive fondness for petrol pumps are members of the Buckinghamshire British Bikers Club. An interesting group, you might think? No. These are bikers who live to bike rather than bike to live. They talk about torque (and forks, exhausts, callipers and brake shoes) for hours. There is even a six-foot, sex-changed transvestite biker, who you would surely put money on as being interesting or entertaining. He/she is neither, having – along with the rest of the guests – turned dullness into an art form.

To be fair to my friend, he is much more interesting than his

guests. He calls a spade a shovel and prides himself on his 'reactionary' pedigree (given half a chance, he comes out with comments such as, 'If women want the vote, they should make themselves useful'), but he is honest, kind and entertaining. It could be because he has a strong personality that his guests are, or appear to be, so anaemic. For me it is the most socially dysfunctional event of the year. Moments after arriving, most people seem to be staring at their shoes and waiting for the end. Or making polite conversation about petrol pumps.

I am not sure why, but this November night is different. I ask one man whether he is still collecting petrol pumps. Not as much as he was, he tells me. What does he collect now? 'Cash,' he replies, before explaining that he is busy installing portable toilets on film sets. 'I did *The Bill* last week,' he says, smiling expansively. Then the neighbour from hell approaches. Drunk, she assumes an inappropriate, cloying familiarity. I have only spoken to her twice in my life. 'Are you still working for newspapers, Roland?' she asks, slurring her words and speaking at the top of her voice. As usual, I decide that alcohol is my best companion, followed by my children. It is only at the end of the evening that I realize what is different: I am scared.

I am scared because I have signed up for a course, starting the next morning, that promises to transform my relationships over a long weekend (Friday to Sunday). It is hard to think of a more appropriate backdrop to a course promising breakthroughs in relationships than my friend's bonfire party. I am not frightened of transforming my relationships with the people at the party (I reassure myself that there is no hope of *that*). What worries me is that I have been told that in about 40 hours this course will break and remake me; it will manufacture a 'conversion' – though not, they tell me, to a religion.

The course offers a new form of 'spirituality' in that it promises depth, authenticity, fulfilment and integrity in all areas of my life. It promises to alter my reality radically and to make my personal and professional (and presumably annual) relationships truly fulfilling and 'authentic'. Some people say that such courses are brainwashing; others say that it will transform and improve my life. Both, of course, could be true. Although I am daunted, however, I want to approach the weekend with an open mind.

A few years ago, I heard about the so-called 'personal transformation' courses and, out of a mixture of curiosity and journalistic research, I attended some introductory evenings. Now my memories are adding to my fears. My first encounter was at a wine and cheese evening with about 20 people in the plush London offices of an organization called Life Training. Two fresh-faced presenters explained that Life Training's aim was 'to radically enhance the quality of everything in your life'. Then a number of initiates testified to the course's dramatic benefits. They all seemed faintly unreal, with the zeal and simplicity of religious converts.

After the presentation we were free to mingle. Suzie, a veteran of nine years, approached me and, in a roundabout kind of way, asked what my problems were. I explained that I was generally overtired. 'This course is exactly what you need,' she piped up.

'But I'm generally content,' I said.

'But that's just it, you're not content with your contentment,' she suggested.

'Erm, I am, really I am,' I said, forlornly. But Suzie was not deterred. After half an hour, I made my excuses and left.

The next introduction I attended was for Insight. About 60 people gathered at the Great Western Royal Hotel in central London. The presenter was an articulate, friendly young woman who drew diagrams to show us that we were stuck in restrictive ways of thinking. She then told us to do something deeply un-English: we were to brag about ourselves to the person sitting next to us. Next we had to heap uninterrupted praise onto each other. I was beginning to enjoy this. Then we were told that, as innocent, loving and lovable children, we had got what we wanted, but, as jaundiced adults, bad experiences had taken away our ability to dream. 'Now, when we

want something kind of wonderful and amazing, it's quite a scary idea,' she said. Before asking people to sign up, she asked us, 'Have you ever had the feeling that you've got something missing?'

Having done my homework on Insight, I felt that there was indeed something missing. There had been no mention of the origins of Insight and its Californian cult leader, who was born as John Roger but latterly preferred to be called Mystical Traveller or Preceptor Consciousness. Insight was apparently created by Preceptor Consciousness after a mountaintop meeting in Hawaii with Jesus, Krishna and other ascended masters. Preceptor Consciousness had also founded an organization called Movement for Spiritual Inner Awareness (or MSIA, spookily pronounced 'messiah'). Many of the Insight leaders were members of MSIA. Was Insight, I asked, an attempt to recruit members of the public into MSIA? No, emphatically not, the young woman told me. Was she a MSIA minister? Yes, but it was just a way of growing spiritually. Had she come to MSIA via Insight? Er, yes.

Other Insight graduates who had nothing to do with MSIA said so quite openly. It was clear that not all Insight graduates became full-blown devotees of Preceptor Consciousness. Yet I later spoke to an ex-member who had been invited to join MSIA on one of Insight's advanced (and costly) courses and claimed that MSIA members believed that John Roger was the messiah. Another Insight graduate was seduced by the facilitator as a way of helping her face up to her hang-ups about men. He was also a MSIA minister and persuaded her that his higher consciousness told him that he did not need a condom! Unfortunately his higher consciousness got it wrong, but as a way of making it up to the pregnant young woman, Insight told her that Preceptor Consciousness would bless the baby on his next visit to Britain. Following this incident the facilitator was banned from running further courses in Britain. The young woman was not impressed and left Insight.

My final introductory session was with Landmark Education, providers of The Forum, the course that I am to take. I remember a middle-aged participant waving her hands in the air and saying with unbridled enthusiasm, 'Drop the life you were living, live another one, I got the magic!' The idea of reinventing oneself seems to be a characteristic of all these groups. At the Landmark session there were about 200 youngish people listening to the leader, a slick, pugnacious, stouter version of Cilla Black. My final memory is of one woman complaining that her husband's involvement in Landmark Education was disrupting her family life because he was away every weekend, helping at courses. The leader's solution was simple: 'Your husband never promised to spend weekends at home. You just have to let it go.'

Nursing a post-bonfire hangover on the early morning train into London, I am nervous, but interested. My mind is agitatedly turning over questions. How is it possible to create such dramatic transformations in 40 hours? Will it be brainwashing and, if so, am *I* open to brainwashing? Is Landmark Education a cult, or has it something real to offer? Testimonies differ. Paul Heelas, Professor of New Religious Movements at Lancaster University, tells me that The Forum is not nearly as extreme as some similar groups were in the 1970s. Personal transformation groups used to be physically abusive and confrontational, he says. Most people claim to benefit from the courses; but psychiatrist Dr Betty Tylden claims that she has dealt with scores of people who have been damaged by them.

I reassure myself that I know quite a lot about The Forum. It was developed by Werner Erhard (whose original name was Jack Rosenberg), a former Scientologist and used-car salesman who founded 'est' (Erhard Seminar Training) in 1971. It was an encounter group made up of a mixture of positive thinking, Scientology, Zen Buddhism and other psychotherapeutic techniques. Est grew dramatically, spreading around the world as well as attracting notoriety when graduates spoke of abusive and controlling behaviour in seminars. Erhard's empire unravelled in the 1980s, when the US tax service charged him with tax fraud, his daughters alleged sexual and physical

abuse, and former employees claimed that he had wanted to be considered god-like and liked to be called 'the Source'.

Erhard went into exile and devised a new course called The Forum, which bears a striking resemblance to est. In the early 1990s Erhard was bought out by his employees, who formed Landmark Education and pay Erhard for the use of his technology. It is unclear whether Erhard still has an influence on the organization. Landmark Education runs other courses based on the same principles and Youth at Risk, an organization with close links to Landmark, runs a similar course for young offenders. The courses attract equally vociferous praise and criticism.

As my train roars towards London, I wonder whether my knowledge will protect me from The Forum's influence. Is protection necessary? I want to be open to the possibility that the course is as good as its enthusiasts claim. It could be that it has received such critical coverage because people have not been willing to face up to what the course offers. There are people who will call any new practice or belief that unsettles them 'damaging' or a 'cult' without giving it a chance. If so many people claim to have benefited from The Forum, then it is quite possible that it has something to offer. I try to hold my fears alongside a resolve to be open to new possibilities, reassuring myself that Landmark's literature says I will not be forced to speak. I mean, what can happen between 9 a.m. and midnight in just three days?

I arrive at an anonymous-looking five-storey office near Euston Station at 8.45 a.m. Scores of people are signing in and picking up name tags. Inside the plain, white and grey auditorium are about 200 participants, about 20 helpers and David Sherman, our leader. Although there is a smattering of elderly people and one or two 18-year-olds, the majority are between 20 and 40, with slightly more women than men. The majority appear to be educated professionals (doctors, lawyers, advertising executives, lecturers and teachers, people in business or the media); others are in sales or the caring professions; there are a few musicians and artists, a few unemployed and retired people.

At 9 a.m. precisely, the doors to the auditorium are closed and David strides down a central aisle to the slightly raised podium at the front. He sits in a director-style chair in the centre, flanked by two blackboards. A little further from the centre are two whiteboards. The window blinds behind the podium are closed. The participants sit in cramped chairs in a semicircle about 12 rows deep, along the length of the room. Behind them, the helpers sit at desks, one on a raised chair directly opposite David's chair at the front. There are three microphone stands, one in the central aisle, the others below both ends of the podium. David has a radio microphone and all sound is relayed from several speakers in the ceiling. On a table at the side are some white plastic cups and three jugs of water.

That is the situation for three days, from 9 a.m. until about midnight. We have short breaks every three hours and a 90-minute meal break at about 6 p.m. We are given 'homework' tasks for the breaks and at the end of the day. Each night I have less than five hours' sleep. It is almost oppressively featureless and bland. Nothing is to distract from what the leader is saying and doing. Yet what occurs during those three days is one of the most extraordinary things I have ever seen. It is impossible not to be affected by it. It is also very difficult (though not impossible) to understand what is happening.

Forty-something, dressed in a powder-blue cotton shirt, patent leather shoes and smart-casual slacks, David sits at the front and smiles over his steel-rimmed glasses. He explains that for the duration of The Forum he will be taking us on a roller-coaster ride and that he is committed to improving the quality of our relationships, our communication and our effectiveness in all areas of life. Yes, he knows we do not believe him, but unless we are wasting our time and the £235 course fee, we ought to give him a chance. He is personable, powerful and articulate and has a no-nonsense manner. 'I'm committed to you having breakthroughs,' he says. 'And to do that I'm willing to be unreasonable. Why? I'm committed to being unreasonable because I'm committed to extraordinary relationships. I think it's worth it. I'm committed to everybody doing The Forum. I believe in it.'

This zealous commitment to transformations is used to justify several disorientating, seemingly arbitrary rules. We are discouraged from going to the toilet during the three-hour sessions in case we lose the 'narrative'. We are not allowed to take notes, eat or talk (unless instructed to). We are only allowed to sit in uncomfortable seats and get up for the odd glass of water. The doors are closed on the minute at the end of the breaks, and to re-enter the room if we are late we have to apologize formally for breaking our word to the Forum helpers on the door. We also promise not to drink alcohol or take nonprescribed drugs (like paracetamol). It is made clear to us that we will be made accountable to these commitments.

Initially, David describes our doubts as our 'Already Always Listening', by which he means the dialogue of sceptical questions and presuppositions that are going on in our minds. He assures us that this is fine, natural even, but if we want to achieve the benefits of The Forum we must banish these doubts. 'Otherwise you're wasting your £235,' he says, assuring us that, if we do not like the approach he offers, we can go back to normal at the end of the weekend. He describes himself as a coach and us as his athletes. We can be taking part on the court or judging from the stands, but the only way to benefit fully from The Forum is to be on the court. To me, this sounds suspiciously as if we are being told to stop thinking, to suspend our judgement and simply accept what our coach says. 'But, listen,' David smiles, 'I'm not saying that this is true. We made it up. You can leave on Sunday and forget all about The Forum. Does it work? Yes. Can it change all aspects of your lives? Yes.'

Quite early on, David takes questions about The Forum. He assures us that it is not psychotherapy or neurolinguistic programming and has nothing in common with them. He mentions Werner Erhard as the 'controversial and successful' originator of The Forum and says that it has evolved over the years. He reads out a passage from a whiteboard which seems to me to have litigation lawyers written all over it. Clearly The Forum has been sued by damaged participants, hence we are told that The Forum is for well people – people receiving therapy or psychiatric care are told that it is not appropriate for them to take part. David announces that people can leave at this stage and receive a full refund. A couple leave.

Through a radical emphasis on personal responsibility for our own lives, deep self-honesty and sorting out unresolved issues with others, David engages us all sympathetically into the 'narrative'. What is odd about The Forum narrative, however, is that they have created their own language to articulate it (I suspect this is because, during the three days, these familiar concepts are slightly skewed and it is harder for us to realize this if the vocabulary used is unfamiliar). What we would normally call a 'hidden agenda' is described as a 'running a racket'. We are told to see all our everyday complaints as 'rackets' and to consider the costs and benefits of such an approach. David invites people to the microphones to describe their complaints, then he shows them that their complaint allows them to be 'right' and to hide behind blaming their partner, for instance. Their partner is probably doing his or her best, but by 'running their racket', they have condemned him or her to being wrong, with the pay-off of righteousness. The cost of this is the removal of any possibility for change in the relationship.

Several people go up to the microphones and share their rackets. Some are peripheral details, petty gripes between couples that have been masking an unwillingness to talk honestly. Others are more substantial. A woman says that she is running a racket in relation to her husband, who left her and took her children. Thin-lipped, she admits that she is furious with him and that she has been 'living off' this fury. David suggests that she had been running a racket even before her husband left. She nods guiltily. He pushes her further: 'You're responsible for your husband leaving you.' He says the 'pay-off' from this racket is 'making him wrong', but the consequence is 'no possibility of love'. She is tearful, but he senses some resistance and says that she is still holding on to her racket. She nods. 'Quit complaining then, you're doing it,' he says. Then he adds, 'You're a disgusting racketeer.' She sits down, resolved to face up to her racket and 'grow up'. There seems to be an uneasiness about this confrontation, but people see the woman's agreement or acquiescence and nothing is said.

David tells us how our past experiences are affecting the possibilities for the future. He tells us that our interpretations of experience are merely our 'story' and that this can really dominate our reality. He speaks for 20 minutes at a time, explaining some theory or psychotherapeutic truism. They are things that we can all relate to and, in some cases, agree with. This is punctuated by people coming to the microphone for some 'coaching'. The coaching often draws the audience into the experience because people are speaking about deeply personal things. They are making themselves very vulnerable. It cannot leave you unmoved.

One woman says that her past has left her feeling completely unlovable. She was the love child of an Irish Catholic and her mother placed her in an orphanage at birth. Years later, her adopted parents disowned her because she got pregnant outside marriage. Now she finds commitment difficult. She smiles with new hope as David tells her that abandonment is her story. (*Could this interpretation not be* his *story?* I wonder.) His manner is a mixture of being understanding and being ruthless and incisive. Sometimes the tone belies the content. 'Don't blame your mother – she loved you totally. In her society, she was doing what she had to do. So were your adopted parents when they kicked you out. "I'm abandoned" is your story, your invention. You weren't abandoned,' he explains. She sits down to uproarious applause.

David's other big idea for Friday is that 'looking good is running your lives'. I know this is laughable and suspect that it says more about the diminutive, slightly portly, overly coiffed David (who tells us at some stage that, before joining Landmark, he was a hairdresser) – but he anticipates my thoughts. 'You're telling yourself that's nonsense, but I guarantee it's true,' he says. Pretty soon a fat man comes out to the front to confess. He is told that The Forum's way to succeed is not to resist, because 'resistance leads to persistence' in the same way that an action causes a reaction. The fat man offloads his angst courageously. Self-consciousness plagues his every move. David coaches him into a state of not wanting to change it and he sits down satisfied. It becomes clear that 'looking good' includes any form of self-consciousness about other people. We are told to share some shameful secret with the person sitting next to us.

One woman questions the idea that 'looking good is running our lives'. 'Your whole life is a sham,' David says.

'Like most people, I care what impression I make to an extent,' she says.

'There you go again. Why did you say "like most people" unless you're trying to justify yourself to look good?' He talks her round to admitting that his premise is right. David is never wrong. Either we accept what he has to say or we simply need to be open to the possibility that he is right. He is an awesome performer: after 15 hours he appears as astute as ever.

At the end of the day he does an exercise to show us that 'tiredness' and 'headache' are both 'story'. A woman with a headache goes to the dais, sits on a chair, closes her eyes and David quietly talks her through a sort of visualization (people with headaches in the audience are invited to participate too), in which he repeatedly asks her where the headache is and how severe it is. After about 10 minutes, the woman claims her headache has virtually gone. David takes the same approach with tiredness. Many people in the audience also appear to feel better, but what strikes me is the pressure for those at the front to say that they have recovered.

We leave shortly before midnight and our homework is to write a letter to someone with whom we have been 'running a racket'. I am exhausted and, as I leave to stay with friends in Holborn, my feelings are mixed. I am unhappy at the forceful interpretations that seem to have been placed on people's

lives, but I admit that The Forum does make us face important issues that we would rather avoid. Some people have been deeply affected.

It is not until the second day, however, when a young man called Paul comes to the microphone, that my misgivings turn to anger. He tells us with tears streaming down his face that he was raped by his brother for most of his childhood. He took David's advice from the previous day and phoned his brother to create a breakthrough. 'I was willing to give up the pain for a good relationship,' he says. His brother put the phone down. David acknowledges Paul's courage and urges him to phone again. 'Rape is interpretation. Brutality is inter-pretation,' he says. Paul *has* to forgive his brother. He *has* to phone again. Paul vacillates. 'Get off your guilt and grow up!' David snaps.

Others are told that they are 'disgusting', that they have hidden agendas in the most innocent of transactions and that they have 'clearings' (Forumspeak for an openness to things which somehow means these things will happen) for abuse. It is clear that, according to The Forum's logic, we are account-able for everything that happens to us as well as our reactions to it. In Forum psychobabble, women are deserted by their husbands because they have a 'clearing', even a desire, for this. One woman is told that she was attacked by a man in a six-hour attempted rape ordeal because she has a clearing in her psyche for men not to be trustworthy. While our interpre-tations of events are discounted as our 'story', David's forceful interpretations are, somehow, gospel. He justifies his ruthless approach as coach by saying, 'I'm always looking for that extra bit of slack in my athletes.'

Why do we allow this to happen? It is not primarily due to the fact that challenging David is difficult because we have to speak in Forum jargon and he is incredibly adept at using it. (When challenged, however, his bottom line is, 'We didn't say this was the truth. We made it up.' He then asks the person if they are willing to try it for a weekend, because, he promises, it works.) There are other factors, but the main reason is that what David is saying is partly true: personal responsibility is good; we do have hidden agendas. We are also sharing on a meaningful level and, therefore, have an 'emotional investment' in the process. We see dramatic and heartfelt 'breakthroughs' – though not, of course, whether they last – and 'new possibilities' in relationships.

A senior surgeon tearfully tells us how he bullied a junior doctor because of her inefficiencies. He promises to write to her and 'complete' (which means apologize and resolve the issue), whatever it takes to track her down. A young woman says she has spoken to her alcoholic father for the first time in years, having ostracized him following years of abusive behaviour. They have arranged to meet for coffee. An advertising CEO announces that he has written a 'breakthrough letter' to a colleague to apologize for sidelining and marginalizing him within the company. He has promised him a new beginning.

The second day is a concerted attempt to insinuate our inadequacy. David speaks about our parents' influence on us: 'I promise you it all comes from your parents.' He introduces the idea of 'winning formulas', which means the qualities that work for us, based on our past experience but which become rigid, like tramlines going into the distance. He assures us that winning formulas are good – they are how we succeed, but they also restrict our future possibilities to more of the same. He is planting seeds of discontent. If we are content, he insinuates, it is because we are dishonest or shallow.

Then he gives up on insinuations. 'The person who wrecked your life is you!' he shouts at one woman. 'Looking good is running your life!' he shouts at us all. 'Your life has been one big illusion!' and 'You've never made a choice in your life!' he tells us, presumably trying to nail any residual self-worth. He has a penchant for telling us what it will say on our gravestones and then adding, 'Then they'll throw dirt in your face, have some drinks and go to the movies.' He bills himself (or Landmark Education) as our 'saviour'. We are told that he is fighting for our lives: 'I'm more on your side than you are,' he says. 'Who you're being as a human being is either racket or winning formula. We have to accept that we're trapped,' he explains.

He then tells us another half-truism, based on what I suspect is a rather quaint 'ethnic myth'. Have we heard about African monkey traps? The trap is a box with bananas in it and a hand-sized hole. As the monkey grabs a banana, its fist enlarges so that it cannot get its hand out of the box while it holds on to the banana. It will not let go, so the next morning it is caught. The idea is that we have to release things, we are not to resist, we are to allow the possibility of change. It strikes me immediately that The Forum's intensity and promises could all too easily become the banana that people cling to. It could trap people.

That evening, during our 90-minute meal break, I visit a local restaurant with a surgeon, a Channel 4 commissioning editor, a lawyer, a telesales woman and a director of a fashion company. These people are not obviously emotionally needy. Most of them have only come on the course because they have been pestered into it by friends or colleagues. They are balanced, humorous and previously satisfied people who are now in search of a 'breakthrough'. We have an accelerated intimacy which is quite refreshing in itself. My companions are exuberant. They have questions, but generally they are happy with the course. My misgivings are on a different scale.

Before we leave for the night, David takes us on an eyes-closed visualization in which we are meant to face and become comfortable with our fears of others. We are to imagine that everyone in the room, then the country, then the world, hates us. I am sure that I have some fears, but this seems too silly to take seriously and by this stage I am resisting the idea of giving my mind to David's promptings. Others seem to have no such misgivings. Within 10 minutes the room is full of strangled whimpers and cries which soon become piercing banshee wails, screams and full-throated sobbing. Then David leads people on to what he says is on the other side of the fear. People start laughing hysterically. Then he tells those of us foolish enough not to see it that the others are laughing because they realize that everyone in the world is as afraid of them as they are of everyone else.

The next morning I wake exhausted. For the past two nights I have fallen asleep at about 2 a.m. and woken with palpitations (which I have never had before or since) at about 6 a.m. It is deeply reassuring to be in my friend's house, where life is simple and good. I am feeling manic but focused. During an invigorating power shower, I decide to challenge David about what I think is happening to people. I write a 'breakthrough letter' in which, according to Forum jargon, I am 'enrolled in the possibility of openness and self-expression'. But the letter is addressed to David and it attempts to explain what is going on. All I have to do is wait for an opportunity to read it. I rehearse with my friend and decide to jog to Euston.

It is a beautiful, crisp Sunday morning as I set off. Heading down Caledonian Road, I fall into the familiar and reassuring rhythms of a run. This is what I normally feel up on the paths by Purtle Springs and the Moon. About 25 minutes later, as I pass Euston Station at 8.55 a.m., I receive a shock. The whole street is jogging with me. About 20 adults are scuttling along Eversholt Street. Commuters late for work, perhaps? Then I realize that these are all fellow course attendees, frightened of the confrontation that will occur if they are late for The Forum. At the end of our breaks on the previous days I have noticed the unholy rush and crush to get in the lift, but this seems ridiculous. I speed past the others, then stop and wait at the entrance. I resolve to be late. When I enter the lift, an out-of-breath man tells me that his train was cancelled, but it is still his responsibility. 'Do you have a "clearing" for cancelling trains?' I ask.

We go into the anteroom. The doors to the auditorium are closed and policed by a number of Forum helpers, whom my Already Always Listening has renamed VFGs (Vacuous Forum Goons). I am met by a statuesque black woman called Marlon. Looking at my name tag, she says, 'Roland, are you present to being late?'

'Yes,' I say.

'Would you be late if you had a plane to catch?'

'No, Marlon, no,' I parrot.

'You gave your word to be on time.'

'Yes.'

'Are you present to the fact that breaking your word is serious?'

'Yes, Marlon,' I say, my Already Always Listening internal grin stretching from ear to ear. I am starting to enjoy this.

'Do you understand that all you are is your word?' Marlon asks. I try nodding, to see what happens. She is not happy with this. 'Do you understand that all you are is your word, Roland?' she repeats.

'Yes,' I concede.

'Are you willing to give your word that you will be early for the next four sessions?'

'Yes,' I say, as the door is opened to me and I am escorted like a naughty child to a seat near the front.

About halfway through the session, David asks for any breakthrough letters. We are reminded to raise fists (rather than hands) if we have not spoken during The Forum. I raise mine and am picked along with several others. I do my best at trying to look fragile and explain that my letter is difficult to read, it is to someone I don't know who has had a big influence, and I ask David if he can hear me out. 'Sure,' he says.

'Dear Dave,' I start, 'I'm on this course called The Forum. People have shown great courage and had amazing breakthroughs in their relationships. I want to honour that. I'm enrolled in the possibility of self-expression and honesty.' I look up at David and continue in faultless Forumspeak. 'To disagree with you is to be in the stands or in a racket. We either agree with you or face the possibility of dying in a coffin that says "Disagreed" as people bury us. You are disrupting thought patterns. You say that you're being unreasonable for our own good; I say that it is deliberately manipulative. You are not a coach with athletes, you're a potter with clay. You have a winning formula: taking The Forum for £40,000 each weekend. [He has said this earlier, but denies it at this point.] You seem more like a salesman than a facilitator, and the extent to which this is true will be proved by how much pressure you put on us to sign up for The Advanced Forum this afternoon.'

By this time I am quite enjoying the release of my words. I know I have to be forceful and honest, I have to talk straight. There is no room for smugness, however, and I do not feel smug (at least, not at the time – though I have revelled in it ever since). I continue: 'You tell people "reality". How dare you! It's not someone's fault that they're raped, they're only responsible for how they react to the event afterwards. It's not in the stars that they should be raped because they've got a "clearing" for it. You say that you made it up, but the implication is that The Forum is the way, the truth and the life. I'm not perfect, but I'm satisfied. The Forum has been one long list of attempts to undermine identity, which creates dependence. Forum junkies. People have to be open to that possibility.'

It is not vainglorious to say that about 200 jaws are on the ground when I finish. David, however, is cool as a cucumber and asks, 'Are you open to coaching?' I am, I say, as long as it does not mean I have to agree with him. He suggests that I have been in the stands. If that means I have been thinking, I reply, then I am certainly in the stands, but I came on the course with an open mind, not an empty one. He tells me that everything I have written is 'interpretation'. I suggest that this is just as true of him, except that I am not in a position to earn rather a lot of money out of it. He starts shouting at me, but, feeling rather cross myself, I stand my ground. David continues to shout, glaring down at me from the dais, trying to drown me out. I ask what he is afraid of. I point out that he has spoken for 40 hours: why is he unwilling for me to speak for five minutes? He invites me to leave the course. I decline and (slightly smugly) say, 'You can always trust a salesman,' and sit down.

People's reactions at the next break are interesting. Several people who have been harbouring misgivings of their own excitedly thank me for my contribution. Those who feel that they have benefited from the course are extremely hostile. One woman says that I have 'vomited' on her. Another uses a more scatological expression. A derivatives trader mutters the f-word in my direction. I have been transformed from nonentity into hero/villain in a matter of minutes. Perhaps more remarkable is how, within a couple of hours, the exchange seems like ancient history.

Later that afternoon we are told that people, because of their past, are 'meaning-making machines', but that actually 'life has no meaning'. The Forum, David says, leads to the knowledge that we are *nothing*. We have to create meanings, and The Advanced Forum ('a hundred times better than The Forum – it's the best we've got') will give us the tools to recreate ourselves and allow us to be 'open to the possibility of infinite human enlightenment'. It is hard sell, but 'pressure', we are assured, is only our interpretation. We are (for the nth time) encouraged to bring people along to an introductory evening and to be persistent in persuading them to attend.

By the end it is clear that most people feel The Forum has benefited them. Many seem euphoric, if exhausted. Some feel that they cannot accept it all, but that there were things that have helped them. A minority are angry with the manipulation and pressure. Several of these say they believe that if I had spoken out again, I would quite likely have been physically assaulted by other participants. Bearing in mind that people's dreams and 'new possibilities' have been so skilfully linked to The Forum, I would not have been surprised to see people become violent. Most people sign up for the advanced course.

When I leave, I am so disorientated and exhausted that I get lost twice on the tube and smoke my first cigarettes in years. Standing waiting for the midnight train, I buy a bottle of brandy and start drinking from the bottle. The only thing I feel clear about is that I am not about to add The Forum to my list of bad habits. I desperately try to phone people to explain what I have witnessed. When I speak, however, it is in the breathless, high-octane vocabulary of Forumspeak. (I feel hyperactive for days, and the language takes even longer to wear off.)

I am shaken by the power of the weekend. As I get on the midnight train out of London, I realize that well over 100 people did experience a transformation in three days. It was not simply a case of self-selection (i.e. of needy people joining The Forum): many were pressurized or badgered into joining by colleagues, friends or partners. The sense of euphoria that such an experience of accelerated community brings is remarkable. Perhaps this is partly why such groups thrive in cities. I was not convinced that any of the breakthroughs or transformations would last in the big bad world outside, but for me to say so in that environment felt like risking being lynched.

The relationship between David and the participants reminds me of Bishop Reid's dominance over his congregation. The Forum's use of shame or inadequacy also reminds me of Christianity. The exploitative relationship of chat-show hosts like Oprah or Jerry Springer with their audience also seems pertinent. People are encouraged to share or confess, and to experience euphoria and the sense of a clean slate once they have done so. Once shared, the isolation or alienation of being human is replaced by a sense of community. Also, to progress in the Landmark Community involves paying hundreds of pounds for further courses.

As the train nears home, I see reassuringly familiar places: woods, fields, street signs, my petrol-pump-collecting friend's house. After The Forum, his firework evenings seem like the most welcome social event of the year.

5

The Wood and the Trees

King Arthur has lost his crown. He has Excalibur, his glistening, four-foot, double-edged broadsword; he has his ceremonial dagger, white robes, green velvet cloak and his white
canvas trainers, but he cannot quite put his hand on his
crown. 'It could be that the Hampshire constabulary nicked it
after the arrest, or it could be the other lot, but they claim not
to have it,' he says. He is making do with a headband of
wooden beads which looks regal enough to me, above his
piercing grey eyes, long grey hair and beard. I had been
looking out for King Arthur in Tepee Valley, but I never
expected such a regal presence to be gulping down cider
in Rajah's Snooker Hall in Cardiff. He is the leader of a
radical druidic order and together with Steve Andrews, his
principal bard (who tells of seeing UFOs and uses a toy spaceship as part of his folk routine), is explaining his beliefs and
practices.

'How many coppers does it take to arrest King Arthur?' King
Arthur asks rhetorically. 'Shitloads,' he replies, opening his
Arthurian Filofax and showing me a picture of him surrounded
by about 30 police and security staff at Newbury Bypass. On
the next page he is up a tree in full regalia, surrounded by more
hapless, hard-hatted security staff. 'That's Arthur's Wood at
Manchester Airport. I turn up, I rally the troops and I get arrested,' he explains. He goes on to tell me about his column in
the *Esher News* and various television appearances. We discuss
his website (www.dragons4.demon.co.uk) which, ironically, is

where I first came across the leader of this most ancient of Britain's religions.

Later in the evening, Arthur is to officiate at a ritual to bring druids and Christians together and I am told that, later still, after some music, there will probably be a knighting ceremony. They are expecting about 100 people to turn up at Rajah's, which is a venue for bands and snooker as well as impromptu investitures. Arthur Pendragon, to give him his full name, was born John Timothy Rothwell, but changed that in 1987 to found a druidic order. 'I'd been in the army for six years, even worked as foreman on road-building projects, but I dropped the mortgage, the whole lot, after I met druids on Glastonbury Tor,' he says. Arthur changed his name (Pendragon means 'battle chieftain', he explains) and shortly afterwards founded his order of druids, the Loyal Arthurian Warband (LAW). The order fight for 'truth, honour and justice' and their principal aim is to save this particular part of the planet. 'We're going against capitalism, against development on our green and pleasant land. Think globally, act locally,' King Arthur says. 'No more Roman roads' is one of his mottoes. Although Arthur once stood for election as Farnborough's MP, he has no faith in party politics now.

'The Loyal Arthurian Warband is the warrior arm of the druid movement. We're the political front; we're all very spiritual, but we're mystics who kick ass!' Arthur explains. There are scores of druidic orders and Arthur is clear that his group is not representative. He is concerned that I should also talk to other orders, and is worried about getting druids a bad name. Other druids do pretty ceremonies but are not so good at fighting for the planet, he says. Arthur has three types of knights: shield knights, who believe that they are the original Arthurian knights reincarnated; quest knights, who are shield knights who do not yet know who they are; and brother knights, who are entering the battle against the forces of Mawdor (the bad guys) for the first time in this life. He claims that there are three periods of knights: pre-Roman, post-Roman and post-Thatcher. I ask if he thinks he is King Arthur reincarnated and he stares at me levelly, then, in his gravelly, slight south London accent, says, 'I *know* that I am.' He adds, 'I don't take myself too seriously, but I *believe* in all this shit.' Arthur also has bards (singers and artists), wizards and faerie queens (wise women who lead three groups of LAW druids). In total, he says, LAW has hundreds of members who put him up as he wanders between protest site and ritual site through-out England and Wales.

After 39 arrests, numerous nights in police cells and many court cases, Arthur's commitment is undimmed. He has served time in prison for refusing to abide by an exclusion order which banned him from being within five miles of any protest site. Some druids criticize him for getting into trouble with the law. 'I reckon that the best place to fight for justice is *in* a court of law – what better place is there?' he says. In one case in the High Court, Arthur resorted to unusual tactics to attract publicity. 'They wanted to take Excalibur off me. I refused, saying that it was ceremonial, but they wouldn't have it. So I took everything off: I went into the High Court stark naked.' On another occasion he announced to the judge, in kingly manner, 'You can't have me, I am the Law.' Then he explained that LAW was the acronym for his druidic order.

As Rajah's Snooker Club fills up with musicians and hip-pies, people cross the room to greet Arthur and buy him drinks – like those 'pretenders', the Windsors, he eschews cash. I notice one woman in a black velvet gown with white nylon wings stapled onto her back. A faerie queen, I suspect. Before Arthur can start his ritual to bring druids and Christians together, he needs a token Christian. Reverend Lionel Fanthorpe, presenter of *Fortean TV* and balding, leather-clad, Harley-riding Church of Wales minister, is late. By the time he arrives, King Arthur is looking a little worse for wear. His cheeks are puffing up floridly, he is swaying slightly and looks more like a drunken Father Christmas than a druidic, eco-warrior chieftain. 'I expect the original Arthur was like that,' someone says. Arthur greets Reverend

Fanthorpe ('Hail, Sir!') and orders people into a circle. We hold hands and he declaims the druidic oath:

> *We swear by peace and love to stand,*
> *Heart to heart and hand in hand.*
> *Mark, O spirit, and hear us now,*
> *Confirming this our sacred vow.*

Then he leads the circle around and we raise our hands and cheer. It is a pretty underwhelming ritual.

After a few songs, about 30 people gather in a circle for the knighting ceremony. Arthur stands in the centre, swaying, chest puffed out, head held high, arms outstretched, Excalibur resting on the palms of his hands. It is about 1 a.m. and Arthur's courtiers seem somewhat blasé about what is to take place. Amidst the riotous laughter, the distant sound of a juke-box, the whorls of cigarette smoke, I notice someone falling off a chair. A small, elderly Asian man in a buttoned-up anorak, with a deadpan expression and a disconsolate-looking cigarette, wanders across the circle collecting glasses. The faerie queen shushes people and the sovereign says, 'Who would like to be knighted?' A leather-jacketed, baggy-jeaned, dark-skinned man approaches him and kneels. Arthur places Excalibur on each shoulder, then on his head, speaking as he does so.

It is hard to hear Arthur's exact words, but it is something about upholding the ancient virtues of truth, honour and justice. The man rises, they hug, and everyone cheers. Then the ceremony begins again with another person. This time it sounds as if Arthur is talking gibberish, but then I realize he is speaking in Welsh. I am surprised to see nearly a dozen people knighted, having imagined that it was an honour reserved for serious druids or environmental campaigners. Some subjects take knighting less seriously than others. One man shouts to his friends, 'I'll be Sir B****cks!' before being knighted. He is almost, but not quite, laughing in the King's face. It is hard to tell whether Arthur notices.

The evening ends and I notice the good King with a shockingly young Guinevere or Morgan le Fay draped around his neck. 'The King's a tart; it's good to be the King!' he admits. He staggers over to me, grinning, and tells me that they are meeting tomorrow to share some rituals. 'I want her, on a bosom level, you understand,' he says. I get the concept, I tell him. 'I'll teach her some rituals … she wants to feel my bits,' he mumbles.

Rajah wanders over and sticks a fiver in Arthur's hand. 'Thanks, it was a good feeling, no trouble, very nice,' he says. The King and Steve, his principal bard, and I wander out into a squally, soaking night and within moments it becomes clear that Arthur is about to start walking into walls. *Shouldn't there be courtiers and minions to cover up for these regal indiscretions and lapses?* I think. All I see are the wet streets of Cardiff at 2 a.m. on a Saturday night.

I am fast regretting their generous offer of accommodation. Steve lives several miles away and taxis seem strangely reluctant to stop. Arthur decides to take things into his own hands. He strides into the middle of the road, holds Excalibur above his head and shouts, 'Halt!' Taxis swerve in all directions but ours. His next kingly line is priceless: 'It's you, Roland, you look too square for the taxis to stop.'

We wander on, trying to keep Arthur out of the road, when a bit of what Arthur later tells me is druidic magic occurs. A 40-something hippy walks past us, heading up to his house. He sees Arthur weaving across the pavement and takes pity. 'That boy needs a black coffee. Come in,' he says to three complete strangers – one of whom is King Arthur, another a dreadlocked bard with a toy spaceship wrapped around his neck, and the third resolutely but unnervingly square. Magical.

We warm up beside a gas fire in the hippy's Victorian townhouse and he tells us that the house is about to be repossessed. 'I was born here, it's always been in the family and before us, Ivor Novello used to live here,' he says with real sadness, slurping down the old opened tins of Special Brew which litter the floor. Gradually it dawns on him that one of the men in his front room is King Arthur. *'That's Excalibur and you think you're King Arthur!'* he says, eyes popping out of his head.

'I *am* King Arthur,' King Arthur says. Our host shakes his long black locks as if unsure whether he is having a flashback. Suddenly he leaps up and screams at his King Charles spaniel. 'Stop scratching!' he screeches. Then he looks at us shame-facedly and adds by way of explanation, 'People think that he's got fleas, then they think that I've got fleas.'

After nearly an hour, King Arthur has sobered up and we are due to set off for a four-mile walk in the pouring rain. Knowing that I have to catch the train from just around the corner, our host invites me to stay the night. It is a difficult de-cision: our host does not appear to be particularly stable, but it is raining hard and King Arthur seems increasingly wary of me. 'I've got a nice spare room,' he adds, and I opt to stay.

He makes more coffee and tells me his sad story again, explaining how upset he is to lose the house that he was born in, now that his parents are dead. He mentions Ivor Novello several times and intermittently screams insanely at his dog. It is after 3 a.m. when he shows me to 'the nice spare room'. It is full of dirty clothes, empty cans, old boxes and broken bicycles. He pulls the blanket back from the bed, and there in the centre of the sheet is a huge pile of dog dirt. 'Stupid dog, had diarrhoea,' he says, screwing up the sheet and throwing it into the corner. 'Make yourself at home,' he adds, closing the door. Before turning the light out, I notice an unused prescription in my host's name for tamazepam. I cannot pretend that I slept well.

The next morning, speeding out of Wales in the reassuring normality of an Intercity 125 with a scalding cup of black tea, I ponder the night's events. The hippy's sadness at losing his house seems pertinent to Arthur's search for his identity in mythology. The rootedness that so many seek seems a factor in Arthur's faith. It is clear that, like many kings before him, Arthur is larger than life. Like some modern royals, however, he seems, if not a media junkie, then at least a dogged self-publicist. Perhaps, unlike some other royals, he does 'walk his talk' – straight onto the battlefield. I resolve to visit other druids. It is what Arthur wanted me to do, and it only seems fair to them and him.

Above the urinal in the café toilets at Avebury are some interesting pieces of graffiti. 'Druids R Cr*p' reads one rather blunt assertion in black Biro. Beside it, a cleverer and more inflammatory 'Burn Again Christians' is penknifed in neat letters into the white gloss paint. They are close enough for it to be clear that one is intended to relate to the other, but it is impossible to tell which came first. The ambiguity over the origins of this exchange of insults, reminiscent of the sort of thing that takes place between Spurs and Arsenal fans, seems appropriate. The origins of druidism are indeed ambiguous, since much of what is left of the evidence was written by their enemies, the Christians and the Romans. We know that druids were pre-Christian Celts who revered nature, and possibly trees in particular. They probably wrote in ogham, an alphabetical system of cuts made on a baseline, also used for divination. Much of the rest of what we know, however, came from their enemies. Imagine an Arsenal fan writing an account of Tottenham Hotspur's footballing skills, and you have the picture.

Outside the café, scores of striking-looking people are mooching around waiting for something to happen. The presence of several men dressed in long white robes tells me that this is going to be another 'square-free zone'. The outfit of choice for the women is a long velvet cloak over a flowing black dress. Some women have rosehips and wild flowers strewn gracefully through their long hair. Others wear brooches of wheat and rowanberry. The men have a penchant for leather accessories (pouches, straps, belts), rough iron buckles, feathers in hats and wooden staves or didgeridoos. Many have intricate, flowing Celtic prints or ethnic batik designs on their T-shirts. Apart from white robes and the odd lurid cagoule, the predominant colours are purple, black, brown, dark blood red and deep green. Rough cottons, velvet and cheesecloth proliferate. They look like a group of extras from *Robin Hood: Prince of Thieves* or *Braveheart*. In fact, they are druids come to celebrate the autumn equinox.

The tiny village of Avebury is set in the heart of a stone circle and earthworks development from the late Neolithic period (between 3000 and 2200 BC). Black clouds, punctuated by glimpses of blue, roll over this archaeologically remarkable area set in the Wiltshire Downs. Silbury Hill, ancient Europe's largest man-made mound, is at one end of the village. Ancient burial mounds or barrows protrude over the open downland slopes. West Kennet Avenue, an eerie line of dozens of standing stones, leads into Avebury itself. There are mysterious earth formations, gullies, ditches and knolls in every direction.

Soon after noon, a man called Phillip, also known as Greywolf, stands on a bench outside the café. Dressed in white robes, he is tall, in his late thirties, with a handsome, friendly face. I expected the chief druid to be a barrel-chested, hairy 'man's man', but Phillip, thin, with neatly cropped hair, the co-leader of the British Druid Order with Emma (also known as Bobcat), is surprisingly flamboyant in his offices. He asks for volunteers to 'hold the quarters' (i.e. to welcome the gods from the points of the compass) in the style of an auctioneer. 'Do I see an east?' he shouts with a twinkle in his eye. Next he asks for volunteers to re-enact the ancient myth of Cerydwyn. 'Nice one, dudes,' he says, mimicking Bart Simpson, as a couple volunteer.

Then, in the role of God, he leads half the group onto the outer earthwork round the circumference of the stone circle. Meanwhile, the graceful Bobcat in her green velvet cloak acts as the Goddess, and walks with the others through the village to a large stone, where the groups come together. I follow Greywolf and about 100 other druids round the slippery outer bank, trying to avoid the attention of a film crew who are scuttling around with that familiar mixture of self-importance and nervousness.

I ask a woman decorated with feathers, berries and flowers what her long, furry grey gown is made of. 'Wolf,' she replies.

'*Real* wolf?' I ask, looking at the coarse, matted material that would not be out of place on a Honeymonster puppet.

'No, no, I wouldn't wear that. This is fake fur, designed to resemble animal fur.'

She explains that today's meeting is a *Gorsedd*, or gathering of bards, and that several druid orders are present. Local druid groups are called 'groves', she tells me. The British Druid Order (with about 3,000 initiates) which convened today's ceremony is the least formal group, with the strongest pagan emphasis. There is no formal hierarchy within the organization, and one can join after initiation into the *Awen*, 'the flowing spirit' or muse. The Ancient Order of Druids is the oldest group, founded in 1781. The more recent Order of Bards, Ovates and Druids is the largest group (founded in 1964, with 6,000 members). There are different levels within this order, although all are of equal importance: bards are people interested in expressing their creativity in various forms; ovates are people interested in healing; druids are those with a more intellectual and philosophical bent. Local meetings of druids often include members of different orders.

We descend from the outer bank of the earthwork down to a large standing stone inside the circle. A woman in a flowing skirt and waxed Barbour coat sits in a cleft in the rock, beaming out at the crowd of druids who surround her. She represents the Guardian Spirit of Avebury Stone Circle and was included in the ritual after Greywolf discovered archaeological records of an ancient burial site in the ditch close by, containing a woman in the foetal position. On the grass in front of her, a smoking 'smudge stick' of sage keeps the bad spirits away. Greywolf kneels before her, gently beating a drum called a bodhrán and smiling up at her.

He turns to the assembly and says, 'So does the wheel of the year turn, so we return to be returned. We make *Gorsedd* on this holy ground of our ancestors. So we gather to celebrate our harvest. The harvest is gathered, so now we gather to make our offerings for future harvests to come and for our children and our children's children.'

The woman responds, 'In the name of the Mother of all Living, the Guardian Spirit of Avebury, and the ancestors of our people, I accept the gifts that you offer.'

Greywolf kisses the woman three times and then he invites the assembly to give their gifts to her. A beery-looking man approaches, kneels, then gives her a cowslip that he has just picked. He stands, she kisses him and he retreats. Next comes a bottle of organic mead, then bags of apples, a handful of nuts and several bunches of flowers, until the Guardian is laden with goods. As I hide pathetically beneath my dark green felt hood (at least I made an effort!), I hear a teenage boy somewhere behind us sneering with delight: 'Look at them!'

The Guardian then invites us into her sacred space, her circle. Greywolf and Bobcat, the priest and priestess, help her to carry the produce through a 'gateway' made between two wooden staves held in the air.

We form a large circle around a ringstone, a low stone that formerly had a hole through the middle for the exchange of rings. Chris and Christina walk to either side of the stone for a handfasting, a traditional druid wedding. Christina, dressed in a green and black ankle-length dress, wears a crown of berries and wild flowers. Chris, despite his green Celtic-print T-shirt, has the look of a civil servant on his day off. They are both beaming as they hold hands.

Bobcat says, 'At sacred times and places such as this, our ancestors clasped hands when they would wed, and such handfastings were lawful, true and binding, for as long as love should last.' I cannot help but admire the cod olde worlde English – but it is well intentioned and has a certain ham-fisted grace.

The druidic liturgy is dimly reminiscent of the King James Bible and echoes the traditional vows one might expect in a Church of England ceremony. Bobcat says, 'As the sun and moon bring light to the Earth, do you, Chris and Christina, vow to bring the light of love and joy to your union?'

'I do,' they each reply.

'And do you vow to honour each other as you honour that which you hold most sacred?' Bobcat continues.

The final vow seems to owe much more to the modern age than to ancient concepts of betrothal: 'And do you vow to maintain these vows in freedom, for as long as love shall last?' The couple kiss. The priest and priestess invoke the blessing of the assembly, the gods and their ancestors, and the assembly cheers: 'So let it be!'

The group now walk across to a small stone and concrete bollard 'circle' (the bollards mark the position of stones long since removed) within the stone circle that surrounds the village. I find myself next to a striking, black-cloaked woman in her twenties. She is a witch and a druid, but druidism has brought out the creativity in her, she says. When she invited the *Awen* in, she grew in confidence as a public speaker. Despite the long black hair and cloak, anyone less witchlike is hard to imagine. She belongs in a Scottish Amicable advert, not a coven. *If all witches were so visually distracting*, I muse, *public perceptions might be different. I might even join.*

Bobcat asks for the guardians to invite the gods from the four compass points to bless us and bring peace. My wiccan neighbour turns in a fluster towards a small church 50 yards away in a northerly direction, flashes her wild, beautiful eyes to the clouds and declaims, 'Oh gods of the north, the spirits of the earth, of the womb of creation, spirits of the night and the snows of winter, deep roots and ancient stones. May we know the power of your blessings. So I bid you hail and welcome.' I wonder whether the 300-year-old church beneath her gaze was placed in the centre of a sacred site as an act of domination. Many churches on mounds are on top of ancient pagan sites – often a Christian way of rubbing pre-Christians' noses in it. The suspicion between pagans and Christians is ancient but still present, as the Avebury urinals testify.

Greywolf now invites children to come and be blessed and a dozen children, aged between six months and about 12 years, join Bobcat in the centre of the circle. They are to be baptized, but the ceremony is remarkably informal. She smiles, whispers and laughs with the children, taking her time with individuals. While this is happening, Greywolf asks for any bardic contributions from the circle. A young man dressed in a green denim tunic, headscarf and jeans volunteers to sing a song that he has written. I wince as he leans on a sturdy staff and starts to sing, but he has a strong, sonorous voice and performs well. Next comes some very, very bad poetry about the harvest moon (it rhymes with 'rune') and the sea (rhyming gloriously with 'we'), followed by some story-telling. A professor of ancient history called Ronald Hutton, in black cloak and leather accoutrements, tells an ancient story of a pompous Buddha who is made to look ridiculous.

Greywolf tells the story of Taliesin, in which Ceredyn, a pagan goddess, chases Gwion, a boy who accidentally stole her magical potion. Gwion shapeshifts from one animal to another in order to escape. Greywolf invites people from the circle to take various parts and delivers the tale in a self-mocking, slapstick manner. Couples act out the chase scenes involving wrens and sparrowhawks, salmon and otters, and various other parts of the food chain. It is a little like an improvised pantomime, but Greywolf has the confidence and panache to pull it off.

Bobcat completes her baptism and I realize that the druidic tug of war with Christianity takes place in their liturgy too:

I baptize thee with fire
So that thy spirit may be purified
And thy days long and bountiful.
I baptize thee with the waters
Of life, the waters that no living
Thing can do without.

Then Greywolf invites forward any adults who want to be initiated into the community of bards and receive the *Awen*, the 'flowing spirit of inspiration'. About 20 initiates form a circle within the circle, looking out at the rest of us. Bobcat walks round them, saying, 'Let us now invoke the *Awen*, the holy flowing spirit of the bardic tradition, and direct its shining stream of inspiration towards those gathered in the midst of the circle, that they may receive its glowing gifts of clear sight, wisdom and strength of spirit.' Once Bobcat finishes, the outer circle chant '*Awen, Awen, Awen*' and recite a blessing to complete the initiation.

The final part of the ceremony is the *Eisteddfod*, a kind of druidic singsong-cum-celebration involving more story-telling, amateur traumatics, bad poetry and the blowing of didgeridoos. This is accompanied by the sharing of bread and mead (a honey wine, passed round in a cow horn) and is followed by the closing of the circle, when the guardians of the circle bid farewell to the respective gods (of earth, air, fire and water). There are prayers for peace in East Timor, Chechnya and other troublespots. Then Greywolf says, 'The *Gorsedd* ends in peace as in peace it began. May the spirit of Avebury, the light of the Sun and the love of our Goddess go with us all as we depart this place, to nourish, strengthen and sustain us until we meet again. So let it be!' The circle cheers, 'So let it be!', a conch is blown and the ceremony is complete.

Later, back at the vegetarian café, I speak to Greywolf and his friends. Like witchcraft, he explains, the druids' spirituality is earth-based. Witchcraft is probably bigger and focuses on the power of magic; druidism concentrates on the celebration of festivals rather than on magic. There are approximately 30 druid orders in Britain and it appeals to him because it is an indigenous, earth-centred spirituality.

Mark Graham, dressed in white robes and deerskin, is the British Druid Order's 'interfaith' representative. He points out that, although there are many druidic gods, the religion is primarily matriarchal. In AD 61, he explains, the Romans forced the druids back to Anglesey before destroying them and their sacred site Venemeton – an ancient grove now on the border between Nottinghamshire and Leicestershire. Mark explains about ogham and the use of these runic symbols as part of the druids' system of divination. He has devised a system him-self, using few (slivers of wood) marked with oghams made from the 20 different trees in the ogham alphabet. Mark's divination is based on his study of ogham and his knowledge of the qualities of the trees (his day job is running nature reserves in Leicestershire). He invites me to visit Venemeton, which is close to one of his reserves.

Apart from ogham, druids did not have a written tradition, he says, and Christians and others subsequently misrepresented them. I mention the toilet graffiti. Mark comments, 'We see the earth as our mother; Christians see it as their possession. They are fundamentally different approaches.' Probably for the first time in 2,000 years, he explains, some Christians and pagans are meeting annually to look at what they have in common.

How much is really based in history, though? Greywolf explains that there are three sources for the knowledge behind the sort of ceremony that he led earlier: the classical Greek and Roman writers, who recorded some druidic rituals, the oral tradition of indigenous legends which were eventually writ-ten down, and archaeological remains. Surely after 2,000 years this is all guesswork? I say. The standing stones probably were not used by druids – they predate them by hundreds, if not thousands, of years. Greywolf and Mark agree, but explain that they are piecing together shards of evidence and putting them into a ritual. 'It is guesswork, but *inspired* guesswork,' Greywolf says. *Inspired by what?* I wonder.

Greywolf tells me that he realized he wanted to become a druid after reading Robert Graves's book *The White Goddess*. He joined a witches' coven and, over time, they all started experimenting with druidism. As a teenager, Greywolf (still known as Phillip at that time) overdosed on Eastern religions and hallucinogenics. Druidism helped him regain control and stability. He spent years researching it, but it is more to him than a set of eco-friendly symbols and ethics. He believes that he has been touched by the supernatural in his druidism. 'It could be coincidence, but I see it as meaningful coincidence, events that have drawn me to *Awen* deliberately,' he says.

Five years ago, he learned the druidic art of shapeshifting. In a sweat lodge he had a vision of a grey wolf. Nine days later, he came across a grey wolfskin at a house sale. 'Later, at a pagan venison feast, with my wolfskin on my back, I felt it rippling with warm energy as the deer meat was put in front of me,' he says, a little sheepishly. Now he feels that he has a 'special relationship' with the spirit of the wolf. Sometimes he becomes the wolf in the forests and valleys of the spirit world. At other times, he feels that the wolf inhabits him in this world. 'Druids believe that everything has spirit, and I meet spirits and fairies in other worlds. I can control it – because it can be awkward at Tesco's,' he says. I nod politely.

Ronald Hutton, Professor of History at Bristol University, is a different sort of druid. We know practically nothing of the original druids and their rituals, according to Hutton. 'All we can say is that druids were an important class of spiritual specialists in the tribes of northwest Europe, probably healers, judges and spiritual leaders. Contemporary druids are modern people; current druidery has little to do with pre-modern culture.' It has more to do with postmodern culture, he adds, a culture in which people reject hierarchy and the pursuit of absolute truth. One of the ways in which postmodern culture is understood is as a 'white noise' of conflicting media signals and images.

It strikes me that the symbols, dress and liturgy of these druids has as much to do with Hollywood depictions of Robin Hood and other 'ancient' Britons as with genuine history. Ironically, our notions of 'ancient people' – for instance as stout, honest, trustworthy folk, living contented, simple lives in harmony with nature – are generated by powerful media conglomerates of which these neo-stout, honest, trustworthy folk would be deeply suspicious. Probably all of us create meanings through filters influenced by the media that manufacture myths and meanings, but perhaps it is because druids focus on a particular period that makes this so apparent.

'Druidery is redreamed with each generation and reflects the preoccupations of the day,' Hutton says. Apparently, the first druidic revival in 1781 reflected the structures and rituals of Freemasonry. More recently, druidism was a philosophical outlook which accommodated other major religions. Those druids saw themselves as producing a set of attitudes to the world which emphasized a single benevolent God, a belief in reincarnation and an emphasis on the relationship between people and the land. 'It's only since 1986 that pagan druids have existed,' he says. Does this mean that druids of different ages simply reinvent the religion in their own image? Hutton believes that this is largely true, but notes an interesting recent development. 'Ten years ago, druids would care a great deal about the authenticity of their rituals. What is more important to them now is that it has authenticity for them in relation to their values.' Hutton acknowledges this 'shapeshift' in emphasis as evidence of a move from truth-orientated modern culture to a more subjective, tentative and ironic postmodern outlook. Greywolf's self-mocking, pantomime manner, and his ready admission that druids have a tendency to create rituals which reflect their preoccupations, bears this out.

Professor Hutton also recognizes that druidism brings people closer to the land. 'It allows people in a high-tech, consumer society to be reunited with the land,' he says. The creative aspect of druidism also has appeal to such a society. 'Druids are generally active in their creativity rather than passive; it feeds the imagination,' he adds.

Hutton is a member of several druidic orders. Does he believe in *Awen* and the pagan gods? 'I'm interested in druids, I enjoy the rituals, but I'm not convinced of the supernatural aspects.' Do they not object to his unbelief? 'No, druids are very liberal-minded. It allows people to believe and disbelieve.' Somehow I cannot imagine such a welcoming, open-minded approach from Peniel's Christians. Could they tolerate an articulate, agnostic member who suggests that their rituals are an act of fantasy? I imagine them locking the professor in a room until he signs away his unbelief with his own blood and starts singing from the same hymn sheet.

Weeks later, while I am visiting Leicester for a newspaper story, a truly remarkable thing occurs. Greywolf would call it a meaningful coincidence; Bishop Reid or T.L. Osborne would probably call it a miracle. Leicester is a city of millions, covering about 30 square miles. Before I set off to see some parents fighting the closure of a school in the centre of a council estate, I phone Mark Graham to see if he can take me to see the site of Venemeton. He says he is too busy at the moment, because he is covering for a colleague running an environmental project on an estate in Leicester. I ask which estate, hoping that I can at least drop by. It is the same estate as the one I am heading for. I tell him that I am visiting an action group based in a half-closed school. For this week only, Mark is based in the classroom next door in the same school.

We meet, and he directs me out along the Fosse Way to Willoughby, a little village on the border between Leicestershire and Nottinghamshire. Venemeton is the Latin for 'sacred space', he explains as we drive past rolling fields, bisected by ragged hawthorn hedges. I park the car and we walk down a grassy lane between tired-looking hedges, ready to drop their leaves. Mark explains that, for him, the razing of Venemeton 2,000 years ago is symbolic of the separation between God and nature. Since then, God has been separated from nature and now, with the rebirth of paganism, the two are coming back together. His grove of druids have occasional rituals at the site, but most druids get more excited by stone circles (which, as I had already observed, predate druidism by at least 1,000 years). He prefers woods, he says, because the word 'druid' means 'knower of trees'.

We reach a stream at the bottom of the shallow valley. There is a tiny cluster of trees: hawthorn, ash, willow, aspen, poplar, oak and horse chestnut. 'Some say that the soil is so dark because it contains the ashes of the ancient grove that the Romans destroyed,' he says. He points out the Fosse Way on the brow of the hill. Lorries and cars thunder along it, belching out fumes as they pass. *No more Roman roads*, I think. Sheep graze in meadows, other fields are ploughed, there is the ghost of furrowed earthworkings in one field. The grey clouds hang over us and, though it is not unpleasant, the scene is resolutely nondescript.

As I look over the empty fields of Venemeton, this seems appropriate. If you wish, the dark soil can be the stain of the Roman legions uprooting God from nature. It could also just be dark brown soil. Historically, druidism is like an empty field. It is a vacuum filled by the radical commitment of King Arthur, by Greywolf's shapeshifting, by Professor Hutton's enjoyment of the bardic tradition and by Mark's gentle, nature-loving thoughts. It is clear that modern druids cannot see the ancient wood for the contemporary trees. But so what? In words reminiscent of an Anglican prayer book, their liturgy says, 'We gather here in peace.' In words reminiscent of Lennon and McCartney, they add, 'So let it be.' So let it be.

6

🛒

God in a Dinner Jacket

I am sitting in the Grand Ballroom of New York's Waldorf Astoria with a sugar-cane shrimp in my mouth, waiting for the Son of God to speak. I am, in fact, listening to a medley of Rodgers and Hammerstein and Lloyd Webber songs and beginning to feel slightly short-changed. The blandly handsome, dinner-jacketed singer struts past the stage piano and croons sentimentally to his oversequinned partner. She flutters her eyelashes and gushes on in a high soprano. I have been told (warned, even) that the man whose words I am waiting for could change my life. All I am experiencing so far, however, is tinkling ivories, sugary melodies and ham-fisted mock flirtation.

About 1,000 people from all around the world lean back in their chairs, politely chatting as they wait for the entrée, but really waiting for the Son of God to speak. Unfortunately, he has not arrived yet. Taffeta is crumpled, cummerbunds are adjusted, pearls dangle, fine glasses clink underneath the ornate gold-leaf cornices and the giant candelabras. The beef tournados, artichokes, shallots and potato ragout arrive and, fighting off guilty thoughts about such food being wasted on me, I tuck in. I think I could get used to these pre-messianic pauses. But there is no substitute for the Son of God, I tell myself. There is no sign of the Son of God, either.

At some point between the hazelnut pyramid cake with liquid chocolate centre doused in pineapple sauce and the *compotiers* (syrupy fruit sweets), he arrives. He climbs on the stage, tall, balding, slightly plump, but immaculately turned out in patent leather shoes and a dinner jacket and looking decidedly sprightly for a man in his late seventies. Immediately the audience is on its feet, ecstatically clapping his (late) arrival. The great and the good are queuing up to tell him how great and good he is. A UN Secretary General of the General Assembly congratulates him for supporting the family as a way of promoting world peace. A former President of Egypt rushes up to shake his hand. An academic gives him a sun-shaped mirror for some inscrutable reason. The Son of God himself says very little.

He grins a lot and waves his arms at his adoring fans. Yet the few words that he does say are something of a shock to the system. The Son of God speaks Korean! Could he not have arranged a more subject-friendly language in which to save us? Then again, this particular Son of God is indeed Korean. Although it seems bizarre, the Son of God receiving the ovations and obsequies at the Waldorf Astoria has 4 million followers and is arguably South Korea's least popular export: Reverend Sun Myung Moon. Indeed, it is due to his reputation for splitting families and brainwashing followers that I have to travel to New York to see Reverend Moon. He was banned from visiting Britain by the Home Secretary at the time, Michael Howard, despite a High Court judge's ruling that the ban was unlawful. I am at a conference convened by the Unification Church (popularly known as the Moonies) to promote the family. Reverend Moon mutters on and I breathe a sigh of relief. Phew! The Son of God (also confusingly known as Father, or True Parent) also speaks pidgin English.

Four Korean women of a certain age mount the stage to receive wedding presents. According to Reverend Moon, they are the brides of Buddha, Mohammed, Confucius and Socrates. They were married (along with 120 million others) earlier in the day at a ceremony at which he officiated, and now he gives them a congratulatory banquet and a gold watch to honour their weddings and presumably to count the minutes, hours, days and years until consummation. The idea is that, once they die, they go to the spirit world where they find their illustrious spouses, consummate their union and so achieve perfection.

As I chew on my fruit *compotier*, it strikes me that there may be one or two anomalies which the Son of God/ Reverend Moon appears to have overlooked. Firstly, Buddha was already married, so if Reverend Moon is right, there will be some sort of celestial tug of war once his Korean bride ascends. It is, however, the wife of Socrates I am most concerned about. Presumably Reverend Moon knows that Socrates was almost certainly a homosexual and quite possibly a paedophile. I have visions of his tiny, sweet old bride chasing him up and down the Heavenly City, desperately seeking consummation. Perhaps Reverend Moon's omniscience was having an off-day.

When you have married over 100 million people in one morning, however, it is probably unreasonable to expect perfection. The so-called 'mass wedding' did not reveal much about why Reverend Moon was revered – he barely spoke – but it certainly re-emphasized the fact that he *was* revered. He filled Madison Square Garden Basketball Stadium with 30,000 people, many of whom were getting married to someone they may or may not have met, *because he said so*. He matched their photographs and personal details 'spiritually' and, by and large, that was that.

It was an extraordinary sight. Thousands of couples stood expectantly in the centre of the Madison Square Garden stadium in immaculate Western wedding clothes. The men were bow-tied in black tail coats and the women wore the sort of white taffeta and lace gowns and veils that normally appear in Pronuptia catalogues. Many, but not all, appeared to be Korean. They glowed brightly under the ultraviolet lights. There was a 2,000-strong inter-church gospel choir warming up on one side, while thousands of well-wishers arrived through scores of entrances. The ceremony was linked via satellite with other places around the world. Millions and millions, we were told, were taking part in the blessing.

The event started with a Mr Larry Moffatt who came on to work the crowd with a bit of warm-up theology. We learned that 'God's plan is to save the world through the family.' Moffatt explained, 'Jesus Christ was sent to marry and to start a new lineage, but people killed Him, so God used this "Plan B" as a way of saving us.' Plan B, I gathered, is Reverend Moon marrying and blessing us so that we can enter a 'pre-fallen state'.

Members of different religious groups then came forward to pledge their support to the family, or to receive awards for their work in the service of the family. There were some rather quaint, jangly rituals with traditionally dressed Hindus, Buddhists and a Russian Orthodox minister. A rather sharply dressed minister from Louis Farrakan's Nation of Islam was followed by the Jewish cultural critic Michael Medved (on video) and by Wyatt C. White, the late Martin Luther King's chief of staff. A Pentecostal minister struggled to give up the microphone. He felt compelled to tell us that he did not like divorce and abortion (who does?) and that we should smack our children with the 'rod of correction'. He thought gays and lesbians were getting a mite uppity and proclaimed, 'The answer to all the world's problems is family values.' *Yeah, yeah*, I thought. My ears pricked up at one point when a minister said, 'The marriages are consummated before witnesses.' Looking around at the demure china dolls standing dutifully next to their upright, serious-looking grooms, I surmised (correctly) that he was mistaken!

These contributions were interspersed with full-throated songs from the gospel choir. After a solemn rendition of 'The Star Spangled Banner', things started to warm up. The air was strangely full of breathless, strangled exhortations of the 'Thank you Jesus!', 'Praise the Lord!' and 'Only Jesus!' variety. Then the lights dimmed and hundreds of men robed in white and women robed in scarlet streamed in, holding candles. The brides and grooms stood still like eerie mannequins. The robed figures surrounded the auditorium and stage and ascended the steps that led from the stage up to 'the gate of heaven', encircled by oriental-looking, golden dragons. A hush fell on the crowd and the True Parents entered, dressed in white robes and tall golden crowns. Gracefully, imperiously, slowly, they descended and sat on their thrones in the centre of the stage.

Reverend Moon sprinkled some of the couples with holy water, and the couples said their vows and exchanged rings. Hundreds of the brides exchanged vows with photographs, because their husbands were apparently unable to get US visas. In scores of Unification Centres around the world, their partners were simultaneously saying their own vows. It was hard to hear Reverend Moon's words, and at one stage I thought I heard him bless Hitler and Richard Nixon, although that can't have been right. He blessed the marriages of the thousands of couples before him and, via satellite, the millions around the globe. I was surprised to see a group of venerable old ladies come forward as brides seeking Moon's special blessing. They seemed a bit old to embark on such an adventure. Then I realized that their husbands were even older – they were dead; long dead; the youngest was 1,500 years old. (These were the brides who were so appropriately to receive golden timepieces later in the day.)

A series of dignitaries marched onstage to pay homage to the good Reverend. I was staggered to see Kenneth Kaunda, Zambia's former President, emerge from the wings. This world statesman (you know, the one with the big smile and the bushy beard who did for safari suits what John Major did for grey) came on chanting, 'One world, one Reverend, through family love.' He thanked Reverend and Mrs Moon for 'uniting the human family'. *Uniting them*, I thought, *in such a way that no one manages to notice*! He then read out a poem that he had written for the Reverend:

Reverend Moon is a moon that shines on us...

I made a mental note to tell him to stick to his day job. Then it came to me that his day job now is being an *ex*-world statesman. *Surely, in a fairer world,* I mused, *writing obsequious doggerel to obscure religious leaders should be left to the likes of Mrs Thatcher.* Mr Moon smiled inscrutably as he listened to Mr Kaunda warble on:

> *To our troubled world, love they have taught,*
> *Undaunted, unblemished, let them continue to love and care.*

As a finale, the Moons were showered with gifts. Then the lights started swirling apocalyptically and the music grew to an awesome crescendo. The True Parents deserted their thrones for the heavenly gateway, where, in a swirl of dry ice, they turned, waved to their followers and disappeared. As 30,000 people cheered and clapped, the choir kicked into a rousing 'Hallelujah Chorus'. I sat deflated, feeling that, whatever messianic qualities the True Parent had, they seemed to have passed me by. I resolved to listen to his speech later in the day with great care.

Sipping decaffeinated tea in the Waldorf's Grand Ballroom, I await the Reverend Moon's words with interest. He starts with the air of a man/God not lacking confidence in the power of his own abilities. His interpreter stands ready. Grinning, Reverend Moon gestures expansively to his audience and says, 'What shall we do? Dancing? Singing? Whatever you choose.' It is a joke. Nearly everyone laughs and claps exuberantly. He then threatens us with a long speech. 'On the contrary, I may give a long speech. You may not know, but Reverend Moon has broken world record of a 17-hour speech.' This is not a joke. I am already anxious on two counts. Firstly, people who refer to themselves in the third person always alarm me. It is as if they see themselves as a phenomenon somehow bigger, grander, of more universal importance than normal people. Maybe that is excusable for God, or even the Son of God, but even so, it seems bombastic and pompous. Secondly, *anyone* – divine or not – who speaks nonstop for 17 hours has to be (a) verbose, (b) boring, and (c) ridiculously self-important. Things are not looking good.

He promises us a short speech, however, and offers his audience a teaser question: 'Do you want everyday talk or a secret message from God?' His fans start screaming out for a secret message from God. I wonder if, hidden amongst the followers, there are one or two people with furrowed brows thinking, 'We'll have the everyday talk, thanks, and just get on with it!'

The secret message from God speech is modestly called 'Let's Build a New World'. Once again, the Reverend tries a joke. 'You look handsome,' he says, gazing down at his elegantly turned-out followers, 'but I look ugly, so close your eyes and listen.' Touché.

Then comes the secret message. The mass wedding we witnessed was an extraordinary event. 'It must be a mystery if Confucius, Socrates, Mohammed and Jesus were married,' he tells us. *Jesus?* I think. *Is the True Parent's omniscience faltering again?* Only half an hour ago he gave *Buddha's* bride an expensive gold watch as a wedding present. The secret message from God is starting to resemble a toe-curling father-of-the-bride speech in which he gets the name of his son-in-law confused with an old boyfriend.

He continues telling us that he will officiate at Adam and Eve's wedding because he is humanity's True Parent in the past, present and future. He explains that Satan has undermined Adam and Eve, and everything since then. That is why everything is so decadent, he tells us. That is why there is homosexuality and lesbianism, that is why there is divorce. 'God can't touch this world because of the lineage of evil.' He rambles on and, though I am taking copious notes, it dawns on me that I am not about to be enlightened. After a couple of hours, he asks the audience to raise their hands if they want him to continue. *Please God, no!* I think. God is not listening.

Reverend Moon carries on, buoyed up by the forest of hands pleading with him to continue his 'secret message from God'. The family is under real threat, he begins to tell us.

Then, by way of a diversionary stunt, he starts asking the audience questions. 'Is your family perfect?' he asks Dr Sidky, the embarrassed former President of Egypt. Moon forces an answer out of him. Next comes another diversionary piece of buffoonery. He starts poking at and mock-punching his translator. He thinks it is great fun. His followers roar with laughter. His translator looks positively thrilled to be punched by the good Reverend. Poke, poke, jab, poke, poke. Hilarious. Twenty minutes later, his speech takes a different turn. He threatens his audience with hell unless they become perfect parents by being blessed by him. 'If you don't believe me, then you must repent,' he storms.

By this stage, several hours into the speech, I have got bored of folding and refolding my napkin. I am silently chanting, *'Ascend, Reverend Moon, please ascend,'* like a forlorn mantra. Self-consciously, I saunter away from the tables on the ballroom floor and, feeling inexplicably obliged to hear him out, climb up to the galleries and balconies which overlook the room. He carries on and on. He is no better from above. Or from the private boxes to the right or left. I return to my table. He is as enthusiastic as ever – so enthusiastic that he forgets himself. He tries to address the audience without his translator. Now *no one* can understand. Ten minutes later he realizes this and reverts to his translator.

One minute he is whispering incoherently, the next he is shouting, his divine spit arching energetically out into the audience's decaff. He tells us that after the war he could have brought the whole world back to God; that God and Satan cannot stop free sex and homosexuality. My thoughts are becoming less generous. The verbs in my silent mantra are becoming unprintable. After about four hours of his 'short speech', I give up. As I start to walk out, I hear him saying, 'When all obey Reverend Moon and all are blessed, he will become the true King of the human race.' By this stage I am taking twisted pleasure in the ridiculousness of Moon's use of the third person to describe himself. I go out in search of several stiff drinks and sane company.

By the next morning, I have given up any hope of finding some sort of enlightenment from Moon's ceremonies or marathon speeches. My family can breathe easily: I am not cut out to become a Moonie. I am keen, however, to find out how he manages to gather such a wide and respected support base for his work, and to listen to what his supporters say about their beliefs and experiences in the Unification Church.

All the conference delegates are staying in the four-star Intercontinental Hotel adjacent to the Waldorf. I join them in the lobby and start chatting to various delegates in a desperate search for irony. I drop the odd hint about the speech being just a weeny bit protracted. Initially this only attracts irritatingly benign and pitying smiles and comments along the lines of, 'Oh, I listened to the Father for 10 hours once.'

Finally, from an obscure academic wedged anonymously against the bar, I get a reassuring response. 'That speech went on rather,' I venture riskily.

'Yes, he's an effing maniac,' the man replies.

Immediately, I feel as if I am entering the gates of heaven. He introduces me to some other journalists and academics. They are all bemused about being asked to attend the conference, not at all sure why they have been invited or what they have to contribute. One was once met on the street by a Moonie and, months later, was invited to travel from Europe to attend a four-day conference in New York – all expenses paid. The same thing has been happening ever since. It becomes clear that many of the delegates and dignitaries are not members of the Unification Church. They may accurately be called 'followers' of Reverend Moon, but only in the sense that they follow him to expensive hotels in exotic corners of the world to eat good food whenever he pays for them to do so.

Unification conferences can certainly boast some big-name speakers. Edward Heath, columnist Paul Johnson and US Defence Secretary Alexander Haig have all spoken at such conferences. They can also boast some tiny-name but big-title speakers: Her Majesty the Queen attended this conference – Queen Toej of the Marshall Islands, that is. His Majesty also –

King Kigeli of Rwanda. The Honourable Mendsaikham Enkhsaikhan, Prime Minister of Mongolia (1983–5), the Honourable Maxine Korman, Prime Minister of Vanuatu (1991–6), the Right Honourable Dr Kennedy Simmonds, Prime Minister of St Kitts and Nevis (1983–95), and the Right Honourable Ramsewak Shankar, President of Surinam (1988–90), are never likely to trip off the tongue as household names. Biggish minnows in a tiny conference pond, maybe? If so, Reverend Dr Phillip B. McPhee, the Bahamas' Director of Fishing, must surely be nominated as the minnows' minnow of the 1998 conference. All of which leaves me asking one question: WHY? It reminds me of Peniel's flirtation with politicians in what resembled a bid for respectability – but was it not Jesus who called the politicians of his day (the Pharisees) 'a brood of vipers'?

All one can say with assurance is that none of the speakers or delegates pays to attend the conferences. Some may, indeed, be paid to attend. It also becomes apparent that the speakers are broadly (with the exception of former President Kaunda) of a certain political hue. One moment the President of the Institute for American Values is calling for a pro-marriage movement; the next, a newspaper columnist is describing homosexuality as 'a disease-ridden, violent life-style'. There appears to be an unspoken assumption that some kind of liberal gay elite is involved in a dirty and sinister anti-family conspiracy. Yet to invite Eliott Abrams, a former Reaganite Senator whose involvement in the Iran–Contra scandal necessitated a presidential pardon, to speak on 'Rights, Wrongs and the Assault on the Family' strikes me as ironic. One assumes that the Nicaraguan families who lost loved ones to the US-funded Contra terrorists might have things to say about Abrams' assault on the family. Reverend Moon's love of the family, however, is only matched by his hatred of communism.

Before the conference ends, I decide to take the time to speak to some of Reverend Moon's followers about their beliefs. Franco, an Italian delegate, explains that Moon is the messiah, come to unite Christianity, to save us from decaying morals and to oppose godless political regimes. He tells of Moon's desire to stop God suffering by redeeming people from their fallen state through blessing them. Being part of a worldwide family of belief, of people who believe in love, is what being a Unificationist means to him.

Feeling guilty, I ask Franco how 120 million people could possibly have been blessed at the ceremony the day before. 'Well, there was a large meeting in the Czech Republic and one in Seoul, and lots of little ones,' he says. Yes, but *120* million? 'Hmm. All who agree with Reverend Moon's affirmation receive the blessing,' he explains, a little embarrassed. I nearly point out that most people would agree with Moon's bland affirmation on the family (read out at the ceremony), and that the idea of those people somehow entering 'a pre-fallen state' beggars belief. I refrain.

Franco, like all the followers I meet, is friendly and warm-hearted, if rather credulous. He is not the stereotyped 'brainwashed zombie' of popular perception. None of them is. These people are the epitome of reasonableness and good manners. Another young woman offers to guide me around Manhattan. I accept and, feeling slightly cruel, I plan to ask her my more difficult questions. What kind of example is the True Parent giving by leaving his first wife? What does she make of the allegations made by Reverend Moon's daughter-in-law that her husband raped and beat her and took cocaine, and that the messiah made no effort to intervene? Why has the Son of God been imprisoned for tax evasion? But I don't ask her these things. I can't. She is too helpful, too solicitous. Instead, I leave New York, sincerely thanking them all for organizing such an *interesting* conference. 'Until the next time,' I almost say.

At 30,000 feet, sampling whiskies, ports and fine wines while reclining in a British Airways Club Class seat, I try to process my impressions of the conference, to articulate why I can say with conviction that I will not be joining the Unification Church. It is not primarily the boring speeches, the hyperbole, or the strange mixture of Christianity and Confucianism which puts me off – though each of these might suffice as a reason. Nor is it Reverend Moon's big idea of 'idolizing' (and idealizing) the family. As big ideas go, this one leaves me with a resounding question: *Haven't I heard this somewhere before?*

Surprisingly, my reasons may have something to do with Reverend Moon's distant past. Moon's family origins are humble. His family were 'commoners' according to the Korean class system, simple farmers, living in a thatched house. They were converted to Christianity by American missionaries in the early 1930s, after shamanic rituals and Confucianism failed to cure Moon's sister of some form of mental illness. He started his ministry as a regular Christian preacher in American-style evangelical churches – his messianic tendencies grew over time. During the Korean War, once again, it was the Americans who saved Moon (and South Korea) from what he described as 'godless communism'. Moon was imprisoned by the communist authorities in North Korea for several years, accused of spreading falsehoods and deceiving innocent people for money. He was humiliated and beaten, but it was American B29s and US troops that forced the Communists to retreat, leading to the prisoners' release. It was also in America that Reverend Moon made it big as a businessman.

It seems to me, therefore, that Reverend Moon's religion comes very close to worshipping the West. This may well owe something to the fact that he was 'rescued' from primitive and ancient shamanism by American missionaries and that he was saved from 'godless communism' by American bombs. It was not long before he abandoned Korean clothes in favour of a smart suit. American-style capitalism (including manufacturing weapons) made Reverend Moon a very, very wealthy man. Moon (not unlike South Korea in general) has embraced the United States, its trappings and apple-pie ideals. Hence the 'family values', the whiter-than-white weddings (largely for Koreans), the anti-communism, the forlorn attempt to unify Christianity (albeit with himself grafted on as the second Son of God). Even the glossy books that the Church publishes have schmaltzy cover photographs (and similarly schmalzy sayings inside) that look as if they belong on a box of chocolates or a Patience Strong calendar. It is all too sugary, too brittle, too unreal. Perhaps it is this unreality that accounts for the statistics which show that, for nearly all converts, the Unification Church is a phase they grow out of in a year or two. Perhaps the dream dissolves, like the Great American Dream, in the lacklustre shades of everyday life.

Unificationists do not seem to me to be a group of dangerous or sinister otherworldly brainwashers. Like Peniel Pentecostal Church, they appear to be distinctly *this*worldly. If I were inclined to worship such a dream, however, I would be worshipping a Porsche or a Rolex watch, not a messiah in a dinner jacket. Call me ungrateful, but the spirituality I am looking for will not be so wrapped up in the American Dream. It will sit less comfortably in the Grand Ballroom of the Waldorf Astoria.

My plane begins its descent over England, leaving the clouds. It touches down at Heathrow. It's raining.

7

On Another Planet

Grey clouds are scudding across the Atlantic above slanting pillars of rain. The horizon is a thin-lipped grimace where sea meets sky. Occasional patches of sunshine glisten onto cold Cornish fields. The muted greens, khakis and browns of the moorland lie brooding beneath the biting wind. Despite the rain, ice covers puddles and frost is struggling to thaw. Across the valley, Rough Tor, a stark, rocky outcrop, rises above the waterlogged moors and bogs where tanks are reputed to have sunk without trace. It is a sullen, desolate, unwelcoming land-scape momentarily transformed by fleeting glances of sunlight. It is late December and the weather forecast is not promising.

I am standing on a two-metre by four-metre rocky plug just below the summit of Brown Willy, the highest point of Bodmin Moor. Manfully facing the western winds, I am hold-ing my forearms up, palms outward, like a cormorant drying its wings. I am inhaling deeply and chanting 15-second 'Om's over the sodden valley. The rock on which I am standing is a holy rock – the rock, indeed, on which extraterrestrial trans-missions were received which declared that the world's next great spiritual leader would arrive in a spacesuit to sort the wheat from the chaff. And in case we weren't interested, his 'magic' would be greater than the armaments of the world's combined armies.

Mervyn Smith, my companion, is assuredly the wheat and, as I watch the gusto with which he hurls his mantras into the freezing wind, I am beginning to realize that I am probably the chaff. Dressed in bright red cagoule, woolly hat and oil-skins, gloved hands in the air, Mervyn calls down the protection of the 'violet flame' on us just as it starts to hail. The violet flame's protective forcefield appears to be malfunctioning in the physical realm, but Mervyn is undeterred as the hailstones pucker his face. '*Om mani padme hum*,' he repeats for about 15 minutes, gradually getting faster before stopping and starting the next mantra.

The wind is starting to wail; the hail is stinging my face. I shift uneasily as Mervyn starts to recite a prayer in declamatory style. He thunders:

O Divine and Everlasting Spirit
We pray that your mighty power
May fall upon the world – NOW!

I scan the clouds for a flying saucer. All I see is an even more ominous black cloud rolling its way up the moor. Mervyn is oblivious to this as his voice changes to a pompous, lisping whisper (quite unlike the everyday Mervyn, who is friendly and completely unaffected). 'Blessed are they who have expended enough energy themselves so that they may know of the Devic Kingdom and knowing this, live in eternal thanks for Its work,' he simpers. It is a voice I am to hear often: the cadences of Dr Sir George King, the man whom Mervyn believes opened up the possibility of communicating with extraterrestrial intelligences. As the cloud drops its load on us, I appreciate the nature of its silver lining: no one else is on the moor to watch me standing in such an unnatural pose beside a man alternately shouting into the ether and whispering nonsense in a lisping falsetto.

I am feeling decidedly chaff-like when Mervyn turns to me and asks if I would like to say some prayers. 'I'll back your prayers up with mantra,' he explains, his voice (thankfully) resuming normal service. Caught off guard, desperately trying to shrug off my cynicism, I say I'll have a go. I am quite touched by Mervyn being so direct. He starts a series of

mantras while I try to muster up some prayers I can say without duplicity. I pray that reason, wisdom and mercy may influence the leaders of Russia in their decisions about Chechnya. I pray for the same qualities in relation to those with influence on the spread of global capitalism. *Have those cosmic intelligences got the foggiest idea what I'm wittering on about?* I wonder. I say a prayer for my family. These faltering prayers seem pathetic, but it feels strangely good to say them.

It is not long before Mervyn reverts to his repertoire of silly voices. In a pause, he offers me coffee and assures me that he will not be offended if I want to get some shelter. I opt for a walk around Brown Willy, now covered in a white sheen of hail which has no intention of melting. Gazing across the frozen Cornish wasteland, I think about the prayers. Throwing forlorn hopes to the four winds is surprisingly liberating. Perhaps we all do this sort of thing on occasion, but it feels like a release. Being close to wild nature seems good for the soul. Mervyn's beliefs may be off the planet, but his sincerity and the wilderness and desolation of this particular patch of our planet (reminiscent of the unspoilt and innocent Tepee Valley) conspire to silence the scoffing cynic within me.

After an hour or so, Mervyn has finished praying. As we descend from Brown Willy, frozen to the bone, teeth chattering, ice covering our boots, Mervyn says, 'Orthodox religion leaves me cold.' *Is he taking the mickey?* I ask myself. 'I came to the Aetherius Society after trying various Eastern religions,' he continues, explaining the background to his beliefs. 'But the difference is that it brings science and religion *together*,' he says with emphasis. 'George King brought the technology from cosmic intelligences on other planets which allowed us to channel our spirituality,' he adds. *He probably isn't taking the mickey*, I decide.

I ask whether Mervyn and other Aetherians scan the skies for UFOs, if the next (and final) spiritual leader is to come from another planet. He scoffs at the suggestion, but concedes that the Aetherius Society does have a UFO hotline and keeps tabs on UFO developments. Has he seen UFOs? 'Yeah, loads,' he says, as if describing close encounters with shopping trolleys. In fact, they were not very close encounters, but lights in the sky at night. How could he tell they were not planes? 'The speed and the sudden changes in direction,' he explains. I am sure that Mervyn is telling the truth as he sees it, but I feel that I have heard this too many times before. Presumably, Mervyn would say this is because that is the way UFOs are.

So, I enquire, is the next spiritual leader due to arrive in his UFO imminently? Mervyn smiles sagely, shaking his head from side to side. 'Could be in the new year, or could be 30 years away. Who knows?' Unfortunately, the last great spiritual leader arrived in a London cab, which he drove, and thus was only recognized by a few thousand people. Mervyn is one of those people, and has vivid memories of Dr Sir George King, the Aetherians' founder and spiritual leader, who died in 1998.

How are they going to manage without their spiritual leader? 'Good question,' Mervyn says glumly. 'I can't pretend it's easy.' He explains that King was the only member (there are 11 branches in the UK alone, and tens of thousands on their mailing list with many more members worldwide) spiritually advanced enough to communicate with extra-terrestrials. Mervyn knew King closely for several years. 'There were so many facets to the man. He did everything to an ultra degree of competence. In his school reports, he was top of everything apart from art. He was the son of a dairy farmer, but he went on to test-drive Jags; he was an outstanding taxi driver,' he says.

'He was the most magnetic and powerful man I've ever met,' Mervyn continues. 'He was a man with a mission, and he worked day and night for it and demanded the same of others.' King was kind, compassionate, determined, with a massive amount of energy, Mervyn tells me. Did he have a sense of humour? 'He had a massive sense of humour, he could have me in stitches of laughter until it hurt,' he says ruefully. 'He wasn't at all like the idea of a peaceful and gentle spiritual leader. He called a spade a spade. Being around him was tough, it built character. He could be harsh for our own good. He expected total devotion to the mission.'

It was King's spiritual qualities that most impressed his followers, however. According to Mervyn, King was a yogic master and could reach extremely advanced Samadhic trances, during which he would receive audible Cosmic Transmissions from the Ascended Cosmic Masters. The ACMs, Mervyn tells me, include the usual list of Jesus, Buddha and Krishna (but no True Parent or Reverend Moon), as well as some other, rather inelegantly named Masters. Mars Sector Six, for example, is a Cosmic Master residing on Mars who controls a spacecraft called Satellite Number 3, which will orbit the earth at set times for the next 1,000 years to allow us to receive colossal amounts of spiritual energy beamed down from it. Aetherius is the more gracefully named Cosmic Master living on Venus who first made contact with King in 1954, proclaiming, 'Prepare yourself. You are to become the Voice of Interplanetary Parliament.' A year later King founded the Aetherius Society.

During subsequent years, King received further messages from space, either while in a trance (during which his voice box would be taken over by the voices of the Masters) or telepathically, along magnetic beams. King was told that humankind evolved from the planet Maldek, which was destroyed by a nuclear explosion after their decadent, selfish habits gave way to a lust for power. Karmic law meant that the souls of the Maldekians needed a home and, in King's words, 'The Earth, being a great Planetary Lord, took merciful compassion on the killers of Maldek and agreed to their reincarnation upon her back.' Despite visits by Jesus and Buddha, humankind has now reached the same state as the original Maldekians and things will only be finally resolved when the messiah-bearing UFO arrives. At this point we will either change our ways or be forcibly transferred to another planet to learn our lesson the hard way.

In the meantime, King gave his followers a number of projects that could help the planet and prepare us for the UFO's

arrival. The projects centre around the idea that the planet and its people are in dire need of prayer power or energy. For each project King developed some hi-tech, pseudo-scientific gadget. Operation Space Power, for example, uses Spiritual Energy Radiators which receive spiritual energy from Satellite Number 3 when it is orbiting. Operation Prayer Power, which Mervyn says 'perfectly combines the essence of science and religion', involves hundreds of Aetherians gathering to pray into special batteries designed by King. The power from their prayers is stored until world disasters occur, at which point it is released via a cosmic ray gun, or Spiritual Energy Radiator, to help the situation.

One assumes that a man must have incredible personal charisma to attract people to such silly ideas – and King did not make it easy to believe. According to Mervyn, King taught that abstention from sex was vital if a person was to grow spiritually. Nevertheless, King's revelations and beliefs began to attract followers in Hollywood and it was only a few years before he emigrated and lived at a ranch bought by the Aetherius Society in southern California.

Mervyn explains that our walk to the Holy Rock on Brown Willy is part of Operation Starlight. Between 1958 and 1961, Cosmic Sources charged 19 mountains (subsequently named Holy Mountains) with spiritual energy. They are now power sources for prayer and the more people pray on them, the more the energy within the mountain multiplies. Because Britain is such an important region for Mother Earth, nine of the mountains are in Britain.

I ask Mervyn if I can see a prayer battery. He invites me to some pre-Christmas meetings with the Aetherians at their European Headquarters in London.

The Aetherius Society's shop front in Fulham Road is not auspicious. There is a scattering of religious tracts alongside a couple of large portraits of George King looking noble, pure and holy, staring square-jawed up to the skies. The style of painting is familiar: it has that reverential, airbrushed piety

frequently found on full-colour religious tracts of a certain age (especially from the 1950s and 1960s). Today the sickly dishonesty of this style of painting is so obvious that it seems quaint and ingenuous. It is the propaganda of a simpler, more innocent time. The one redeeming feature fronting the European Headquarters is a multicoloured neon UFO, jauntily hung at an angle above the door.

Inside are about 30 people, many dressed in green robes with large gold medallions dangling from green ribbons. I am met by Christopher Perry, the organization's Communications Officer. Like all the Aetherians I meet, Christopher is open and friendly. Robes and medallions apart, he seems a remarkably conventional-looking man to be involved in such an eccentric organization. People start to move to the back of the room and down some stairs. Christopher whispers, 'We're going into the room in which George King received the Cosmic Transmissions.' As people descend into a crypt-like basement, a hush falls. Each person waits for a few moments at the entrance, walks across the darkened room to a large brass cross encrusted with big polished stones, turns to it, bows and then finds a seat in the congregation.

Fifty or so people are now in the room, and soothing classical music is playing as they sit quietly. Around the room are illuminated pictures of George King in various poses (painted in the same style as the pictures in the shop window), as well as various strange hieroglyphs which I am later told are Sanskrit. The room also features a Christmas tree, tinsel, baubles and other incongruously normal decorations.

A woman walks to the front wearing a strange mitre with floppy ear flaps, and invites the violet flame to enter and protect us. This is followed by a chant of *'Om mani padme hum'* and various other mantras that were frosted into my subconscious on Bodmin Moor. People stand, hands raised, palms outward, to release the spiritual energy of the prayers. The mantra gets faster and louder until the darkened room is full of pulsating, deafening sound as the congregation, eyes closed, robes swaying, reach an almost sexual crescendo.

95

One of Sir George's speeches is then read out from the front. The reader reminds me of Mervyn: he affects a silly voice and says something about Mars Sector Six. A little later a deep, portentous voice fills the room. I realize that this is the source of all silly voices – it is George King himself. Or, more accurately, it is a lisping Saint Goo Ling (who inhabits the Devic realms, a spirit realm in the atmosphere) followed by a whispering, ponderous Master Jesus, top-heavy with his own significance.

'Jesus' sounds ridiculous, each agonizingly slow word drowned in a sort of hallowed resonance. It reminds me of the pictures on the walls. It also seems to go on and on in a clumsy approximation of the English of the King James Bible, which reminds me of the druids' liturgy. This, however, is far more incoherent: 'Thrice Blessed are they who provide the Devas with the Spiritual tools, so that They may build Their empires upon the rock of balance. Oh Children of Earth, walk ye into the night and thank your God for it. Walk ye into the dawn and thank your God for it and you will be helping the Silent Workers to preserve balance for you. Thrice Blessed are those who have done this – and this is NOW – NOW. SO ENDETH THE THIRD BLESSING.' Thank Master Jesus for that!

Next Dr Ray Neilson, a diminutive, chirpy man in his sixties, gives a sermon. It is a résumé of the year, the first year since the Primary Terrestrial Mental Channel (Sir George) died. My conversations with Mervyn about the Aetherians after Sir George's death left me thinking about them as a dying star, slowly petering out in a quiet, benign corner of the universe. Dr Neilson is more optimistic: 'I can't remember a year since 1960 in which we've been so active. It's been a spiritual express train. If you were a visitor, say, to this world, you'd see one organization that ran with a concept to communicate to as many people as possible about a spiritual belief.'

The problem, however, is not with visitors from other planets. It is the visitors from this planet who seem a little underwhelmed. Dr Neilson appears to be thrilled, however. During the year the society has had 556 new attendees, and their national Paranormal Tour attracted 546 people and sold 423 books. The financial takings for the society were £16,000. The society does not appear to be reaching for the stars and, though they do not seem to realize it, they are hardly going to rock the world with such negligible achievements. Admittedly, they have bought and refurbished a new building – the Inner Potential Centre – but Dr Neilson's optimism seems misplaced.

'There aren't many organizations that can respond within a few hours to disasters,' he chirrups. 'Within hours our machines are activated. Others tut-tut, but don't do anything about it. And people respond to our breadth and downright logical approach. What other organization has contact with Cosmic Masters from space as we have in Operation Sunbeam?' Luckily the question is rhetorical, and Dr Neilson moves on swiftly. The service ends after a few more mantras, prayers and a visualization involving a white flame. People stand and quietly leave the soothing, dark crypt.

I speak to Dr Neilson after the service. He joined the Aetherians 40 years ago. 'I was playing in a band, but part of me was searching,' he explains. 'A band member invited me to meet Sir George and I came along here and knew that it was my destiny.' I suspect, once again, that the charisma of King was a factor. What impression did King make upon Dr Neilson? 'He had such spiritual authority. You felt so confident in his presence, you just felt that he knew what was going on, what was needed.'

The more he speaks, the more I suspect that Dr Neilson might not, in fact, be a doctor. I have been aware from the start that the 'Sir' in Sir George might be a little aspirational too (even with *his* charisma, I cannot imagine the Queen bestowing a knighthood on someone who claims to be the Primary Terrestrial Mental Channel for Mars Sector Six and other assorted cosmic ne'er-do-wells).

It is a tricky subject, and I feel embarrassed asking such questions. Nonetheless, putting my tact into Warp 9 cosmic overdrive, I ask, 'Is, er, your doctorate an internal qualification, recognizing your work within the Aetherius Society?' Dr Neilson blushes and comes clean. 'What about Sir George's doctorate?' I venture bravely.

'He was given the doctorate by a theological college in California,' Neilson mumbles. My embarrassment is mounting. 'Is it honorary? Is it widely recognized?'

'It's certainly recognized by cosmic sources,' Dr Neilson counters.

'And, er, did the Queen knight Sir George?'

'It's not only the Queen who can knight people, you know. He was knighted by Knights of Malta and other orders of chivalry.'

'Ah, of *course*,' I almost say. 'Yes, yes, the knights of Malta and other chivalric orders. How silly of me.' I stop myself.

I would not have thought any less of George King or Ray Neilson without their doctorates, but it seems odd that they felt the need to tack them on in a bid for credibility. Ray is a bit embarrassed, and I feel for him. 'Our leaders are highly qualified people,' he says. 'Christopher Perry was a Department Head in Debenhams and Richard Lawrence [their Executive Secretary] was a school teacher.' He goes on to describe King's ability in the field of radionics. *Radionics*? 'The science of metaphysics, the manipulation of subtle energies,' Ray explains. 'George King introduced us to the science of direct action. To us, prayer is an active application of science.'

He describes the batteries and prayer radiators that King designed. Can I see them? Ray looks doubtful. 'They are on site here, but the whole science behind our radionics is strictly classified, for obvious reasons.' I can certainly think of some obvious reasons, but I do not think they are the same as Ray's. 'In the wrong hands it could be dangerous,' he adds. He tells me that I can see a prayer battery at the next Operation Starlight meeting. I might be able to see a photo of a radiator, but only Aetherians of a particular pedigree can be present at a transmission, for fear of contaminating the prayer energy.

A couple of weeks later, I visit the recently opened Inner Potential Centre (also in Fulham) in search of the elusive prayer battery. On the way into the futuristic orange foyer which stretches up through three floors to the heavens, I pick up a copy of *Cosmic Voice*, the journal of the Aetherius Society. On the cover are three men wearing sunglasses, baseball caps and ties featuring the Sanskrit Aetherian symbol, beneath the headline, 'The Saturn Mission Phase 39 Successful!' They resemble something from a Peter Sellers film and, for a moment, I wonder whether they are showing signs of humour, or even self-parody.

I walk into the large rectangular meeting room on the upper floor in a break between mantras. The room is sunshine yellow and sky blue, with six futuristic chandeliers. On each side of the room are 25 people in scarlet robes, with another 20 or so at the back. They all face towards a gold-framed picture of George King. Beneath the picture I find what I am looking for: a prayer battery on a tripod. The battery may be state-of-the-art radionics equipment, but it looks like something from a Blue Peter programme, knocked together out of cereal packets, drinking straws and sticky-back plastic. It is square, with the sort of grille found on old-fashioned radios, and a series of tubes stick out of the front. To the left of the tripod and battery stands a mantra leader, and to her left a man sits at a desk with a clipboard, pen, stopwatch and some charts. A man with white rubber gloves sits on the right. His job is to put the battery in its numbered container without contaminating it.

A robed man calls a prayer team of three out to the front. The prayer director announces the exact time, stopwatch in hand, and the next round of mantras starts. The mantra leader, swaying slightly, moves her arms as if conducting. She starts intoning '*Om rama rama*', as the congregation stand, raise their palms cormorant-fashion and follow her lead, slowly building up volume. Once the mantras have reached an appropriate intensity, the man in white rubber gloves lifts a flap on the back of the battery. Then the prayer team get to work. They take it in turns to strike a kung-fu-style pose, one leg stretched dramatically behind the other as if for balance, their left hand held in the air with the fingers and thumb in an equally unnatural-looking position, the flat of their right hand placed on the battery. Then, in a variety of silly and more normal-sounding voices, they pray into the battery. The prayers are taken from 'the 12 blessings of the Master Jesus'. This goes on for about 20 minutes, after which they have a break.

The next session starts with variations on *'Om Om Om Brahma'*. I join in for a while, but my arms get tired and, not surprisingly, I get a bit bored. Sitting down, I open my copy of *Cosmic Voice* and read a description of the Saturn Mission's latest phase. These missions take place on an area thought of as a psychic centre on Lake Utah (Loch Ness has also been used). The idea is that, at these centres, Aetherians can open their prayer batteries and, miles above, a spacecraft from Saturn, usually under the control of an Adept called Nixies Zero Zero Five, beams down immense amounts of spiritual energy. The effect of this energy is to remedy and stabilize the spiritual imbalances on the planet. *Cosmic Voice* describes a rather comic episode in which one member of the team tried to soothe the wind Devas (spirits that inhabit all aspects of nature) by blessing them so that another member could steady the prayer battery to enable Nixies Zero Zero Five to direct his energy beam at the battery opening.

Further on in the magazine is a transmission from Mars Sector Six, broadcasting (via George King) on Satellite Number 3 in the Magnetization Terra Orbit. After the usual pseudo-scientific nonsense ('terrestrial man has at his command quite some Units of Energy to use ... the Absorption Factor when Satellite No. 3 vacates Terrestrial Orbit will be 5.62 Units'), Mars Sector Six starts haranguing the terrestrials about their lack of faith and reminding them that George King is King, so to speak. Mars Sector Six says, 'This is the weakness of terrestrial man. He is a born doubter. Even though before you lies a proof second to none... May I remind you too of something else. Search as you will throughout the world we refer to as Terra, you will never find greater

Teachings, more simply given, a greater Truth with less distortion than you find in and through Mental Channel Number One.' Call me cynical, but if I were an Aetherian, I would be a bit suspicious about this sort of transmission. It is a bit like sending oneself a Valentine card and opening it in front of wavering admirers. Nevertheless, I am relieved that Mars Sector Six seems to eschew King James English.

The *Cosmic Voice* magazine also details meticulously the number of prayer hours stored safely away in batteries and the number of prayer discharges sent to various trouble spots. Operation Space Power collected 436,560 prayer hours and London released 2,200 prayer hours in weekly release. NATO's bombing of Yugoslavia was accompanied by discharges of prayer, and the Northern Ireland peace process also received a discharge. In the time since King's death, the Saturn Missions have saved 450,000 people from death or serious injury due to averted natural disasters.

After another two sessions of mantras and rotating prayers, I see Mervyn approaching. He talks about the prayer battery with me and explains that it is full of crystals and gold, radionics specially designed by King. He cannot really explain the science behind it, he says, because it is complex and Sir George was the real expert in the field. The man with white gloves takes the battery and places it in a case which looks as if it should hold radioactive fuel rods. Mervyn explains that the man sitting at the desk to one side is a prayer assessor, whose job it is to grade the quality of the prayers channelled into the battery and fill this in on his chart. This helps them to estimate how many hours of top-quality prayer energy they have stored. 'Most of our prayer teams get AA+,' he says. 'They are highly advanced prayers, they've all done tests.' I ask what would get a D or an E. 'Someone cussing into the prayer battery, but it hasn't happened,' he replies.

As I leave the Inner Potential Centre, it strikes me that the prayer batteries are symbolic of the group. If I am to call their prayer batteries wishful thinking, then I must be open to the

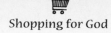

possibility that the same is true of New Age visualizations or the prayers of Christians. The distinctive thing about Aetherians is their faith in their technology. In his book *Cults of Unreason*, psychologist Christopher Evans has described this use of science in religious groups as 'black box' technology. His idea is that people know what the input is (graded prayer hours) and the output (peace and harmony wherever the radiator is pointed), but God knows what goes on in between! That is faith. The attempt at dressing up in scientific garb the belief in gods in space originated with King. And King's followers believe it. It is unfair to say that the Aetherians are weak-minded (though on my visits they appear to be an intellectual-free zone), but, let's face it, this is not rocket science.

As sci-fi cults go, the Aetherians are all fiction and no science, but they are benign and harmless people. I note that there is an unusual amount of men for a religious group (more than half the congregation), and this is probably because of all the technological imagery that Aetherians embrace. Their lack of education may also signify. Clearly they embrace a spirituality which incorporates the value of quantifiable science and technology. It is a touching, ingenuous faith in science which would be impossible in a more sophisticated and educated seeker (a druid or New Ager, for example) who would be more likely to find divinity in a *rejection* of science and modernity, in the wild myths of the ancients.

Unfortunately, science does not offer much succour in relation to the big religious questions. It is, after all, scientific materialism which for many undermines notions of after-life, soul, spirit, the comfort of the omnipotent or a higher purpose. Nonetheless, to place wise, omnipotent, technocratic deities in spacecraft, offering us purpose and meaning, satisfies both the spiritual impulse and an inclination towards science. It is ironic that those spiritualities whose rituals and beliefs are based in pseudo-science and future technology are the ones that now seem passé, unsophisticated, sleepy – on a par with head-in-the-sand creationists. Perhaps we can make scientific sense of this by reminding ourselves that, when we gaze at the stars, we are, quite literally, looking into the past.

It strikes me that a similar faith is also present in non-religious UFO-watching groups. Members of the British Unidentified Flying Object Research Association see themselves as scientific researchers, but aspects of their quest have religious dimensions. Some of their members describe encounters or myths of encounters in awed, reverential terms. They are seeking an ultimate meaning, the big picture which takes us out of the mundane and into a 'truer', more intense understanding. Sadly, however, the big picture may well be encompassed by the big screen: the history of sci-fi in the cinema.

To understand both religious and non-religious UFO-orientated groups, it is worth knowing about the key dates of science fiction texts and UFO mythology. The first UFOs in fiction were in the shape of airships (soon to become reality) in the writings of Jules Verne and Edgar Allen Poe at the end of the nineteenth century. The early sightings of UFOs were strangely similar. In the 1930s, UFOs of various shapes were popularized in American pulp cartoon magazines. The term 'flying saucer' originates from the alleged sighting in 1947 by a pilot, Kenneth Arnold, of nine glowing craft, travelling at 1,700mph over the Cascade Mountains in Washington State. Although the craft he described were not round, journalistic shorthand described them as 'flying saucers' in newspapers across the USA. Days later, sightings of 'saucers' were being reported elsewhere. Four years later, a glowing flying saucer flew across Washington DC in Robert Wise's film *The Day the Earth Stood Still*.

This film (and others) included aliens who contacted humans. The shape of aliens has also changed over time. The benign, handsome, 'human' alien (Klaatu) in *The Day the Earth Stood Still* led to a number of 'contactee' stories in which people were met by beautiful, polite aliens, offering rides in their spaceships whilst warning (as Klaatu did) about the danger of nuclear weapons. Interestingly, the most famous of these contactees, George Adamski, who published *The Flying Saucers Have Landed* in 1957, had also led a Californian religious group called The Royal Order of Tibet and failed at writing science fiction. Following the release of *Close Encounters of the Third Kind*, alleged alien sightings also resembled the aliens in the film. 'Greys' with huge eyes, expressionless faces, long necks and thin bodies seem to originate from Spielberg's film. The release of box-office sci-fi hits leads to a corresponding increase in UFO sightings or reports of contactee and abductee experiences. The relationship is symbiotic: the public seem to respond to film and fiction, and Hollywood responds to public interest by incorporating UFO mythology into its films.

It not surprising that the Aetherians and a number of similar groups sprang up following the early films and fictions in the 1950s. Scientology, like the Aetherius Society, was founded in the mid-1950s by a science-fiction writer. The late L. Ron Hubbard started this 'religion' as Dianetics, a 'science' of the mind. Perhaps by emphasizing Scientology's self-improvement aspects (as opposed to the cosmic spirituality), Dianetics caught the *zeitgeist* of the time and expanded rapidly. Nearly 10 million people (including 100,000 Britons) have paid for Scientology's self-improvement courses (one researcher reports that it costs £150,000 to complete all of Scientology's courses) and Hubbard died with a reported personal fortune of $500 million.

Yet Church of Scientology 'theology' is reminiscent of the Aetherians' beliefs. The central belief is that all humans are 'thetans' who were the creators of the universe, but whose traumas (known as 'engrams') caused them problems which could only be eradicated by 'auditing'. Auditing sometimes involves a technological gadget known as an 'E-meter' (others describe it as a 'voltmeter', but it is essentially their 'black box') and usually costs money. Like the prayer battery, the science of how it works is not discussed.

The higher courses involve details of our cosmic history. Participants are told of Xemu, a despotic ruler who controlled 76 planets 75 million years ago, who captured thetans, froze them in alcohol and glycol, flew them to earth, chained them to volcanoes and dropped hydrogen bombs on them. It was Xemu who captured us and implanted 'sexual perversion' and 'religion' in us. The 'theology' is almost charming in its naive unreality. Perhaps it is no coincidence that in the hyper-reality of Hollywood such quaint theologies have gained considerable currency (in all senses). Tom Cruise, Nicole Kidman, Demi Moore, John Travolta and others earn their living by entering into fantasy. It only seems right, perhaps, that they should tithe to a fantastical religion like Scientology. The therapy rather than the fantasy seems to be the real attraction, however, and this is why Scientology, Insight and The Forum leave the tiny Aetherius Society fading like a quietly dying star in the forgotten corner of the galaxy.

8

🛒

Magical Mystery Tor

The idle rich have a lot to answer for. Be they members of the aristocracy or the moneyed merchant class, fading celebrities or sports stars, leisure for them is a dangerous thing. If they cannot be encouraged to litter the land with ill-conceived follies or start collections more ludicrous than petrol pumps, they start to develop ideas. These are not the sort of ideas that normal, hard-working people have (*Let's get a greenhouse*, perhaps, or *Let's go abroad this summer*, or *Shall we try decorative swags below the pelmets?*), but ideas that become all-consuming *raisons d'être*.

One significant difference between the idle rich and the idle ordinary is that the idle rich have money to spend on propagating their ideas. Lord Brocket supported the Nazis, Brigitte Bardot supported seal cubs, Prince Charles argued for 'traditional' architecture, David Icke (I am assuming he is not penniless) even developed the idea that he might be the Son of God. All of which makes me think that banning fox hunting might be a bad idea. At least it keeps them occupied.

The reason for this outburst is that, had Alfred Watkins been a little busier in the 1920s, I suspect that my visit to Glastonbury might have been slightly less painful. Watkins is the inventor (I choose my words carefully) of ley lines. The owner of a wealthy milling firm in Hereford, he was an all-round accomplished dilettante. He was a keen photographer (inventing a light meter), walker and amateur historian. While indulging all three hobbies in June 1921, he had an idea. He noticed that a view from Bredwardine in Herefordshire was made up of a series of alignments of ancient sites, monuments and churches. He found similar alignments elsewhere on maps and started to do some fieldwork, examining these features and, where possible, taking photos of them.

Watkins started to talk about the alignments at local naturalist clubs, calling them 'leys' and suggesting that they were ancient pathways. The archaeological establishment was unimpressed, but his idea gained popularity and publicity via his book *The Old Straight Track*. Nonetheless, his theory was (and still is) all rather vague. You would think that a definition of a straight line would be simple, but sadly there is still debate over the definition of a ley. Some say that it is four alignments; others say five. Some say the alignments must feature over a period of five miles; others say 50 miles or more. Some say that leys are found on maps; others that a visit is necessary to sample the energy.

Following Watkins's 'invention', societies of ley-hunters started poring over maps to find ley lines, and groups of 'landscape detectives' took to the fields. You might think someone would have pointed out that, if you stick a long ruler on a map, things are likely to form alignments. It would be statistically spooky if this were *not* so. And, yes, maps have lots of old things marked on them and sometimes they align. In fact, Watkins's theory was so contorted that straight lines were an inevitability. Trees, marker stones, earthworks, ponds or other stretches of water, mounds of earth, churches, tracks and place names could all feature in his alignments. At this stage, however, ley lines were still simply the quaint invention of an eccentric old man with a surfeit of money and leisure.

It was in the 1960s that Watkins's ideas were revisited and sent well and truly off the straight and narrow. New Age writers started to suggest that the ley lines were lines of unmeasurable energy. They said that one could dowse for ley lines with twigs, that UFOs used them for navigation ('Er, Captain, that trip from the Constellation of Orion was pretty straightforward, but we've got leaves on the line and I just can't make

out if that's the King's-Lynn-to-Avebury ley or the Uckfield-
to-Droitwich ley down there…'), and that Gaia, the Earth
Spirit, has chakras along the leys. Basically, anything old and
weird in a straightish line (though some say leys move in
curves) anywhere from Peru to Pudsey could be a ley line
or an energy channel/point/field. Not surprisingly, entrepre-
neurs saw this sort of scenario as a win-win situation and the
New Age economy was stimulated. No one, strangely
enough, has studied the number of banks on ley lines.

So, to be fair, it is only partly due to Alfred Watkins that I
find myself at the bottom of a hill, standing between Gog and
Magog (two ancient oak trees) and staring up a ley line. It is
only partly due to Watkins that I am accompanied by Neil
Stevenson, a ley line enthusiast and geologist who really
should know better. 'I sometimes imagine druids landing here
on a boat and walking up towards the Tor between the oaks
that formed an avenue up the hill,' Neil says. A robin perches
on a hedge and hops inquisitively to within a couple of feet of
us. 'I've had robins land on me,' he adds. 'It's those kinds of
thing that confirm that the area is magical. It's like living in a
bubble – the outside world lives in a different way.'

We are on the edge of what the locals call the Isle of Avalon,
but which is more commonly known as Glastonbury. The
town and the Tor, which overlooks it, rise above the Somerset
Levels, a flood plain stretching west towards the Severn
Estuary. Before proper drainage ditches were put in centuries
ago, it was quite literally an island above marsh and water. It
is an area swathed in mystery, myth and, as Neil points out,
magic. I am walking with him to see if any of it rubs off on me.
We are going to follow several ley lines via the church tower
on top of the Tor, the point that some say has the greatest con-
fluence of ley lines in the world.

'As a scientist I can't explain it, but I do feel an energy
when walking on these ley lines,' he says. I am not optimistic.
As we walk uphill towards the foot of the Tor in the bright
morning sun, however, I admit that it does seem an enchanted
place. *En route* to the Tor we pass strange earthworkings, one

of which resembles a serpent. 'That's part of the mystery,' Neil says. 'As a geologist I can say that's not natural, but we don't know what it was.' We cross an old orchard draped with mistletoe. Neil explains that the Glastonbury Order of Druids use it for ceremonies in which they cut a sprig of mistletoe with a golden sickle.

We start to climb the Tor and arrive at the Wishing Stone, a massive egg-shaped stone, hidden beneath a hawthorn tree. The tree is festooned with coloured scraps of cloth, representing people's wishes. 'I come here to reflect. It's a strangely peaceful place; it helps clarify things for me,' Neil says. He explains that this sunny hollow looking down on the River Brue is also seen as the entrance to the underworld. The Arthurian underworld, I suggest, brimming with sturdy knights ready to save the kingdom? 'No, I mean the subconscious,' Neil explains. One day, he tells me, he found a sleeve of a pinstriped shirt ripped off and tied onto the tree. 'Perhaps they were trying to escape the rat race for the Isle of Avalon,' he muses.

We continue up the steep sides of the Tor and Neil explains that the terraces are not natural. He tells me that there is a labyrinth going up, round and down the Tor which takes several hours to complete. I opt for the simple route and we climb on. The view from the top is exhilarating. The Mendips rise out of the flood plain to the north, while the River Brue flows by, the banks rising a full metre above the flatlands. To the east, the flatlands rise up to the fields that host the annual rock festival, and to the west is the graceful old town and its abbey ruins. By now I have plodded obliviously across several ley lines, but surely on top here I should be feeling an energy rush? I could do with one, as I am distinctly out of breath and my legs ache. When I recover, I am ready to admit that the Tor's dramatic rise out of the flood plain does have an eerie aspect.

Neil points out Chalice Hill, an adjacent hill below us which aligns with Glastonbury Abbey and the Tor. As coincidences go, it is a minor one. Chalice Hill holds its own legends, however. Some say that beneath it lies the chalice that Christ used at the Last Supper (also known as the Holy Grail). A local we meet tells us that one lady living on the hill became convinced that the chalice was buried beneath her kitchen. She hired builders to dig up her floor. Seven feet down and Grailless, they downed tools and refused to go on. Neil then tells me that my druidic friend and king, Arthur Pendragon, once hired a JCB and started digging up a roundabout on the hill. He struggled to operate the JCB and ended up disconsolately bashing a lump of tarmac with a hammer. The Somerset constabulary were not impressed.

We amble down the narrow path along the spine of the hill that brings us out between Chalice Hill and the Tor. A little later we arrive at a lane which separates the Tor from Chalice Hill. Two springs rise there, one on either side of the lane. The spring from the Tor is crystal clear; the one from Chalice Hill tastes of iron and stains the lane orange. People are filling containers with water. 'They have healing properties,' Neil explains.

Beside the springs is the Chalice Well, a garden built around an ancient well which supplies one of the springs in the lane. In the garden, one woman stares motionlessly into the sun, another alternates between putting her palms on a tree and hugging it, and a man meditates cross-legged by the well stream. The wellhead itself is a little lacklustre – a sort of spiritual manhole cover. Once lifted, there is water to be seen. It is nice water, but it does not shine or cause a tremor in my spiritual ethers. Despite the alleged healing properties, no one has yet been ready to go public about it, I am told. The high point of the visit is the Chalice Well guidebook, which bans smoking, alcohol and mobile phones and sensibly adds, 'Remain clothed whilst in the garden.' I am definitely inside the Glastonbury bubble, I realize, but I am likely to keep my clothes on.

Once we are off the ley line, Neil departs after asking me, 'Was that just a normal walk in the English countryside?' Well, yes it was – apart from the maniacs.

I wander off down Glastonbury high street. It is a surreal experience. Every other shop seems to be selling New Age bric-a-brac. The shops have names like Psychic Piglet, Dragons, Speaking Tree, Crystal Star, Gothic Image, Growing Needs, National Federation of Spiritual Healers Shop, Outer Limits, Spiral Life, Crystals, and Another Lovely Crystal Shop. Windows shimmer with exotic crystals: ameythst, rose quartz, malachite, topaz. *Does anyone*, I think to myself, *consider the appalling conditions of the workers, the child labour or the environmental damage involved in the strip-mining which provides these feel-good crystals?*

Glastonbury high street is a New Age supermarket with spiritual paraphernalia spilling out onto the road. Everywhere I turn I am faced by healing centres, vegetarian restaurants, incense-filled craft shops, crystal shops and bookshops selling volumes on angels, fairies, ley lines, witchcraft, runes and aromatherapy. Half way down the street a man with a multi-coloured woolly jumper, an ill-disciplined floppy hat and a middle-distance gaze is leaning on a crook. He has the look of someone who is trying rather too hard to look simultaneously content and profound. Still, it beats working for a living.

I pop into a café for a tasty cashew and peanut korma. In one corner a bearded man plays 'Greensleeves' on a harp. Delicate filigree notes rise and fall, plangent thrums hang on the air. His playing is hypnotic and soothing as, in melodramatic fashion, he gracefully lurches over the bounds of restraint. After my meal, I walk to the bottom of the hill and find another odd figure. A besuited man in his fifties is preaching to the wind. 'Crystals, New Age healers, Tarot – it's all deception and superstition. Salvation rests only on Lord Jesus Christ!' he shouts as people walk by. Some teenagers skateboard past him. A man in white robes resembling an Indian guru walks past him without a glance. The besuited man is undaunted and continues his rant, but nobody is listening.

The whole town reflects a kind of hyper-reality, a bohemian yet rarefied spiritual ambience. Wandering along the street, I note that Glastonbury does not have 'Kill Your Speed' signs.

Instead, drivers are told that they are entering a 'Traffic Calming Area'. Even the payphone LED emits what must be an unusual message: '30% off calls to India.' I decide to spend the night in Backpackers, the local hostel and pub, where I discover that the dog is called Merlin.

That evening I meet Palden Jenkins, a tall, bearded, 40-something gentleman who is intelligent, tolerant and a gentle enthusiast for the town. He says that, for a town of 10,000 people, Glastonbury is remarkably cosmopolitan. These days it is less polarized between hippies and Somerset yokels, because people are realizing that the alternative approach to food, agriculture, health and spirituality is bringing the town employment and wealth. So is it a New Age supermarket? Palden prefers an alternative metaphor: 'I see it as more of an exhibition town, showing a model of personal growth and social evolution.' He concedes that it does attract extremes (and not a few mental health patients), but believes that tolerance is what is being learned, an openness to alternatives that is rarely found in rural Britain. That, however, does not take account of the exploitation masquerading as mythology and healing. 'People aren't really excited about getting rich,' he explains. 'That isn't their motivation.'

Later on, in the Backpackers bar, I meet a woman who makes medieval wedding dresses. How would she describe the town? 'As a playground for adults,' she says enthusiastically. She tells me that it is a place where adults can experiment and enjoy without having to conform to society's expectations. She also concedes that it can become a religious war zone. When the Christians' preaching outside gets too much (or too amplified), she tells me, members of the New Age community gather African drums and literally drum the Christians out of town.

Next morning I rise early to sample as many spiritual experiences and healings as I can afford. I set off to the Ramala Centre, where the public are invited to join devotees of Indian guru Sai Baba. The centre, a converted stable block and old stone house, is quiet and peaceful as I take my shoes off at the door. A notice directs me into the meditators' room, where two women sit in the lotus position and one young man reclines in a chair. Eyes closed, they sit serenely beneath a large signed and framed photograph of Sai Baba, hung above the mantelpiece. Dressed in a bright orange robe, Sai Baba smiles broadly beneath the mother of all Afros. The sun streams in onto daffodils arranged on the mantelpiece, candles burn beneath the portrait, a joss stick's lazy trail of smoke rises to meet the guru's gaze. I sit down, close my eyes and breathe in the tranquillity.

About 20 minutes later, one of the women reads a thought for the day from Eileen Caddy, the founder of Findhorn New Age Community. It is not particularly original or inspiring: 'Be yourself and do not try to be like anyone else. It takes all sorts to make a world. I do not want you all alike, like peas in a pod...' She then hands me a card with one of Sai Baba's *bons mots* on it:

Duty without love is deplorable.
Duty with love is desirable.
Love without duty is divine.

I am not sure how long I am supposed to meditate on these profundities, but after a couple of seconds I am fidgeting inside. The woman brings a box of fine brown dust over to me, spooning a little into my hand and rubbing some onto my forehead.

When the others rise to leave, I follow. 'What is the brown dust?' I ask.

They laugh. 'That's not dust, it's *vibhuti*,' one says indulgently. Sai Baba frequently materializes this sacred ash, she adds. Sometimes it materializes between the glass frames of his portraits.

'Surely *that's* dust?' I say.

They disagree. 'It has healing powers too. That young man had cancer, but we think he's been healed now,' one says. *What do the doctors think?* I wonder but do not ask aloud. 'We put *vibhuti* on your forehead to take bitter thoughts away, so that you only see purity in others,' she adds smiling.

Unfortunately, my work as a journalist makes it problematic for me to view Sai Baba with such purity – I have spoken to too many disappointed devotees and heard too many allegations. Who knows, though? Perhaps the *vibhuti* will purify my thoughts on the rest of my spiritual trawl round Glastonbury.

Walking down the road, I am struck by a large modern bungalow with paintwork ugly enough to make your retinas peel off and die. It is built on a hill and has a 10-foot wall which is coated in garish turquoise paint and covered in bird droppings and scabrous white blisters where the plaster has burst. Anywhere but Glastonbury, this toothpaste-coloured monstrosity would lead to a civil war with the neighbours. This, however, is the Berechah Colour Healing Centre.

Inside I am met by Jan Billings, colour therapist and owner of the centre, who offers to explain colour healing to me. She takes me into her vivid lilac treatment room and turns on an illuminated screen displaying about 100 bottles full of brightly coloured oils. Each bottle contains two separate coloured oils and she explains that each combination relates to particular characteristics. She asks about people's favourite combinations to get in touch with their core personalities. 'It's non-intrusive. You choose the colour and I tell you what the colours represent,' she explains. The colours vibrate at particular frequencies which, when applied, regenerate, revitalize and rebalance the human aura. It is primarily for personal growth, Jan says, but physical healings can also occur.

Jan asks me which bottle jumps out at me and after a couple of minutes I choose olive green and coral pink. 'That's called gretel,' she says. 'It represents feminine leadership, someone who knows themselves very well, who has conquered fears and turns difficulty into an opportunity for personal growth.' I am beginning to enjoy this. 'This person has an open heart and many deep insights and speaks from the heart. He is happy with himself and lives with integrity,' Jan continues. I could listen to this for ever. My second choice is less flattering, however: blue and orange, Jan tells me, represent the clown or joker and emotional junk.

A treatment would involve applying the oils and massaging them onto certain chakras. The healing continues by surrounding oneself with appropriate colours. Jan shows me a variety of coloured rooms where people can stay as part of their treatment. The treatment technique, known as Aura Soma, came from a blind psychic herbalist from Lincolnshire. *The blind leading the colour-blind*, I think, before banishing such impure and closed-hearted thoughts from my head. The strange, pseudo-scientific faith that links particular colours with character traits and then with healing frequencies is slightly reminiscent of the Aetherians' prayer batteries. As personal growth goes, however, colour healing certainly beats The Forum. At £25 a session, it is a lot cheaper, too.

I amble down the high street towards the abbey and into The Orthodox Way, a shop full of paintings of religious icons and various saints. Behind the counter is Father John Ives, a gaunt, bearded man with long, bedraggled hair, thick glasses and the black robes of an Orthodox priest. He grins at me nervously, with the look of someone who is not overburdened with customers. 'Doing much trade?' I ask. He titters under his breath, perhaps at the vulgarity of referring to his calling as a trade. He tells me that he paints some of the icons himself and shows me his latest, Christ of Glastonbury. 'Glastonbury is important as a Christian place, not because of all this New Age nonsense,' he says. The Orthodox Church wanted a centre in Glastonbury, he explains, because it was where Christianity first arrived in Britain via Joseph of Arimathea (the man in whose tomb Christ was buried). There is no real evidence to suggest that Joseph of Arimathea came to England, but I nod politely.

I ask where the Orthodox congregation meets and Father Ives grins conspiratorially and takes me through to the back of the shop, up some stairs and into a small, narrow room, barely big enough for a table-tennis table. The room is a tiny, ornate

Orthodox church, complete with altar, candles, icons, tapestries and altar-piece triptych. There are four chairs facing the altar. 'We don't have many members,' Father Ives explains. He points to a painting and explains that a couple from Atlanta bought one like it and the hands and feet started secreting perfume. 'I can't guarantee that it will happen every time,' he chuckles. How was he drawn to the Orthodox Church? 'It was a gradual process,' he explains, 'but when the Church of England admitted women priests, I knew that I had to leave.' Does the Orthodox Church pay him? 'No, they have very few stipendiary ministers. I'm paid through the shop's income.'

Just round the corner, past the East West Centre, the Bridget Healing Centre, a crystal shop and several bookshops, is Glastonbury Abbey. Legend has it that the abbey was built close to the church that Joseph of Arimathea built when he – allegedly – brought Christianity to Britain in AD 63. Some even believe that, when he was a child, Jesus visited Glastonbury with Joseph of Arimathea, said to be his wealthy tin-merchant uncle. And, yes, some say that Jesus and Joseph started a church here – before Jesus started his ministry in Palestine; before the concept of Christian churches existed, in fact. Maybe not.

Another legend says that King Arthur and Queen Guinevere are buried in the abbey grounds. Strangely, this story first appeared in the twelfth century, at a time when the monks needed money because their abbey had burnt down – money presumably gained from the pilgrims visiting the 'burial site' of a much revered king. The tale about Joseph of Arimathea's visit with Jesus originated in the same period. There is a problem with these theories – namely, a total lack of evidence. It is not known that Joseph of Arimathea was Jesus' uncle, nor that he was a tin merchant, nor whether he ever left Palestine. The arrival of the boy Jesus on these shores is the sort of myth to make even the dourest Bible scholar break into a belly laugh.

It is clear that Glastonbury's Christians are in no position to point the finger at the New Agers' myths and exploitations.

The stories of the Grail, Joseph of Arimathea and the boy Jesus were the original exploitative myths, and there is no more evidence for them than for the healing properties of the Chalice Well or the energy of ley lines. Such myths can still be dangerous in the wrong hands, however. In Victorian times, the British Israelites developed the idea that Britons were the 'chosen people', the 10 lost tribes of Israel. They incorporated the myth of Joseph of Arimathea's visit into their theology. The group still exists. It has links with racist groups in the USA. These ideas even fed into William Blake's poem 'Jerusalem':

And did those feet in ancient time
Walk upon England's mountains green?

Er, no. Forget it. Don't even think about it.

In Glastonbury it is probably best to start with what can be seen. I see the abbey's huge, headless columns stretching up to blue skies, vaulted arches without glass and one-metre-thick walls that really must have taken some dedicated vandalism to destroy. The reality of this evocative ruin is rather prosaic. Henry VIII's troops destroyed the abbey in 1539 after the dissolution of the monasteries, when he founded the Church of England and told the Catholics to leave because they disapproved of his serial marriage habit. The abbey was a wealthy Benedictine monastery (probably founded in the tenth century) when it was attacked, and the abbot was hanged, drawn and quartered. All that is left now are huge arches reaching gracefully up to the heavens and thick yellow columns, dotted with gruesome gargoyles, cut off by blue sky. It reminds me of T.S. Eliot's line in *The Waste Land* symbolizing the complexity of the collapse of faith as 'sunlight on a broken column'.

There are two other things of note at the abbey. One is a hawthorn tree held up by several iron poles. Legend has it (again) that this tree is descended from Joseph of Arimathea's staff, which started to sprout when he placed it on the verdant fields of Glastonbury. It is a type of hawthorn that flowers at Christmas and also grows in Palestine, and it attracts visitors from far and wide. Like the rest of Glastonbury, it begs the question: Is nothing *not* sacred?

The second noteworthy thing on the site of the abbey goes a little way towards answering this. It is a heap of rocks piled up in a rectangular form. There are a couple of gargoyles that have had the grimaces wiped off their faces, and the rest is ruined chunks and blocks of abbey wall. It *could* be a UFO navigational aid; it *could* be where Jesus discovered his calling; it *could* be an earth chakra on a ley line – but thankfully it is simply a pile of rocks. No doubt it is an alignment waiting to happen, but so far it has not. I am tempted to sacralize it, to start a myth, to bow down to it, to put up a notice offering healing stones or gargoyle therapy, but I do not. I leave the fallen rocks in their state of pre-fallen innocence.

Opposite the entrance to the abbey is a side street that leads to Chislett's All Tools and Plant Hire. It is reassuring to see somewhere so earthy, so grounded, so full of Kango hammers, chainsaws and JCBs. I notice a couple of thick-set, bearded types in T-shirts and dirty jeans. Just across the road, in a converted chapel, is the Archangel Michael's Soul Therapy Centre which offers angelic realignment and shambala education. Outside are images of angels and strange wire geometric shapes. Perhaps the elusive energizing alignments that I have been seeking will be *inside* me, I think, as I go through the door.

I am met by a barefoot, middle-aged woman in maroon and gold robes. I tell her that I am researching different forms of spirituality in Glastonbury. 'You've come to the *right* place,' she whispers, leading me upstairs with a serene smile. We enter a light, airy room with football-sized wire cuboids, triangles and pyramids hanging from the ceiling. There is a strange droning voice submerged in bells, drums and too much echo effect which also seems to be coming from the ceiling. On the shelves are six-inch crystal rods, partly wrapped in copper wire, with geometric shapes on the end. The walls are covered in brightly coloured prayer flags and tapestries of Eastern deities. 'He is here; he is among us,' the woman says, looking deep into my eyes. I realize it would be a mistake to ask who she means.

She starts telling me about the strange shapes hanging from the ceiling and positioned on the shelves. 'They are *vajras* which transmit healing energy when you pick them up,' she says with suffocating calm.

'Do you make them?' I enquire.

She tells me that only a handful of people in the world are qualified to make them because of the complex radionics.

'*Radionics*? Are they the work of George King?' I ask.

She has not heard of him. 'Radionics is the science of etheric energy,' she says with a knowing glint. 'I think it is best to let you experience,' she continues, gesturing around the bizarre room.

The peace is disturbed by a phone. Someone shouts upstairs, 'Who should a banker's draft be made payable to?' and my companion disappears in a rushed blur of maroon and gold robes.

I nose around the rooms upstairs. One has a bed with a diamond-shaped mat on it, underneath a 10-foot pyramid frame. Another has a seat in the centre of a pentagram-shaped framework, crowned with a small pyramid. I pick up a leaflet and it explains that this is a Buddhist centre and the 'he' to whom my companion referred is His Holiness Tulka Buddha Maitreya Rinpoche. The leaflet suggests that the woman, who was reluctant to give her name (for fear of indulging in egotism, I suspect), is a levitating nun and that Tulka Buddha is also served by other levitating nuns and lamas in Tibet and California. The *vajras*, pyramids and 'metatronic mats' are designed by the Buddha. The hand-held ones sell for hundreds of pounds, the larger ones for thousands.

Then I see his photograph. This Buddha has a most disconcerting appearance. Stripped of his orange robes, bejewelled golden mitre, pyramid and accompanying wings (which hang beside his ears), this man, surely, belongs at Chislett's All

Tools and Plant Hire! He has the moustache, shortish beard, fat jowls and surly expression that should be selling six-inch nails and Hammerite, not crystals wrapped in copper wire. His belly should be propping up a counter, not a pyramid; his thick, muscular hands should be holding Black and Deckers, not *vajras*. I am not surprised to learn that Tulka Buddha is an American. However, when my levitating nun friend said, 'He is among us,' I suspect she meant that he was on a retreat somewhere in California rather than moonlighting at Chislett's.

I sit down in a leather chair in one of several white booths along the side of the room. Each seat has a special copper-lined healing mat, two *vajras* to hold and some headphones. It is supposed to be a total healing experience. I pick the *vajras* up and close my eyes, trying to empty my mind. All I hear is terrible, out-of-time thudding on drums, accompanied by random bongs on random bells and the excruciating drone of chants and 'wise words' with layers of swirling echo. A notice tells me that this formless din is pure, unadulterated Tulka Buddha.

I pick up the headphones, press play and hear a similar, truly distressing cosmic cacophony. It is divine music to make your ears bleed, but the final twist of the knife is its claim to have healing properties. If that is not enough, then piled on a shelf by the booth are dozens of tapes and CDs *for sale*! Beside them a notice says, 'Planetary and Personal Soul Therapy is invoked by the Sacred Songs and Music of Buddha Maitreya. The songs are invocations of Angels, Buddhas and the Saints of Christ.' *Tulka Buddha – don't give up the day job*, I think.

My levitating nun returns. 'What did you experience? Did he have an effect?' she asks. Her physical feet may be firmly on the ground, but in a metaphorical sense they are some-where outside the stratosphere.

'It was very soothing. I felt peaceful,' I lie. I cannot bring myself to tell her to turn off the awful din.

She asks me to pick a *vajra*. I choose what I think is a dodec-ahedron. '*That*,' says my non-levitating levitating nun, 'is the sacred geometric pattern of human consciousness.' She goes on to explain that certain geometric shapes have deep spiritual significance. She tells me that holding the octahedron *vajra* (£263) while wearing the crystal ascension pyramid (which, for £333, fits snugly on the head) while sitting on a metatronic mat (£768) beneath a Metatronic Pyramid Ascension System (hard to work out the price, but very expensive) would be most beneficial.

My maths has never been great, but the significance (and cost) of all these geometric shapes is confusing me. They are, I am told, for the healing of my aura, in order to release the angelic nature inside me. Tulka Buddha is telepathically overseeing the development of these metatronic sciences, to heal individuals by contacting the angel that is our true nature. The non-levitating levitating nun gets out an Etheric Weaver to show me how it works. This is a laboratory-grown coloured crystal on a chain. She holds it above the palm of my hand. It rocks slightly, then, with a slight movement of her finger and thumb, the chain starts to move, pulling the crystal in a dramatic pendulum swing across my palm.

I am not supposed to notice the movement of finger and thumb. I am supposed to believe that Tulka Buddha has found some damage in my aura and that the Etheric Weaver helps to sew it back up again, so that the angel in me is free to *be*. The nun asks me how I feel. I cannot really say that I feel nothing, so I comment on the peacefulness of the 'music'.

She smiles. 'It always has a healing effect, even on newcomers.' She then goes on to tell me that I have to be discerning on my spiritual search. 'This Celtic New Age stuff is garbage. In Glastonbury there is a lot of vampiric energy,' she counsels.

'The master is not ready to reveal himself,' she tells me. 'He will wait until he has 140,000 followers. This time he is not here to be crucified; *we* will suffer for him.' He has followers in Tibet, Europe and America and as soon as he gets 140,000 he will be back as quick as you can say 'His Holiness Tulka Buddha Maitreya Rinpoche'. Yet the Antichrist is also among us, deceiving people, and he has a bigger ashram than Tulka

Buddha. *Hey, size isn't important,* I want to say. I hazard a guess as to who this Antichrist might be, and the nun is awed by my discernment. I rub my forehead hastily, checking that Sai Baba's thought-purifying dust has gone. As a reward for my spiritual insight, she tells me when the Antichrists and deceivers will be exposed (the year 2035, in case you were thinking of setting up as an Antichrist).

A robed lama interrupts us and the nun leaves, saying that a payment of £5 is normally expected for sitting in the healing booth chairs. And would I like an Etheric Weaver? She can give me a £20 discount on it and I can have it for £80. I explain that I only have loose change. 'How much change?' she asks.

'Two or three pounds.'

'It's just that not to give after healing can damage your karma. For your sake, leave it in the bowl by the door,' she adds. Foolishly, I do.

I leave Glastonbury along a street leading to Wearyall Hill. Wearyall is a narrow hill which rises above the flatlands. On it is a windblown thorn tree, but it is not, my guidebook tells me, a direct descendent of Joseph of Arimathea's staff which sprouted here 2,000 years ago. From the hill I can see over Glastonbury and back to the conical Tor. In the other direction lies the flood plain leading to the Severn Estuary and, naturally enough, I am standing on a ley line. It is a beautiful and striking situation, but I do not feel a rush of spiritual energy. I am weary, and keen to leave the rarefied Glastonbury bubble. I glance at my guidebook and am irritated to see that I am now walking into the Glastonbury Zodiac (I won't bore you). I suspect, however, that this Zodiac can only be seen by very intelligent people. I see nothing. My guidebook tells me that I am looking at what would have been a beach and a megalithic village. Try as I might, all I can see is a Safeway's car park.

9

Chant and Be Happy

Some people seem to believe that pain, self-denial and humiliation lead to God. This can be self-inflicted (of the 'Watch me hang breeze blocks from tender parts of my body' sort – a timeless favourite of Japanese television), or it can be accidental (of the 'M'Lud, since being locked up for mugging old ladies, I've found God' sort). It would be easy to interpret this Route 666 as a quirk of modern times, a sort of reaction to our consumer-cosseted Western lifestyle. Yet General Unpleasantness, self-inflicted or not, as a path to spiritual enlightenment has been around for some time.

It goes back at least 5,000 years to aspects of early Hinduism (anything that could be enjoyed, they banned, and when this got boring they started inflicting wounds on themselves) and rears its ugly head in the Book of Job and the parable of the Prodigal Son, in Buddha's cheery Fire Sermon (*everything* is burning with lust, greed and ignorance) and in all sorts of self-flagellating types ever since. It is both a catholic and Catholic practice, if you like. (You will have gathered by now that most modern, New Age beliefs tend to be pain-free zones.)

Quite why we pursue pain, humiliation and self-denial with such zeal is puzzling. Perhaps we confuse it with the more laudable practice of selflessness. Or do many of us feel an innate unworthiness which leads us to believe that unpleasantness is our just dessert? The German theologian Dietrich Bonhoeffer seems to me to have got this right. The church that played on people's weaknesses and guilt was ignoble and un-Christian, he said. When did this revelation come to him? It came to him while he was in a rather unpleasant situation himself: in prison awaiting his execution for conspiring to assassinate Hitler.

All of this has given me cause to wonder if pain and humiliation have ever led to inklings of spirituality in my own life. I remember once humiliating myself by chatting up a girl on a bus, then falling off the bus and breaking my arm. I was drunk at the time and, though the pain got pretty bad, divine revelations were not forthcoming. No, the most painful and humiliating thing that I can remember happened more recently on an operating table. I should have realized that I was in a lose-lose situation when the surgeon had my testicles in his hand and twisted them.

I was escorted through to the operating theatre in my regulation-issue NHS apron – looking, perhaps, like an ascetic monk in search of gratifying hardship. I was introduced to Dr Akbar and his team. Karen was the reassuringly named 'scrub nurse'; Mark, barely out of his teens, was a sort of embarrassed assistant's assistant. However, the sack of burning coals poured liberally over my head was called Jean, the 'escort nurse'. It was her job to talk incessantly about nothing and to distract me from my vasectomy, which was the job in hand.

When I was lying back under the bright white lights, Dr Akbar pulled back my apron and exclaimed, 'Why, Mr Howard, you have a remarkably small scrotum!'

Choking back a mixture of embarrassment and shock, I muttered, 'Actually, I'm feeling rather tense. It's contracted.'

His solution was to start pummelling my testicles with the palms of his hands. 'This should do the trick,' he said, kneading away. After a few muted yelps from me, he decided that maybe some local anaesthetic was in order. A glistening, two-inch needle was duly sunk into the depths of my scrotum as I stared fixedly at the patterns on the ceiling tiles. You might think that, if there is a direct link between pain and spirituality, I was due a divine visitation.

No. Jean, in her role as 'escort nurse', chose this moment to go into conversation overdrive. However hard she tried to talk about plans for Christmas, I was having none of it while a cold needle was being thrust into my private parts. Four injections later, I was there: my testicles were swimming around in some giddy, painless delirium. Perhaps now my pain and humiliation was complete, and I was ready for the brush of angel's wings?

No. Dr Akbar explained that the anaesthetic only worked on the surface. A couple of incisions later, he was making this abundantly clear as he poked around inside with what felt like the blunt end of a tent pole, looking for the sperm ducts. Meanwhile, the conversation went something like this:

Surgeon to scrub nurse: 'Pull the tube out.'
Scrub nurse to surgeon: 'You know me, I'm cack-handed.'
Escort nurse to me: 'How are your children getting on at school?'

You might think that if the humiliation–holiness theory has anything to it, then I would find that I had transcended the material plane and discovered holiness.

No. Two days later, my testicles were the size of tennis balls. Just sitting up in the morning was excruciating. The final humiliation, however, came several months later. I was told that the operation had not worked. I would have to return for a second attempt.

All of this is no proof, as such, of the absence of the spiritual side of suffering, but it does provide enough of a straw for a coward to grasp. Perhaps my analgesic life has prejudiced me against pain, but the trite phrase 'No pain, no gain' always leaves me wanting to respond with a deadpan, 'No pain, no pain.'

It is not that pain cannot be productive: Martin Luther King, Gandhi, Nelson Mandela and countless unknown campaigners and workers have clearly grown spiritually through pain. What I find more discomfiting is what one might call the *pain fetishists* – those who seek out pain with the same zeal with which others seek pleasure. This seems like an inverted form of decadence. Some have no choice. I am not saying that self-denial is always bad. Perhaps it is a matter of distinguishing between vanity masquerading as long-suffering and fulfilment within the strictures of measured self-denial. Perhaps the latter really can lead to enlightenment.

It is with this challenge to my nature in mind that I decide to sign up for a weekend with the ascetic monks and nuns of the International Society for Krishna Consciousness (ISKCON), more commonly known as the Hare Krishnas. The weekend that I join them is not just any weekend: it is a celebration of Lord Chaitanya's birth. This celebration is not just an excuse for a 4 a.m. rise for chanting and prayer, a day's fasting without food or drink (except water) and a street procession through the heart of London. No, they also have to fit in several hours of chanting and *japa* (meditation) in between the partying. At the end of the day, when the moon rises, they get to chant some more, then eat a vegetarian meal.

It is early Friday evening when, feeling a little daunted, I arrive at Bhaktivedanta Manor, a large house set in several hectares of rolling fields near Watford. I will be staying in the men's ashram, living with the monks, participating in their devotions – but how will I cope? I know embarrassingly little about their beliefs, apart from their enthusiastic chanting and their equally enthusiastic abstinence from tea, coffee, tobacco, alcohol, meat and sex. Will this abstinence open a tiny window in my bloated soul? Will the chanting lift me onto another plane? Or will I, in the words of my mother, 'be brainwashed'?

At the main door to the mock Tudor mansion (which George Harrison bought for the group in 1973) is a large shoe rack and instructions to remove shoes before entering. It is the first of many Hindu traditions that are rigidly adhered to by the devotees. Inside, about a dozen men (shaved) and women (scarfed) dressed in orange or white robes are chatting or looking at books. One man drifts around the room chanting *'Hare Krishna'* under his breath. In a nearby room I can hear the tinkling of cymbals, muted chanting and the quiet beat of tabla drums. The air is laced with the cloying, sweet smell of incense. I am reassured, however, by the relaxed, friendly faces.

I am met by Vikunta, a young Croatian monk who is in charge of accommodation in the ashram. Like most devotees, he has adopted the spiritual name given to him by his guru. He is shaven-headed, and wears the orange robes that denote celibacy. He leads me through the manor to another exit. This presents the first problem with this sort of asceticism: if you cannot wear shoes indoors, and there is more than one exit, then you need a pair at each door. You also have to remember where you left them. I follow Vikunta past a bakery and shop to an outbuilding, where he leads me, barefoot, upstairs to a Spartan loft conversion which houses seven monks. Everywhere I hear whispered chanting: *'Hare Krishna, Hare Krishna, Krishna Krishna, Hare Hare, Hare Rama, Hare Rama, Rama Rama, Hare Hare.'*

I am given a bed and introduced to Roland, a Slovakian monk in his twenties who is still waiting to be given a spiritual name. He is a recent convert, at the manor for the weekend and hoping to be allowed to live there permanently. He tells me that he arrived in England as an au pair, then started studying Social Policy before failing his exams. He had been interested in spiritual matters for some time. He was a vegan, so it was not a big step to become a devotee and ISKCON member. He is friendly, but a little too earnest for my liking. He has the knowing half-smile of the initiate who feels impregnable and looks down with amusement on any pitiful sceptics around him.

I wander back into the manor to retrieve my shoes. I visit the toilets and discover that they leave courtesy flip-flops there, to avoid any monks paddling in urine. I also note that each toilet has a jug of water (I am told later that Hindus use water not paper). Then I walk through the gardens and woods that surround the manor house. I follow a path around a small, tree-lined lake, noting wooden plaques displaying up-lifting thoughts or chants. The scene and the plaques seem like a Hindu version of a Patience Strong calendar. I come to some wrought-iron railings and look through to a typical Home Counties village street, complete with duck pond, old pub, flowers and cottages. It seems a world away. On the other side of the manor are acres of vegetable gardens, pasture and a big barn with 'Cow Protection' written in large letters across it.

Back inside the manor, Pancha Pandova, a 40-something divorced ex-engineer, explains about the beliefs of ISKCON. The four pillars of the religion are truthfulness, mercy, cleanliness and austerity. Each one of these relates to four regulating princi-ples which are slightly weaker as selling points: no intoxication (which subdivides into no alcohol, caffeine, nicotine, illegal drugs or chocolate), no meat, fish or eggs (but milk and cheese are fine), no sex unless for procreation (and then only if you are following a lower spiritual path) and no gambling. 'We're for simple living and high thinking,' Pancha explains.

He tells me the story that led to him giving up alcohol, nicotine, coffee, chocolate, meat, fish, eggs, gambling, sex and his marriage (he is now a celibate). 'I was managing leisure centres when I got interested in vegetarian cookery and went to classes run by devotees. I started visiting the temple with my wife. I was 40 and asking questions about the meaning of life,' he explains. Gradually he started chanting and visiting more often. Pancha wanted to live by the regulatory princi-ples, but his wife did not. They split up amicably, and he joined the temple.

So what is it about chanting? 'When I'm chanting, I feel joy and awe and reverence for Krishna, I get closer to him, get engrossed in the name,' he says. At any given moment in the manor, one can hear chanting: either the whispered *japa* chants or the full-blooded song chants. Pancha explains that they have to do a certain amount of chanting each day. There are set hours for worship in the temple throughout night and day, as well as several hours of *japa* to be completed. The communal chanting and dancing is called *kirtan* and is for pleasing Krishna by pleasing each other.

Pancha tells me about the significance of Lord Chaitanya to ISKCON. He was the Hindu equivalent of Martin Luther (they lived at the same time), and challenged the religious leaders of his day for keeping the Vedic teachings in their temples, away from people. Chaitanya took the teachings to Hindus regardless of their caste, and started a movement of devotion to Krishna. Many Hindus worshipped other deities, but Lord Chaitanya was the first of a line of teachers to emphasize Krishna as the fullest expression of the godhead. The founder of ISKCON, Swami Prabhupada, was the last. In 1965 he took the teachings to the West, starting with New York. Over the next 12 years, before his death, Swami Prabhupada founded hundreds of temples and colleges and graced hundreds of thousands of *Bhagavad-Gitas* (his translation of Vedic scriptures) with his prune-faced visage on the back cover. As increasing numbers of Westerners were drawn to his teachings, the press branded him a brainwashing cult leader. George Harrison was his most public follower.

Pancha takes me to the suite of rooms upstairs where Swami Prabhupada stayed. They are kept exactly as they were on his last visit nearly 30 years ago. In the plush bedroom is a glass cabinet containing items that he used on his last visit: a Gillette razor, Phillips milk of magnesia, Monsieur Lanvin shaving mousse and Boots nail clippers. His picture adorns the walls, flowers are placed on his duvet. Do they consider him to be an avatar, a visitor from God? 'He's not really an avatar,' Pancha says, 'merely a signpost. A holy man on a high spiritual level.' In the en-suite living room is a life-size plastic mould of Swami Prabhupada. He is revered, but not worshipped.

Later, after some vegetarian curry and salad (served on paper plates with plastic cutlery, and eaten while sitting cross-legged on the parquet floor), I hear drums, cymbals and communal chanting. It comes from a high-ceilinged ballroom which has been converted into a temple. The room gradually fills up, men on the right side, women on the left. The musicians and lead chanter are at the front, facing a large silver and gold shrine with several black-haired, white-faced statues dressed in fine, elaborate and colourful clothes. They have beatific smiles, unnatural poses, and are draped with garlands of flowers. To be honest, I think they look silly and irritating with their accentuated expressions of innocence and purity. They are deities, however: most of them are Krishna at various stages of his life or in different incarnations. Candles and incense burn in front of them, and a bare-chested man in a loin cloth wafts them with a large ostrich-feather fan. Another sprinkles them with water from a silver tube.

Devotees at the front stand motionless, gazing at the deities or whispering a prayer. Most are walking back and forth to the rhythm of the tabla drums, chanting. The music gains in speed and rhythm: it is becoming ecstatic. The expression on people's faces reminds me of the charismatic worship at Peniel Pentecostal Church several months earlier. These people are giving themselves with total abandon and joy. They are completely focused on Krishna, waving their arms in the air, regardless of what onlookers might think. Perhaps it is a testament to the Hare Krishnas' superior rhythm section (or it could be all sorts of other factors), but these people are more communal in their dancing. Sometimes they join arms and whirl round in what looks like a Scottish jig. Although it is intoxicating, I stand at the back, self-consciousness intact.

The music rises to fever pitch and then tails off into more soothing, restrained chants. After about 40 minutes, people sit down, get out beads from bags attached to their wrists, and quietly start to chant *japa*. I give it a go, but like so many religious rituals, I find it boring. Watching saints pray is the spiritual equivalent of watching paint dry. Until the significance of the rituals is unlocked to me, this sort of thing is a waste of time. I creep off to bed, ready for an early-morning start and more communal worship. As I drift off to sleep, the '*Hare Krishna*' chant is reverberating around my head.

At 5 a.m. I am woken by a monk chanting at the top of his voice as he applies his make-up. I roll over. Another joins in. I pull the covers over my head. It is too late to get back to sleep, however, so I go to join the worshippers in the temple. They are whizzing round the room like dervishes. The chanting, the drumming and the enthusiasm are infectious. For such an anti-sensual religion, what I am witnessing looks positively ecstatic. There is a clear build-up, a crescendo, then the kind of lull when you might have a cigarette and roll over for a sleep. It is probably unfair to say that these celibates are sublimating sex into wild, abandoned chanting, but the idea does cross my mind.

Later, after half an hour of deeply tedious, whispered *japa*, a portly, white-robed Asian man sits cross-legged on the floor in front of a microphone. He reads a passage from the Vedas and embarks on a sermon. He talks about Krishna slaughtering soldiers, about Lord Brahma and suffering, about karma and past lives. Apparently, Krishna shook hands with Lord Brahma and creation started. As origins go, I quite like the idea of the whole shebang starting on a handshake. After about 40 minutes, he says that Krishna's concession is giving us the *'Hare Krishna'* chant. Thanks. We can chant our way to Krishna-consciousness. Nothing else will work, he tells us, eyes closed in the half-light of the temple. At the end people ask questions, and I slip out for a bit of sleep. It is nearly 7 a.m.

I wake at 10 and wander down for some breakfast (more vegetarian curry). Afterwards I walk out to the barn with the 'Cow Protection' sign. In it are cattle stalls with ornate, multi-armed Hindu deities overseeing them. They are empty except for a couple of calves. On the walls are details of ISKCON's work protecting cows around the world. They protest against the live export of cattle, against bullfighting and against the destruction of the BSE herds. 'Such inoffensive animals are symbols of religion and should be protected,' a notice says. But the crux of the matter, it seems to me, is that Krishna protected cows *as a cowherd*. Ever since, of course, they have been sacred cows. ISKCON have rescued several cows, and a notice tells me that they are now grazing in the neighbouring fields. I wander past the byres for a view of these spiritual creatures. Dozens of long-horned bulls graze in peace. One is quite close. Its soggy nose, saggy face, blank expression and long eyelashes, though inoffensive, could more easily be described as 'stupid' rather than 'spiritual'. I don't think I'm in tune with this whole thing yet.

At 11 a.m. I join two devotees in a mobile soup kitchen, which is known as their Food for Life project. They take vats of curry, rice, fruit and whole-food products from their bakery and distribute them six days a week on the streets of north London. The food is *preshnam*, food that has been offered to the deities. David, an ex-security guard in his late thirties, drives the van and Tomaslav, a younger Croatian, joins us. Both were drawn to ISKCON because of its 'higher values'. They were, they tell me, yearning for a deeper meaning, and they believe that they have found it. When I ask about the tough regime, David explains, 'Krishna means "the enjoyer", but we enjoy more deeply by living a moral life.'

Both are enthusiastic about the 'soup run', and their clients have a good relationship with them. We make several stops and I really enjoy slopping out plates of good food to interesting, hungry people. Some are young homeless, others alcoholics or people with mental health problems. Some are very middle class, others are asylum seekers. There are a couple of prostitutes and several people with glazed eyes and bruised arms. One young man in a trench coat and woolly Russian Army hat stands in the queue with a book under his arm. He mumbles a request for food and David asks what he is reading. The young man looks up with an unhinged grin and replies, 'I read about conspiracies. It helps to keep me paranoid.' All are polite and thankful. I think I am beginning to understand what David called ISKCON's 'higher values'.

On the way back up to Watford, I ask David and Tomaslav how they fit such altruism with their belief in reincarnation. Weren't those people on the streets because of bad karma from their past lives? I ask. They agree. So, if they were *destined* to be on the streets, are David and Tomaslav not going against Krishna by intervening? 'It would be useless to feed them if this was normal food, but it is spiritual food, it will help their karma for their next life,' David says.

I press on. Does Tomaslav really believe that the refugees from the Balkans are there because of bad karma? Karadic, Milosevic, all politicians are the same, he replies. They need Krishna. But it is these people's own karma that brings them to the streets. They deserved it from their past life. Hmm. Did the Jews, I ask, deserve Auschwitz? Er, yes, they tell me. The 'higher values' are slipping down the karmic ladder pretty quickly. I change the subject.

Back at the manor, I have yet another vegetarian curry and find Indriesh, the monk in charge of ISKCON's education programme (i.e. school visits). He is a quietly spoken intellectual with a hollow face and a crooked grin. He is so thin it hurts. One of the oldest residents at the manor, he is refreshingly honest about life in community. I have noticed that the European Hindus seem rather more serious in their asceticism than the Asian ones do. He agrees. Community is difficult, he explains. They now have an introductory programme to see if would-be monks can cope. Not all can manage the higher path of celibacy. So is sex dirty?

'Sex is good to have children,' he says.

'No fun practising, then?' I ask.

'The body is very beautiful, but strip the skin off, and it is not,' he replies.

The whole idea is to transcend this reality, and part of this is to sacrifice our bodies to 'purity'. Everything has to be done in a spiritual way to improve our karma. Six hours of chanting is exactly for this purpose. Indriesh tells me that they do not use the sitar because it is too sensuous an instrument. No sex, no alcohol, no tobacco, no meat, and the countless other rules, are all to improve karma. Part of the idea seems to be that, if one can die while chanting (and, therefore, while thinking of Krishna), it leads to a kind of karmic jackpot in which one

skips a division and goes straight into the Premiership. That is, you are more likely to be reincarnated as a saintly human than as a threadworm. You might call it a kind of sublimated spread-betting.

It is clear that they see themselves as being on an ascetic treadmill in which a good life leads to a slightly higher 'incarnation' on the route to oneness with Krishna. They have hundreds of lives, Indriesh explains. It reminds me of those twee T-shirts which say 'Life is not a rehearsal' – except that Krishna devotees would wear one reading 'Life IS a rehearsal'. Indriesh assures me that they are not living in fear of karma, but simply want to transcend this world and achieve bliss and oneness with Krishna.

The next day (Lord Chaitanya's birthday), transcending reality would have come in rather handy. After rising at 4 a.m. with only a drink of water for sustenance (even fruit juices are banned on this fast), I spend several hours in the temple. It is heaving with people in the dim light, as the deities blaze in resplendent innocence from their golden shrines. Half-naked men are wafting incense with ostrich-feather fans; others sprinkle blessed water from silver salvers over the pulsating, chanting crowd. At times the worshippers are a frenzied, whirling mass of devotion as hundreds chant and wail and dance. Then the deities are washed in oil and water before the curtains are closed. After more chanting, the deities reappear in new clothes, draped in garlands of bright hyacinth petals. There is more *japa* chanting, followed by a guru waxing lyrical for far too long, then an hour's extra chanting. Finally we walk round a sage plant, have a flame placed near our head, and smell some flowers.

I take my place on a double-decker bus into London for the procession down Oxford Street. By this point (about 11 a.m.), I am feeling really rather hungry. I am also noticing my all-too-thisworldly vanity coming into play. What if someone recognizes me? What if I am caught on camera, dancing and chanting my way down Oxford Street? Generally I pride myself on not caring what people think, but this is truly pushing the boat out. I begin to notice odd glances being thrown from overtaking cars at the robed and shaven monks on the bus. I start to wish for bad weather.

As we arrive by the London Temple in Soho Street, the sun beams down and the streets are full of shoppers. Fifty or so devotees are waiting outside the temple. Most people head upstairs to the shrine and temple proper. There is a massive pile of shoes outside. The room – coloured candy pink, pastel green and pale orange on intricate wooden cornices and fretwork – is crammed with dancing, chanting devotees. It is all more of the same, and I have had more than enough of that, even if it offers me shelter from the gaze of curious shoppers. I leave and find a quiet park where I wait for the procession to start.

When it begins, I wander behind at a discreet distance, nipping into the HMV store, WH Smith's and various souvenir shops *en route*. The devotees appear to be completely blissed out as they chant and drum into microphones, leading the float carrying a shrine of Krishna and a model of a flying swan. Shoppers wander by bemused. There is no meaningful communication with them, beyond the fact that female devotees hand out sweetmeats (*preshnam*, no doubt) to those who will take them. I continue to shadow the procession, maintaining a respectful distance.

I stroll along in an awkward limbo, feeling increasingly guilty at disowning the people who have been so hospitable and good to me for the last few days. Surely I should just plunge myself into the midst of the devotees, wave my arms from side to side and chant my heart out? I also feel my stomach contracting into a tight ball as I realize that my last meal was about 16 hours ago. Even the thought of another vegetarian curry seems rather appealing. The procession continues down Regent Street. Gradually it dawns on me that I am passing an *inordinate* number of Angus Steak Houses. I start to inspect the menus with guilty glances: sirloin steak with pepper and cream sauce, rump steak in white wine... *Impossible*, I think. *Those cows have sacred credentials*. Anyway, it would take too long. I would lose the procession.

The thought gnaws at my stomach like a temptation that will not let go. It is only when I see the statue of Eros, sensuous god of love, at Piccadilly Circus that I know I am pierced by his arrow of temptation. In the corner of my eye, I also see a Burger King. I sprint ahead into the vice centre of the UK (Piccadilly, that is, not Burger King) and rush in for a quarter-pounder of cow with cheese, large fries and (to placate the ascetic that I know lies dormant inside me) a Diet Coke. I find myself a nice first-floor seat and look down on the procession feeling a little like Orson Welles at the top of the big wheel in *The Third Man*. Mmm … food does taste better after fasting.

I rejoin the devotees at Leicester Square and they are gathering a crowd to watch some street theatre in front of the float. In terms of quality, it is definitely *sub*-Christian street theatre, which is something of an achievement in itself. Let's just say that the sketch involves a train journey which starts at Human Body Junction and makes its way to Blissville, with branch lines to Fleeting Pleasure, Lower Species, Old Ageton and Diseasechester.

Perhaps it is a reflex reaction after so much wincing during the drama, but as the procession starts on its way back to the bus in Oxford Street, I throw myself into the part. Arms waving above my head, my whole body swaying to the drum beat, I chant ecstatically at the top of my voice:

Hare Krishna, Hare Krishna,
Krishna Krishna, Hare Hare,
Hare Rama, Hare Rama,
Rama Rama, Hare Hare.

I am aware that I am sublimating my ego in rhythm and chant and, sure enough, it works. I am transcending reality – or ego-reality. I am not converted, or even persuaded, but I can at least see that it is possible to let myself go and, in the words of the Nike Corporation, 'just do it'. I do it all the way back to the bus.

Later, back at the ashram, something else falls into place. I put on my running shoes and go for a jog around the estate.

After passing lots of people looking into the evening sky for moonrise (at which point they can start their feast), I approach the road beside the fields. My burger lurches and swills around in my stomach as I jog past the cows. After five minutes beside the undulating green fields, I find my rhythm.

Then, as often happens when I am running, I have a minor realization. It is this: jogging is quite similar to the experience I had while chanting on Oxford Street. When I run, I let myself go, transcend ego-reality and start to have more penetrating thoughts. It is strange that a religion which so robustly rejects physical reality as illusion should use physical activities (chanting and dancing) so centrally to transcend reality. I know that jogging leads to this state, as the clutter of bric-a-brac in my mind dissolves, leaving the bigger picture in view. I also know that the painful physical strictures undergone by the devotees could lead to the release of endorphins and a similar 'spiritual state'. Of course, the fact that something can be explained physically need not discount the possibility of a spiritual interpretation also being true. Nonetheless, for a religion which appears to dislike the body so much to use such markedly physical rituals seems contradictory.

On my return I notice many of the Asian Hindus tucking in well before moonrise. One leaves the bakery carrying bags full of cream cakes, whole-food crackers and cans of drink. He hands things out to his family, all in their best clothes to celebrate Lord Chaitanya's birthday. It is, to them, a traditional Hindu feast day, much like Easter or Christmas is for Christians. He picks up another bag from the bakery and I notice the slogan on the side, which seems to sum up the weekend: 'Chant and Be Happy'. Chanting may give these good devotees a sense of transcendence, but I think I need a more physical transport. A pilgrimage, maybe?

10

🛒

Snapshots from Paradise

Oban, the tourist centre on the west coast of Scotland, is not an auspicious place in which to start a pilgrimage. It has two chippies, a quayside greasy spoon, a clutch of hotels, some dour, granite-faced churches, a Woolworth's and a conurbation known as Tesco's. McDonald's must be just round the corner. There are tourist shops with Oban rock, pubs with pub rock (or 'traditional Scottish music') and bookshops selling booklets of Scottish jokes/recipes/proverbs.

This is perhaps a little unfair. The town is pretty enough and, on a sunny day, like lots of places, you might call it beautiful. More importantly for a would-be pilgrim, it has the shops and amenities that allow one to stock up before leaping back in time to a simpler, more pious past. Oban's role as 'gateway to the isles' makes it the perfect place to begin such a journey. Ferries run to remote islands on the west coast archipelago, where time appears to have stood still. These boats deposit passengers or cars (or both) on deserted piers in tiny island hamlets whose largest and newest structure is often the pier itself. There are over a dozen islands, where life is held in varying degrees of aspic, all just a ferry ride away. I am probably a gullible fool, but I have been told that the people on these islands hold a simple, genuine faith that has much to offer.

The luxurious, hi-tech boat hardly prepares me for the imminent shock of the old. Relaxing in the swish video lounge, watching President Clinton's confession-cum-public-relations exercise concerning Monica Lewinsky, seems an incongruous way of travelling back to a simpler, more honest past. I go out on deck and look west at the watery horizon. A school of dolphins come alongside as we sail towards the sunset. This seems more in keeping with my romanticized ideal. My destination is Barra, five hours west of Oban.

I disembark in darkness, leave Castlebay village and find myself driving through a steady drizzle as I cross the tenuous causeway from Barra to Vatersay. Lurching round corners in the pitch black, I am terrified. There is *nothing* to be seen except a tiny ribbon of single-track road. You simply don't get darkness like this in modern Britain. When the road comes to an end without warning, I have no idea where I am. Suspecting that I cannot be far from the Atlantic, I pitch my tent and fall asleep.

The next morning I wake in the muggy, claustrophobic atmosphere of a tent that has been in the sun for too long. I shrug off my lethargy and unzip the flap to crystalline open skies. I am next to a deserted beach in a bay between two barren, rocky hills. A few cows wander from the machair (verdant, fertile meadowland by the dunes) down to the beach. It is like a scene from an Enid Blyton novel: a romantic and dramatic landscape, innocent, inviting and adventurous. There is even a mysterious plane lying wrecked beside the road (it crashed in the war and was never recovered). An old man is chuntering along on a Honda 90 with his shopping in a washing basket strapped on the back. I came here in search of a durable spirituality, and have found myself in a scenic heaven. I stroll over a hillock and realize that I am camped on an isthmus with a beach on either side. There are half a dozen council bungalows sheltering beside the dunes, and that is it. I spend the day searching for eagles.

The Outer Hebrides are deeply reminiscent of the immediate post-war years in the rest of Britain. These are islands where doors are left unlocked, where sweets are sold in jars not packets, where Nike ticks are far rarer than chunky Arran sweaters. The people even speak an inscrutable, ancient language – Gaelic. Here Post Offices are in garden sheds; mobile shops and banks perch precariously on the back of old Transit vans. As I travel up the string of islands, piles (not bales) of hand-scythed hay fill the fields, beside rusty red tractors. Crofters go beachcombing or cockling on endless beaches – although one of these is an 'airport' from which old propeller planes fly to Glasgow. There are no cyber cafés, cinemas or arcades. Instead, locals hold ceilidhs in weatherbeaten village halls.

Strangely for an isolated string of islands often seen as a single entity, there is a religious divide nearly half way up the archipelago. Vatersay, Barra and South Uist are firmly Catholic islands, Benbecula – which houses Army and Air Force missile ranges – is a kind of buffer zone, and North Uist, Berneray, Harris and Lewis are increasingly staunchly Free Presbyterian and Calvinist. The Church of Scotland is also present on the islands, offering a milder version of the Reformation tradition. The Free Presbyterians (known as the Wee Frees) seem to enjoy a good schism, because between 1843 and a more recent spat which surfaced in 1998, they have split six times – all over what to outsiders look like theological niceties. The Free Church of Scotland, Free Presbyterians and various subsections or splinter groups are broadly united in their theological hatred of Roman Catholicism. The northerly islanders may secretly think of the southerners' faith as an expression of the Antichrist and the southerly islanders may secretly think of the northerners as dour and miserable, but there is no real visible conflict, and everyone seems to have a strong sense of shared traditional values.

Some of these values are quaint, if contentious. The Co-op in South Uist, for instance, was boycotted until they stopped selling condoms. Campers on Berneray are told not to hang out washing on Sundays, to avoid offending locals by working on the Lord's Day. In many newsagents north of Benbecula, the main seller is not yesterday's paper (it takes a day to deliver newspapers to the Western Isles) or even *People's Friend*, but the evangelical *Christian Herald*. In Lewis and Harris, some people eschew Christmas as a pagan festival. The locals are disarmingly friendly, however, and their faith is one of the factors that helps them to resist modern culture.

A few days after my arrival, a shopkeeper gives me another insight into the Hebridean temperament. 'We're having plenty of *weather*,' he remarks, meaning plenty of wind and rain. We are, but it strikes me that the harsh, changeable weather probably affects their gritty, unpretentious attitudes. Nature will have no truck with modern self-indulgence. It will not even let the trees grow! The shopkeeper's comments also convey a sense of contentment. There is no hint of complaining: the weather is as it is, and that is all there is to be said about it.

That evening I pitch my tent on a desolate Barra beach, yards off the single-track road, before climbing a craggy hill in search of a chambered cairn and people to talk to. I walk by small cottages, smelling the sweet scent of peat fires as I follow the track through the tiny village of Craigston. Further up the hill, after the track becomes a path, I come across a preserved croft cottage (a croft is the term for a smallholding's land and cottage). The curator, a local, rolls up a cigarette and tells me the cottage's story.

A couple of years ago, the former owner, by then in his seventies, herded a few cattle, made butter in a pail and slept in the bed in which he had been born. The cottage had no road, no electricity, no sanitation and a bare mud floor. The old crofter was healthy, but was a worry to the health services. One winter, they decided to take him into new social services accommodation based around the mountain in Castlebay. Just days later, he died. I look at the butter churn, paraffin lamps, hand-made clothes, an old Bible and leather-bound notebook. Almost certainly, the crofter lived a hard and poor life, but the curator said that he was a happy character. It seems sad that he could not have been left in his cottage and died in his own time, in the bed in which he was born.

This story presents a powerful image from a different time – a time when people were so rooted in landscape, family and community that a sense of the spiritual was indistinguishable from the warp and weft of everyday life. 'It was all he'd ever known, and he was happy enough,' the curator explains. I try to ask about people's spiritual beliefs. 'We're nearly all Catholic doon here; up there they're Wee Frees,' he says. That is the way it is and always will be, he seems to imply. For him there is nothing to explain. The unquestioning approach seems almost pre-Reformation in its outlook.

Continuing up the hillside past a large chambered cairn, I think about the old crofter as a sort of metaphor for the islands. The wrong sort of modernization could ruin them. I also realize that patronizing, romantic southerners' yearning for a simpler, more spiritual past is pretty offensive. I pass the huge pile of stones forming the cairn and soon arrive at the summit of Beinn Mhartainn. The view is spectacular. Vatersay, the Uists, Benbecula, Sandray and other tiny islands stretch out to the north and south. I see a smudge on the horizon that could be St Kilda. Below are tiny crofting communities, heather and sand, the single-track road glistening in the sun. This is living history. The people on these beautiful islands actually live this way. I breathe it all in. It affects me deeply, in an ineffable way, but I cannot pretend that there is not an edge of melancholy to my feelings. I have to accept that this way of life is dying.

That night I lie on the machair reading until 11 p.m. (the island is so far north that it is only fully dark for about four hours in the summer). I drift off to sleep with the Atlantic swell lulling me into unconsciousness. At about 6 a.m. I wake to the steady hum of drizzle on canvas. It sounds as if it is there to stay, and a glance outside confirms this. The tent has to be taken down from the inside to keep things dry. It is the first time I have been in this tent in heavy rain, and the meaning of 'dry run' hammers its way into my head as the moisture seeps through my clothes. I manage to dismantle everything successfully, but it feels a bit like trying to take off your underwear while wearing trousers. Here I am, on the romantic edge of civilization, in the land of myth, getting soaked to the skin.

My feelings are becoming rapidly de-romanticized. I drive off through fog and wind.

My next destination is Berneray, an island of under 100 inhabitants. I reach it after another ferry journey and a long drive across several islands. *En route*, the weather improves and I wander lazily among the ruins of a pre-Reformation abbey, discover a deserted stone circle on a heather hillside and saunter among the multicoloured seaweeds on the sandy shore, which stretches out of view in both directions along the west coast. I walk across causeways with aquamarine water and white sand on either side. I munch sandwiches on a grassy verge overlooking a loch beneath craggy mountains. Then I take the small ferry to the tiny island of Berneray, where I am to stay in an old crofter's cottage converted into a basic hostel.

The wind howls across the sea outside, buffeting the bluff white stone walls of the cottage, tugging at the thatch, rattling the windows. The electricity cables are down and the spluttering Aga seems incapable of making a pot of tea. It has been difficult to leave the cottage for two days now, as the wind teeters on that meaningful razor's edge between gale and storm. Things are *not* going according to plan. This crofter's cottage, jutting out into the Sound of Harris by a fine, platinum beach on the tiny island of Berneray, was supposed to be the idyllic spiritual and scenic heart of my pilgrimage. It was supposed to be the place where I could meet the locals, go to church with them and see if I could breathe in their sanguine ways. Instead, I am learning any new card games that my fellow hostellers can teach me. Two-hour sessions of blackjack, whist, pontoon and some European variations are losing their appeal.

Then there are the hostellers themselves, stuck together in the same room for hours on end. The three cyclists and the two Dutch women are a pleasure to spend time with. Not so the pugnacious, mountain-sized woman-hater who appears to think that he owns the place, nor the fresh-faced scout-master type who oscillates between breezy 'seize the day' exhortations and tut-tutting because I have left a saucepan out to drain dry. No, these are surely from a pilgrimage to Hades. As for the quiet couple who insist on practising yoga, furrowing their brows over *The Tibetan Book of the Living and Dying* as the rain lashes at the windows – do they really have to be *so serene*?

The twist of the knife, however, is neither the weather nor my fellow travellers: it is the beauty of the surroundings that we are missing. 'Berneray is stupendous, very good,' Anke, one of the Dutch women, says to me. 'It's the best place in Britain,' says the woman-hater. The sea and a sodden white beach are a mere five yards from the front windows.

On Saturday the gale subsides slightly and I push myself through the wind around the bay to a Portakabin that is the island shop. 'The weather's not so good,' says Mrs Macauley. I ask how long it is likely to last. 'Och, who can tell? Probably not long.'

'Will there be a service tomorrow?' I enquire.

'Oh, certainly, yes.'

'Do all the islanders go?'

'We do, yes. There's a few elderly that can't get there now, you know. The minister visits them.'

I ask why Christianity is so popular here, while church attendances are dropping on the mainland.

'We hold to it very much. On the mainland there are so many distractions, things have gone badly. They've lost their way without the Lord. But they would be better to follow our example,' she says. She *knows* that the islanders are better off with their communal faith and way of life, and it seems hard to argue with this. True, the islands have a few alcoholics, but that is nothing compared to mainland angst and social problems.

The next morning I try to dress reasonably neatly for the Presbyterian Church of Scotland service. As neatly as a cagoule allows, that is. The gale has nearly blown itself out. As I approach the village, a church bell is ringing and it does seem as if the whole community is on its way to the service. Everyone is dressed in Sunday best – women generally have formal dress or skirt, blouse and cardigan; men are in dark suits, polished black shoes and ties. They file from the road that skirts the bay, along a road leading half way up the hill to where the squat church stands. It is shaped like a church hall, but is solidly built of brick and grey plaster, with a raised bell above the gable end. It could not be less inspiring.

Inside is a small porch and a bright white room with wooden pews. There is an elevated pulpit with a small stand in front of it. There is nothing else. The room is deliberately plain. There are no pictures, crosses, candles or prayer cushions – just wooden pews and whitewash. A man known as a precentor walks to the front stand and starts to sing a psalm. He works his way through it in a kind of pious drone, and I can barely hear the words. Instruments are not allowed: as with the Hare Krishnas, they are considered too sensual and worldly. I quickly see that a Road to Damascus experience is looking unlikely. People stand up and the precentor starts another psalm. The congregation follow his intonations, this time in Gaelic. After several more psalms in Gaelic, a black-suited minister enters the pulpit. Unfortunately, he speaks in Gaelic too. The service ends with some Gaelic prayers.

At the end, I wait outside the porch to meet people. It has stopped raining, but the heavens are about as grim as the service and the wind is still strong. I feel just a little foolish, having sat through a service in another language. I sidle up to Calum, a big man in his forties. 'I didn't understand much of that. What did he say?'

'It was about keeping Sunday special,' he says, then adds by way of explanation, 'the ferries are trying to do crossings on Sundays, but the Bible says we should keep it as the Lord's Day.' I cannot help admiring this. He does not mince around with comments about Sunday rests giving a better quality of life, or about protecting workers' rights. He is quite plain: Sunday is the Lord's Day, and that is that. Calum is not harsh or judgemental in manner. He is friendly and matter-of-fact.

He tells me that he works on the oil rigs. 'On Sundays?' I ask.

'Only sometimes, in emergencies,' he says.

An elderly lady called Mrs MacLeod introduces herself with a wicked grin. 'You speak Gaelic, do you?' Then she tells me that they had an English service last week – they have them every fortnight. She tells me that she enjoyed the service. 'On the mainland anything goes, but out here we follow the Lord's commandments,' she adds.

'Why are there no decorations or adornment in the church?' I ask.

'We want to concentrate on the Lord and his Word, not all the finery and distraction of some churches. Our faith is simple.'

I wonder if she is referring to the Catholics, but probably she just means most other Christian groups. I can see that she is a benign, content lady, but I cannot help wondering if that sort of rigidity is helpful. If life is good, dogma does not matter, but I am reminded of a similar form of Christianity where life is too often bad: in Northern Ireland. While I am thinking this, Mrs MacLeod changes the subject, and I notice both the simplicity of her faith and how undemonstrative she is about it. It simply *is*.

On my last evening on Berneray, I walk to a stone circle overlooking the whole island. I survey the archipelago with mixed feelings. The lush pasture, the endless beaches and dramatic, craggy mountains make these islands a kind of paradise. In the sun they are sublime, and in the rain (as long as one is not blown away) they are brooding and dramatic. They are certainly invigorating. Yet the people are living in a cocoon, a hermetically sealed time capsule. The world is moving in as surely as lack of jobs is moving their young people out. Things might be better if the world were this simple, but to retreat to this enchanted enclave somehow seems like cowardice.

Back at the hostel, perched above the beach surrounded by lush machair, with seals basking on the rocks across the bay, I meet some kids playing football in a field with goalposts made out of rough timber and fishing net. They ask me to join them. Where else in Britain could this happen? The memory of playing football in a gentle breeze, looking out across the Sound of Harris towards the massive blocks of bare gneiss rock that form the mountainous eastern seaboard of Harris, will stay with me for a long time. The sense of open space, of wildness and wilderness, of civilization being far over the horizon, is hugely refreshing.

A little further up the islands are the Hebrides' real mountains. Clisham on North Harris is the best part of 3,000 feet high. These mountains are formed of Lewissian gneiss and, according to geologists, contain some of the oldest rocks in the world which date back nearly 3,000 million years. Harris is simply a string of tiny lanes winding around the grey, gnarled, lunar landscape. On the east are rocky coves below small cottages and rusty outhouses in which crofters make Harris tweed on hand looms. On the west are acres of mint-green meadows, skirting dunes and miles of deserted beaches. Driving by these meadows, I notice a painted wooden sign: 'No golf on Sundays.'

Surprisingly, in the village of Tarbert – Harris's main port – there is a small Pakistani community of two families. Despite their Muslim faith, by all accounts they are completely accepted by their Calvinist neighbours. Presumably this is because they share many conservative, 'traditional' values with the other islanders. It reinforces the sense that shared values create community much more than shared dogma does. The northerners may view the southerners' theology as suspect, and vice versa, but, although the trappings (or pronounced lack of trappings) are different, they seem pretty similar in their friendly contentment and their suspicion of 'the mainland'.

If the mainland is their devil, then he manifests himself differently to each religious community. In the Catholic isles it was condoms that were banished; in the Calvinist isles it is

Sunday trading. If a group of libertarian hippies were to arrive in the Outer Hebrides, rest assured, they would not settle happily. It would bring out staunch grimaces as hard and durable as Lewissian gneiss. To me, this sort of intolerance is intolerable. It is not necessary to eschew morality or ethics in order to believe that consenting adults do not *have* to marry to have sex. Hanging out one's washing on a Sunday is *not* going to have a domino effect on the island's moral rectitude that ends in unbridled lust and orgies. This rigidity is no advert for the islands' old-time religion. Flexibility might be a greater sign of strength.

Before I leave these strange islands, I stop off at the pre-Christian Callanish Stones on Lewis. They are tall slivers of silvery stone, coincidentally in the shape of a Celtic cross, which stand gracefully over the surrounding moorland and sea. An avenue of stones leads to a burial chamber in the centre. They certainly suit the wild, romantic landscape more than the grim, squat, rectangular Free Churches which are dotted around. The stones are mysterious and beautiful; the churches are functional and ugly.

My last afternoon is spent in a café in Stornoway, waiting to board the ferry to Ullapool. Stornoway is disorientating. It is a kind of culture shock to see a town: a place with street lamps, a council estate, a Woolworth's. It may contain a roundabout, or even some traffic lights! Outside the café, it is raining with Hebridean determination. I do not resent this: it is part of the raw beauty of the Hebrides and, like the islanders, I have learned that you have to accept the less appealing aspects of its wildness along with the sublime. Struggling through a gale is no hardship if you can see the weird, sand-blasted sculptures it creates on the beach. Sombre, grey skies are worth it when you can sit undisturbed on sand, heather or rock, gazing into the wild heart of the Atlantic. The relentless rain is worth it when it gives way to days of crystalline sunshine. The unpredictability is part of the appeal. In this far-flung corner, there are no half-measures – and it has had an effect on me.

I cannot remember finding a place in which I have ever felt closer to nature, in which I have ever felt freer inside. Yes, this feeling is spiritual, but it has nothing to do with the islanders' simple Christian piety. Neither can I call it paganism. Certainly it has something to do with awe and reverence before nature – an 'otherness' which strikes deep. I leave the Hebrides sad, but touched by nature, raw, wild, beautiful and serene. I also respect the islanders' uncomplicated lives and, in some ways, their unquestioning spirituality. But my fondness for the people and place also has something to do with nostalgia. My visit was like walking back into a golden age: the 1950s.

It is a place of innocence, but I suspect this has as much to do with the world outside as it does with the intrinsic qualities of these islands or their inhabitants. The islanders may feel that they are under siege from modern mainland culture, but the reason that they have not yet been conquered is not simply their indomitable spirit. They have maintained their innocence because the influence of consumerism has not yet forced its way onto the islands. The reason for this is simple: the islands are a costly boat journey away and there are few people to make money out of. The possibility of profitability in these islands is less than marginal, hence they have been left in a 1950s' time warp. They are protected because there is so little return to be made on them; they are uncorrupted, with distinctly limited exposure to good and evil (though they also miss out on the more positive aspects of progress). Although it seems desirable to be in this Eden, however, the snake will find its way in. Already there are web designers in Stornoway and it has to be good that e-commerce gives jobs in such remote places. It may go against the grain in such a place, but it seems to me that this is what capitalism does: it increases efficiency and does some collateral damage along the way. One cannot base a spirituality on running away from the world.

While I am on the boat to the mainland, the sun sets over the islands. Looking out across the boat's wake, I think of two sights I saw on the islands that encapsulate their relationship to the past. I was standing on the North Uist shore looking across an empty beach and past the nearly completed causeway to Berneray. The causeway, funded by European Union and local council money, seemed like a symbol both of prosperity to come and of the loss of innocence: two-way traffic. In the background was the glistening Roineval, South Harris's highest mountain. Roineval, made of Lewissian gneiss, one of the world's oldest rocks, also stands as a symbol. A quarrying company wants to blow it up, take it south in barges and sell it cheaper than gravel from pits in the Home Counties. The locals are split: some want the jobs, others want Harris to be left unspoilt. The maintenance of their simple, innocent outlook will depend on how the islanders manage incoming offers of money. Their piety is part of the equation, but so are the sorts of compromises that they will fashion with investors and government agencies. Spirituality always has a rate of exchange with commerce.

Ultimately, the spirituality of the Hebrideans is unlikely to transform a modern Briton. The lifestyle and the beauty might be tempting, but the almost wilful unquestioning of their faith is, for me, untenable. It would be beautiful as a 'holiday-cottage faith', but is not robust enough for a permanent dwelling in the modern world. That is why I turn my back on Paradise and look, instead, to the skies.

11

To Boldly Go

It is a beautiful, sunny Sunday morning in spring and I am sitting in the boardroom of the Cruising Association, a yachting club, overlooking a marina in London's East End docks. It is a part of the docklands whose history and character has been erased and replaced with futuristic glass, yellow brick and chrome towers, arching gracefully into the skies. It is a cityscape from sci-fi cyberspace except for the street names: Horseferry Way, Shoulder of Mutton Alley and The Highway. In the marina, the sun glints on plush yachts and angular, pristine motor cruisers. The parking area is filled with dozens of sporty two-seaters – Alfa-Romeos, Porsche Boxsters, BMWs. Cars pull up intermittently and I peer intently at the occupants, but each time they walk into the marina. Rather guiltily, I try to rehearse my false name and story, and wonder why no one has arrived. For a moment I wonder if I am being watched. I open a cupboard door to check.

The reason for my deception is simple: I am waiting for a meeting of Raelians, a UFO cult, who do not appear to like the idea of me writing about them. Earlier I wrote to the group explaining my intentions. Then I e-mailed and left messages. Each time I was ignored. I was told that they were secretive and very wary of outsiders, and decided to ignore them – until I saw a notice on their website proclaiming that all were welcome to public meetings. So I gave it another shot with a different name and no reference to doing research. Within a day I had an e-mail inviting me to a meeting.

The reason why the Raelians are so wary could be due to bad experiences with the press, or because of their controversial beliefs. Of course, the two could be related. There are several distinctive aspects to the Raelians' beliefs, but one which stands out is called the 'cosmic orgasm', the idea that couples can achieve sublimely satisfying sex with a little help from the Elohim – our creators, orbiting, a little voyeuristically, in space. Perhaps with a view to reaching this experience of the 'infinite', Raelians are relaxed about sex, seeing it simply as an expression of beauty with no strings attached.

They are a religious group who reject the notion of God or the soul and describe themselves as 'an atheistic religion'. Their leader Rael teaches that the only hope of immortality is through scientific regeneration. Through an initiation ritual called Transmission of the Cellular Plan, new members sign a contract which allows a mortician to cut a piece of bone from their forehead. This bone is then frozen, until the Elohim, our alien creators, arrive to regenerate it. They also believe that, during four annual festivals, the Elohim fly overhead to record the Raelians' DNA codes on their computers. Some have suggested that the Raelians are fascists because of their rejection of democracy in favour of the rule of the most intelligent – 'geniocracy', as they call it. These beliefs were all revealed to Rael who, like George King, claims to be the last prophet before the UFOs arrive.

Rael (born Claude Vorilhon) was a French journalist with an interest in car racing when, as he claims, he encountered aliens in 1973 while walking in a volcanic mountain range in France. Over a period of days, an alien told him that humans were in fact created in their laboratories in space and that he must tell humankind to choose between destroying themselves with nuclear weapons or following the path of higher science offered by the Elohim. Rael claims to have been taken to their planet and says he received several messages. One of these was that he was the product of his mother and an alien. Another was that the Elohim want to return by 2030 and must be welcomed at an intergalactic space embassy, to be built in Jerusalem.

There was a problem with this scheme: the Israeli government had no intention of letting this group of overventilated space cadets set up an embassy. They would become a global (and possibly intergalactic) laughing stock. Another blot on the Raelian copybook was the fact that, apart from white clothes, early Raelians liked to wear a medallion shaped like a Star of David with a swastika in the middle. This did not endear them to the Israeli government either. The medallion has subsequently been changed out of sensitivity to the Jews.

As I sit waiting in the boardroom, therefore, I am feeling both apprehensive and bemused. Why are they 10 minutes late? I am aware that these sorts of organizations have a reputation for inhabiting a conspiracy-laden, paranoid universe. Could they have grown suspicious and called it off? Just then, a clapped-out rust heap pulls into a space among the Porsches and Alfa-Romeos. Out jumps a bald man in his fifties, rummages beneath some decorator's dustsheets and pots of paint, and pulls out a ghettoblaster. He walks into the building, comes into the boardroom and introduces himself as Paul, the Assistant National Guide of the Raelians. I introduce myself as Jesse Cohen and find out that the only other person coming is Eric Bolou, the National Guide. When Eric (a tall, warm, articulate French African) arrives, I realize that, however unfriendly they may be towards writers, I have misjudged them: these two are open and friendly, and not in the least bit sinister. And they are desperate to tell me about Raelianism.

They tell me that the Elohim are Hebrew-speaking humans who live in Gondwanaland (another planet). Their scientists and artists created everything that is on the earth. Jews, however, are a chosen people because they are part-Elohim and part-earthly human, and so are more advanced. If they continue to refuse permission for the Elohim's embassy to be built in Jerusalem, however (and it is suggested that they have recently been offered their last chance), they will be dispersed. Rael's half-nature (as an Elohim–human hybrid) means that the Elohim speak through his mouth and see through his eyes. 'He's the humblest, the most innocent, childlike person you'll ever meet,' says Paul, reminding me of Mervyn's breathless descriptions of George King.

Raelians are honest about sex, Eric explains. They have rejected the churches' guilt-laden teachings, and believe in having sex because it is good. They reject traditions and taboos. 'We live wholly, fully, in love, peace and harmony. We live in the *now*,' Eric says. Their only ceremonies are the Genetic Code Transmissions and partying – they do not worship as such, because the Elohim are not divine, simply more advanced. Both men keep stressing that this is not really religion: it is hard science. Rael still has a penchant for motor racing, apparently – mainly, they stress, to get publicity for his beliefs. He has raced a Dodge Viper in the USA and is hoping to race in a Ferrari. They tell me one of Rael's *bons mots* concerning spreading the word about Raelianism: 'Somebody selling Ferraris doesn't have to talk.' They keep talking, however, give me a book and invite me to a European convention. On my way out, I pass Paul's rusty, 1970s Ford Escort. It seems a more appropriate metaphor.

About six weeks later, I head off to their European convention in a lecture theatre at University College London. It is, appropriately I suspect, 1 April. When I arrive, the room is about a quarter full and it is clear that nearly all the attendees are continental (as opposed to British) Raelians. Closer inspection reveals a surfeit of young or youngish women with long hair, short dresses and sultry foreign accents. Eric walks onto the low stage at the front and introduces the conference by welcoming visitors and describing Raelianism as a 'science-based spirituality' which 'fits with the twenty-first century'. Worldwide, it has 50,000 members in 84 countries, he says, and it started in the UK in 1977, four years after Rael received his first revelations. He reminds us that the movement is *for* contraception, abortion, euthanasia and male and female priests.

Eric sits down and is replaced by a tight-trousered, long-haired Frenchman in a white shirt and shiny black suit who inexplicably starts singing karaoke over a backing tape. His performance is wonderfully overblown. He strikes dramatic poses for the extended notes, and makes louche, smiling eye contact with women in the audience. He sways to the smoother rhythms, arms aloft, head back, eyes closed. To rockier songs, he waves to the audience, jumps in the air and claps his hands above his head: a kind of one-man stadium rock band. He leaves us with an enigmatic 'Enjoy your life', before stepping off the stage.

Next comes a film introducing Raelianism. The film is judderingly low-tech, like a very early sci-fi film. It tells us that UFOs are mentioned in the Bible and early Sanskrit writings, and that we were created by scientists who decided to make us in their own image. It debunks evolution, but argues in favour of genetic experimentation and human cloning. It shows Rael dressed in white, futuristic clothes with clumsily large shoulder pads, his circus-clown frizzy hair sticking out as he walks, surrounded by followers. It also mentions 'sensual meditation', a 'religious ritual' which includes sex or, at least, masturbation.

In Rael's snappily titled *The Extra-Terrestrials Took Me to Their Planet*, he describes what sensual meditation is: 'If you want to reach a high level of harmony with infinity, arrange a place of sensual meditation. Place in it works of art, paintings, reproductions, tapestries, posters, sculptures, drawings, photographs or anything else that is intended to represent love, infinity and sensuality for the enjoyment of the eyes.' He then advises on scents, foods, cushions and music and possibly the right person (or persons) for 'physical union' and an experience of 'infinity'.

After the film, several Raelians give testimonies. Lara, a blonde American in her thirties, tells us how Rael's book brought her love and self-acceptance. With dreamy eyes and a quiet enthusiasm, she says, 'I'm totally unique and different; I'm free to be who I want to be.' We are then introduced to various National Guides and to Rael's assistant, a smooth-looking man in a black suit and polo-neck sweater. They have nothing of interest to say, except that the rest of the meeting will be a party. Oh, and tomorrow new initiates will be having their DNA transmitted to an orbiting space craft. Sadly, I cannot be here for that.

The party is wonderfully eccentric. Lara comes on dressed as a clown, flirtatiously telling the audience that she is going to teach us to play. She then croaks her way through a song, sticking various body parts to the fore. A Frenchwoman in her thirties with a more assured voice stomps out a celebratory song called 'Viva' (sadly, the gist of it is about celebrating life, not about the 1970s' mid-range Vauxhall car). Another young woman sits Eric centre stage and rubs herself against him while she sings seductively. He grins, stroking her inner thigh as she bends over him. This is all slightly sleazy, but also very dated. It is tacky in the same way that 1970s' disco music is tacky. It is stage-managed and slick in the manner of a team of Redcoats at a Butlins holiday camp. They are trying too hard to party and, to an outsider, it looks quaint and a little insincere. Perversely, they round the party off with a dirge to the Elohim which sounds more like a Methodist hymn.

As I leave, Paul (the Assistant National Leader with the rusty Ford Escort) greets me. He stresses what a scientific religion Raelianism is. 'In fact, it's not a religion, it's 100 per cent scientific fact,' he says. *Gondwanaland is fact?* I think. He hopes that his DNA will be safe with the Elohim on their spaceship. It strikes me that the idea of his DNA being safely tucked away on a spaceship is his reinterpretation of the idea of eternal life. What is fascinating about Raelianism is the strange mixture of 'science' and myth. After all, if they believe in Gondwanaland, they might as well believe that the sacramental wafer is literally the body of Christ. It would be so much easier (though admittedly without the perks) to belong to the Catholic Church. On the other hand, if they believe that their only hope of eternal life is via their DNA rather than their spiritual essence or soul, why not plump for scientific materialism, along with probably the majority of our society? The fact that Raelians reject notions of God or the supernatural in favour of science testifies to science's victory over religion –

yet they have created an anti-religious religion, a pseudo-scientific spirituality with the empirical credentials of Ali Baba's magic carpet.

My next journey into London is to meet a cutting-edge exponent of scientific rationalism whose little-known organization has been seen by some as religious. Like the Raelians, the group are materialists in the sense that they do not believe in God or spirit. Unlike the Raelians, they are empiricists who only believe what they have scientific evidence for, even if their predictions and prophesies are optimistic and speculative. Nick Bostrom, a doctoral student in philosophy and science at the London School of Economics, vehemently denies any religious aspect to the organization which he co-founded, but admits that the World Transhumanist Association satisfies some spiritual urges and answers many religious questions.

Nick has just finished his doctoral dissertation on 'observational self-selection and probability in relation to quantum mechanics, extraterrestrial life, the existence of God, evolutionary biology and traffic planning'. He is busy preparing for Britain's first Transhumanists' Conference (Transvision) before he goes to lecture at Yale in September. Transhumanism is an intellectual movement that embraces the idea of fundamentally changing the human condition and human nature through the use of technology. They do not just mean making prostheses. Transhumanists are intent on creating perfect humans, even post-humans and, to top it all, eternal life in an internet heaven.

We meet for a beer in a Cuban bar with salsa blasting away in the background. Nick is in his late twenties, a gangly Swede with an eager smile, a slight nervous tic and a firm handshake. He tries to explain his breakthrough in observational self-selection by describing a series of hypothetical experiments in probability. It is interesting, but the probability of me following it all to the accompaniment of screeching, ecstatic trumpets and pulsating marimbas is low. 'Because there are infinite universes, then this San Miguel bottle must be somewhere in space,' Nick says. I want to say that, if there is a San Miguel bottle or, indeed, a petrol pump complete with collector, or prayer battery, or anything else, in space, then I reckon that the odds on God or Gaia being out there are looking pretty good. Instead I suggest a different venue for our conversation.

At a quieter bar, Nick explains that Transhumanists first met on the internet. They were generally scientists with an interest in discussing the exponential rate of change and what the future might bring. 'It was no accident that we met on the internet, because that is exactly the sort of technology that we were discussing, as well as being the sort of technology to allow communication and to encourage people with similar interests to gather at a website,' he says. You might say that it was the primordial soup which allowed them to come into being, because they see humankind as the beginning of creation rather than its end and crowning glory. Pretty soon, the group realized that science could allow them to fulfil many of the functions usually left to God or Gaia. 'Advances in artificial intelligence, in nanotechnology, in pharmacology and neuroscience mean that we can design ourselves and change ourselves and become part-human, part-machine,' Nick explains. 'Transhuman', it turns out, is short for 'transitional human'.

At its most basic level, this means using technology to lengthen life span. This could be explored via diet, genetics or cellular rejuvenation. Nanotechnology, the science of building with atoms, should, Nick believes, make the creation of organisms or partial organisms possible. The ultimate aim is control over, and expansion of, our choices. 'Pharmaceuticals currently under development promise to give an increasing number of people the choice of drastically reducing the incidence of negative emotions. These smart drugs could target particular emotions like shyness or jealousy and eliminate them. They could go beyond changing behaviour – they could be used to modify personality,' Nick explains.

How will we be able to make judgements about who we want to be if we are not ourselves? 'We must be cautious initially, but these drugs and gene therapy could enhance our capacity for empathy, courage or emotional depth,' he continues. If you see courage or emotional depth as a chemical mix, moving around our brains, then Nick is right. I am just not sure that I do see it that way. When I confronted the lovely David at The Forum, it was a choice based on who I was, not a chemical cocktail. Of course, the choice and my nervousness will have had chemical components and consequences, but they were not *just* chemicals.

Is there not also a danger that people will become increasingly homogenized if they can design themselves in this brave new world? Will everyone not want to be confident, witty, extrovert and beautiful? Will they not all aim to be like television personalities? To me, an identikit world sounds like a bland new world, like living on a perfect but vacuous American film set inhabited by stereotypes. I point out that, if we truly become masters of our selves, we will lose the eccentric, the vulnerable, the hesitant. Nick thinks that this will be up to individuals. The hesitant probably do not want to be hesitant, but others, he believes, might want to accentuate their differences. I envisage a sort of hyper-reality, peopled by angular, intense but completely different personalities and crowds of television blands.

Another aspect of Transhumanism is the use of artificial intelligence and computer implants. 'Superintelligence is an intellect that massively outperforms the best human brains in all fields, including scientific creativity, wisdom and social skills, and to implant these chips into people would transform their potential,' Nick enthuses. I feel I can cope with a cyborg being better at cogitating than I am, but some unctuous cyborg trying to charm my socks off is likely to get a spanner through the skull/C-drive.

What about the abuse of power, I ask, when only the super-rich can afford superintelligence? 'Transhumanists aren't really political, we don't have an answer to everything. There will be problems, but society will learn to cope.' Nick has libertarian tendencies (anti-state, and far right in relation to commercial and individual freedom), but does believe in the state to the extent that it could intervene to stop abuses of power. Is this not just a little bit optimistic? Surely every step of this decision-making process needs a multiplicity of checks and balances, particularly since Nick envisages private enterprise pushing back these boundaries.

Some Transhumanists believe in 'strong superintelligence', or intelligence that is not only faster but qualitatively better than human intelligence. Of course, it is impossible for us to imagine what this might be like. The best metaphor we have is the mind of God. This is a perplexing thought. All I know is that I would not trust someone with superintelligence. Neither would I like to compete with them in a job interview. Increased efficiency is the Transhumanists' priority, not equality of opportunity.

Transhumanists see no distinction as such between man and machine. Indeed, once the technology is present and people have transformed themselves into post-humans (i.e. human 'descendants' who have changed so far that they no longer qualify as human), some might choose to get rid of their tedious bodies and live as digital information patterns on super-fast computer networks. 'To make a moral difference between natural and artificial is equivalent to racism,' Nick says. 'All beings that are capable of wants and desires should be of equal value; we can treat computers as we wish because they can't suffer at present, but this may well change.'

So what is the essence of a person? Nick feels that all behaviour is ultimately chemical. 'Higher-level values might be your essence rather than basic instincts, though,' he says. 'The technology will give us the choice to be what we want. Traditionally we have only chosen whether to marry or where to live, and the new range of choices may take some getting used to – but I believe that we will manage eventually.' Identity is something in constant flux. He points out that our 'essence' cannot be consciousness, because people are still themselves when in deep sleep or under anaesthesia.

The transference of one's personality onto the internet is called 'uploading' by the Transhumanists. Eternal life in cyberspace. Many Transhumanists have left their life insurance to Alcor, a cryonics company that freezes people after death, in the hope that they can be rejuvenated once the technology makes it possible. To 'upload', Nick explains, all they need is the technology to record digitally all the synapses in the brain and place this information into a computer. 'The idea is that you survive as long as certain information patterns are conserved, such as your memories, values, attitudes and emotions. It matters less whether they are implemented on a computer or in that grey, cheesy lump inside your skull.'

Would that really be *you*? 'Yes, I think so,' Nick says. But what happens if you are uploaded twice? Which is *you* then? 'Uploading presents some philosophical problems and anomalies,' Nick replies. You could also spread like a virus, or be deleted. 'If you're smart, then you'll have a back-up,' he says. But who will put that back on the net? I suspect that the answer to this is 'someone who has been paid a lot of money to do so'.

Surely this 'uploading' idea is just a substitute for the traditional religious pursuit of an afterlife? Nick agrees that Transhumanism is meeting some needs traditionally met by religion. 'I see it from an evolutionary, biological point of view: people needed a survival instinct so that their genes could survive, and when people died they needed a mythical afterlife to help them psychologically,' he explains. 'So we are left with this desire for an afterlife when there is no God, and we look to science to give it to us.'

Despite Nick's optimism, reaching this state is a long, long way away and probably impossible. Digitally recording the one thousand million million synapses, or the one hundred thousand million nerve cells, might prove more difficult than colonizing Mars, travelling at the speed of light, proving if the universe is flat, or operating the timer on a video recorder. But Transhumanism has an answer: they appear to have a scientific equivalent of cosmic consciousness or transcendence, a

kind of technological 'rapture' when the faithful are transported to a future beyond their wildest dreams.

It is called 'singularity' and is the point at which scientific
and technological progress is so advanced that it progresses at
an exponential rate (the sort of thing that *Star Trek* fans refer
to as 'Warp 9 overdrive' in terms of speedy space travel).
Naturally, we cannot imagine what will happen at this point,
or even whether it *will* happen, but in the Transhumanists'
harsh but happy universe, it has become an object of faith. In
their favour, it has to be acknowledged that the capabilities of
computers are said to double every 18 months, and 50 years
ago PCs, palmtops or the internet would have been unthink-
able. Some estimate that singularity could be just 50 years
away. Others consider it a juvenile, adolescent fantasy.

Of course, in the world of post-humans we are entering an
all-too-well-trodden path of science fiction writers who create
techno-monsters that run amok. If scientists make technological superintelligences, who is to say that they will do what we
wish? Should progress not be creating servants rather than
masters? We could, in a very literal sense, be creating our God.
Nick believes that, so long as the parameters are set, even self-
knowledge or consciousness will not send post-humans off
the straight and narrow. 'We know that we like sex because it
is hard-wired into us so that the species survives – but this
knowledge doesn't put us off sex,' he explains. Yes, but if we
are able to create something that we do not understand, then
how can we be sure what will happen?

So, what practical steps has Nick taken towards becoming
a transhuman human? He eats carefully and takes fatty acid
supplements and vitamins to keep his health at its optimum.
He chews nicotine chewing gum, because research shows that
nicotine leads to enhanced intellectual performance. He has
not yet paid a cryogenics company to freeze him once he dies,
but he will do so in the future.

Are Transhumans mainly scientists, or has its appeal broad-
ened now that fewer people put their faith in an afterlife?
There are about 10,000 Transhumanists in the world, including

up to 1,000 in Britain. 'They are mainly young, highly-educated males working in business, science and technology, but we have authors and artists too,' Nick says. The majority are in the USA, where Transhumanism evolved on the internet sites of futurologists, philosophers, scientists and sci-fi writers. Europe is now catching up and Nick hopes for considerable interest in Britain's first Transvision Conference.

As I catch the train home, I feel confused. I am an admirer of science and all that it has done to improve humanity's lot, and yet I feel uneasy. It also seems that there is a strangely religious aspect to the Transhumanists' approach. Their extreme position seems fundamentalist and simplistic (however complex their science may be), their boundless optimism is reminiscent of religious faith (though different because it is faith in reason and humankind rather than God), and the individualism reminds me of the personal piety of some faiths, revolving completely around 'I'. Nick himself is not narcissistic, but the zealous simplicity of his beliefs is almost monk-like. Some would say that this was the kind of zeal that led to the Third Reich's eugenics and Hitler's murderous desire for a 'master race'.

Several days after my meeting with Nick, Prince Charles adds to the debate going on between the synapses, dendrites and nerve cells in my 'grey, cheesy lump'. I cannot pretend that I am happy about it. This uneasy dialogue between science and spirituality has already reminded me of Prince Charles's fulminations on the subject. I make studious efforts to avoid taking seriously anything that the royal family say, however, because in my view the main (and only justifiable) function of the royals is to stop us thinking about the things we really *ought* to be thinking about – i.e. to give our grey, cheesy lumps a break.

Nonetheless, I have to admit that, however chippy I might feel, Charles has made some points that help to clarify my thinking about Transhumanism. 'PRINCE SLAMS GM FOODS' is the gist of the headlines. Closer reading of the

reports reveals a more carefully nuanced speech. He discrimi-
nated between the 'science of understanding' and the 'science
of manipulation', and argued for working 'with the grain of
nature'. The 'science of manipulation' reminds me of the control and domination at the heart of Transhumanism. Perhaps
a little unfairly, Charles also said, 'Wisdom, empathy and
compassion have no place in an empirical world, yet traditional wisdom would ask: *Without them are we truly human?*'
Wisdom is an overused word, but for Transhumans even
sentimentalized qualities are chemicals and, of course, they
would argue that there is no such thing as 'truly human'.
Although it is a metaphor that we cannot pin down and do
tests on, 'the heart working with the head' is what most
people feel at ease with. And I agree with them.

Charles's speech rooted this more natural approach to
science in a sense of a created universe, or at least a universe
that we should learn from and revere. This approach has been
lost in rationalistic utilitarianism, he argued. The 500-year-old
spat between religion and science is enlightening, or a revelation (depending on your viewpoint), or both. It starts and
ends with the stars, and with a rather brave Pole called
Copernicus who only dared go into print on his deathbed, followed by Galileo, who built on Copernicus's work in suggesting that the sun was the centre of the universe and that the
earth was moving around the sun. Galileo was met by the
Inquisition, called a heretic and given an offer he could not
easily refuse: change your mind or die. He was kept under
virtual house arrest until he died in 1642. The Vatican may be
a cumbersome administrative beast, but it is still remarkable
that they took until just a couple of years ago to apologize for
their error! That little papal memo inscribed 'Sorry, pal, we
cocked up' didn't just collect dust under piles of papal edicts –
no, it travelled round the sun 368 times as well.

In the early days, therefore, science was boxing above its
weight. Then, in the late 1700s, came the Enlightenment, or
Age of Reason. French philosophers and writers attacked the
Church and monarchy on the back of the French Revolution

and at this point the idea of 'progress' was born. Prior to this, 'reason' was to understand the way the world worked (particularly the Church, monarchy and aristocracy). Afterwards it was a tool to be used to improve things. For the first time humankind was at the centre of the universe. Some jettisoned God, most took him along, but the Church was now on the back foot. Once unleashed, progress happened as science, medicine, trade and industry transformed civilization and massively improved humanity's lot.

The philosopher Jeremy Bentham swung a few killer punches, arguing that morality had nothing to do with God. Morality was what did 'the greatest good to the greatest number'. Then came Charles Darwin and the theory of evolution (and the Church's silly campaign, 'Don't let Darwin make a monkey out of you'), and finally Nietzsche (admittedly no great fan of science) brought the Church to its knees. 'God is dead,' he said – we simply had to grow up, throw off our dependence on the Church and act powerfully and 'truly' without the Church's morals. The Church may have been declared dead with little sign of resurrection, but in the last few years of the twentieth century, while science was swaggering around the ring and the Church was out for the count, God – or spirituality – was experiencing a renaissance.

As Charles pointed out, people are now asking questions of progress. It is seen as cold, powerful and mechanistic. It may be the post-Hiroshima knowledge that science's advances have made our slaughters more efficient; it may be ozone depletion, genetics, cloning, or simply rising crime and the increased alienation of modern life, but people are worried about where we are going. And people do not trust experts, authorities or scientists, or, quite often, reason itself. Like Charles, they trust their intuition and have nightmares about men in white coats with syringes and electrodes. After its struggle against the all-powerful Church, science itself seems to be abusing its power, seems guilty of the sort of hubris that weakened the Church's hold on people. The problem is that the Church could only control people's hearts and minds, but

science has much more power. The Church could talk ominously about the end of the world; science can bring it about.

I am reminded of one of Nick's more chilling views. 'We should push back the frontiers of science regardless of the consequences. Even if our survival is at risk, we should continue, because, if Western democracies don't proceed, smaller governments or groups will,' he said. Er, surely the point of science is to make life better? Surely Nick's adolescent optimism about the process of achieving Transhumanism's goals and their benign application has metamorphosed into jaded pessimism about the chances of any form of regulation for science? (Perhaps, I wonder ironically, he swallowed a smart mood-altering drug.) This lack of balance, this simplistic rationalist fundamentalism, is precisely what is making people fearful. The heartless, mechanistic angles of the Transhuman world, dominated by Über-nerds on vitamins, are frightening and make me more inclined to take spiritual things seriously.

Nick would probably ask me exactly what I mean by 'heart' and 'heartless'. Well, I can't tell him. I just know that, if he explains it in terms of chemicals, genes or neural pathways, it will not do. He would probably argue that heartfelt feelings (like compassion, empathy, courage, anger or love) developed on the African savannah 200,000 years ago amongst some primeval people and led to an increased survival rate and, because they survived, we are their descendants and that is why we feel these things. (This approach is called 'evolutionary psychology' and is no more empirical than the efficacy of Buddha Maitreya's quartz crystals.)

One problem with this is that certain genuinely inspiring actions clearly do not lead to survival. Take self-sacrifice, for instance. It makes no sense scientifically, but when I see someone like Gandhi or Martin Luther King knowingly risk their lives for the sake of others, I am impressed. Tolstoy sacrificed his land and wealth and gave it to the peasants on his estate so that they could improve their conditions. Nelson Mandela sacrificed much of his life (spending 27 years in prison) to bring apartheid to an end. Smaller examples are equally moving: adults risking their lives for their children (evolutionary biologists would say this was because they wanted their gene pool to continue through their children), soldiers knowingly facing death in the cause of opposing despots, instinctive acts of bravery at emergency scenes. My father, living in wartime Holland, sacrificed a law degree because he would not sign up as a National Socialist. Utilitarians would try to call these acts examples of 'enlightened self-interest' and evolutionary biologists would have some clever way of explaining them away, but these deeply unscientific acts truly *inspire* me.

During our meeting I asked Nick who inspired him, and he said Eric Drexler, the pioneer of nanotechnology. Nick is no doubt impressed by Drexler's hard work, but primarily it would be his intelligence that Nick finds inspiring. I do not find intelligence remotely inspiring in itself; it is simply the muscle of the mind. For me it is the equivalent of being inspired by a body-builder, or by someone who, through an accident of birth, is born beautiful. What matters is what people *do* with what they have got and, more importantly, how they use the power that they have. Offloading power makes no sense at all from a mechanistic point of view, yet it is for me the most inspiring human behaviour. It resonates with the sort of emotional depth that a smart drug cannot supply. It is irrational, yet in it I hear echoes of an otherness that I cannot pin down or measure. This draws me on, away from the scientific and towards the spiritual.

12

🛒

Men Behaving Godly

'I'm a man, I'm a man, I'm a Holy Spirit man, I'm a winner!' shouts Noel Stanton, leader of the Jesus Army, as he mounts the stage and takes the microphone. Seven hundred men clap and cheer as one. They sit in a darkened, semicircular auditorium at a Northamptonshire girls' school listening to the man with wispy grey hair, painstakingly brushed over his bald pate. With whispered intensity, Stanton goes on to explain the stifling effect of Church tradition. 'The Church has been held back from its real virility in Jesus,' he says. He urges the men to share with the brothers sitting beside them. 'You must hug one another and get into the same bonding that the men of the New Testament days had,' he adds. He struts forcefully across the stage, chest puffed out, and concludes, 'We're men. *We're* the glory of God! Get it? Women are the glory of men – it's in the Bible! All men are biblically to take leadership; they are to be leaders.'

The scene is a Men Alive For God conference organized by the Jesus Army, the Northampton-based Christian community. Women are barred from the meeting, but I am perched nervously in the middle of the crowd, half expecting to be swatted down as some effete, namby-pamby, sitting-on-the-fence observer. The men are petitioning their Heavenly Father for shelter from the ravages of feminism, which they believe has marched straight out of the workplace and into the Church. The aim of the day is to help men find a role in today's pitiable, emasculated Church. They sit in jeans, regulation-issue Jesus Army Day-Glo camouflage jackets, T-shirts and baseball caps.

Lurid slogans are emblazoned across the Jesus Army gear: 'Freedom in Jesus', 'Bleeding Life', 'Jesus Revolution' and 'UK People We Love You!' I am beginning to get the message. In their baseball caps, epauletted jackets and bright combat fatigues, I cannot help seeing them as charismatic Christianity's answer to *Thunderbirds*. As they call on God to reaffirm their masculinity and bless their brotherly bonding, it registers that this is a Saturday afternoon. Should these men not be watching *Grandstand* or buffing their cars with turtlewax?

Not according to Duncan Centamore, mechanic and van-driver. Standing in the foyer after Mr Stanton's speech, Duncan has clearly learned his lesson. 'It's OK to be a man. I want to grow into my maleness, into leadership. We are made as the glory of God,' he says. He points out that he works with a 'big, butch, lesbian feminist' and that equality is OK in everyday life. 'But spiritual life and leadership is different,' he explains. Jim Redman, a young labourer wearing a standard-issue Day-Glo combat jacket, adds, 'The Church has been dominated by women, and men need to grow in stature, to find their place in the Church.'

The women have clearly found *their* place: in the kitchen. They are washing up and serving coffee and biscuits behind a counter as the poor, beleaguered brothers sip Nescafé during a break before the seminars. Barbara Motherheart (her 'virtue name', given to her by the Jesus Army community) says, 'We're really serving the saints today. It's a real pleasure, but they need us to do the catering.'

Her sister with the scrubbing brush, Fiona Gentlespirit (another 'virtue name'), shakes the suds from her gloves and laughs, 'They couldn't open a tin of biscuits without us.'

'There are a few women along, otherwise we wouldn't eat,' says Mick Haines, the leader of a seminar for 'Men Needing to Find Their Masculine Role'. (I am not sure of his virtue name, but Unreconstructed has a certain ring to it. Or Largebigot, perhaps?)

John Campbell, Jesus Army Press Officer and the day's organizer, tries to put a more egalitarian spin on it. 'Men don't

often fit into church. They are ill-at-ease with the emotional aspects of worship and prayer which women tend to respond to. We want to show men that church is a place for action and ethics, boldness and integrity, as well as emotion and compassion,' he says. I sip my tea, looking at the throng of exuberant, noisy males crammed into the foyer. Despite the gaudy uniforms, it is clear that the range of men is broad. Pensioners mix with skinheads, accountants with labourers. There is a raw intensity about them that would melt turtlewax and turn any *Grandstand* presenter into a pillar of salt. I have to admit that I am glad about this. But I am also struck by the fact that these anointed Action Men are like sheep. Campbell interrupts my reverie. 'We believe that the main leadership should be men's, but that there's room for women in leadership underneath the men,' he says. Stifling a chuckle, I realize that dogma is their shepherd.

This dogma comes from a particular reading of the New Testament. The Jesus Army vision is unique, not because it is based in 'Scripture', but because of how far they take it. Originating in the 1960s, the Jesus Army (or Jesus Fellowship) was very much part of the charismatic movement, which came out of the American Pentecostal movement and was characterized by a fundamentalist and literal view of the Bible, together with a belief in the power of the Holy Spirit to heal, exorcize and enable people to prophesy and speak in tongues. The Jesus Army's inspiration from Scripture went beyond these gifts and into the idea of setting up a Christian community based on New Testament principles. They learned from hippy communes at the time, but their main influence was the New Testament. 'We weren't trying to re-create New Testament history, but were trying to look at how we could meet today's needs, based on principles found in the first-century Church,' Campbell says.

The community grew out of a small Baptist church in Bugbrooke, on the outskirts of Northampton, where Noel Stanton was minister. The congregation was made up of an unusual mixture of people. Campbell says, 'The "straights"

parented the "freaks" into a more ordered lifestyle, and the hippies convicted the middle class by their simple, radical lifestyle.' The congregation started to share possessions, doing jobs for each other and buying food in bulk from the cash-and-carry. In 1973 some families took in single people to form 'extended families'.

Certain neglected passages in the Acts of the Apostles inspired them to pursue this vision of radical community:

> With many other words he warned them; and he pleaded with them, 'Save yourselves from this corrupt generation' ... Everyone was filled with awe, and many wonders and miraculous signs were done by the apostles. All the believers were together and had everything in common. Selling their possessions and goods, they gave to anyone as he had need ... They broke bread in their homes and ate together with glad and sincere hearts, praising God and enjoying the favour of all the people. (Acts 2:40–46)

Another passage focusing on the social aspects of the first-century Church that influenced them was this:

> All the believers were in one heart and mind. No one claimed that any of his possessions was his own, but they shared everything they had. With great power the apostles continued to testify to the resurrection of the Lord Jesus, and much grace was upon them all. There were no needy persons among them. For from time to time those who owned lands or houses sold them, brought the money from the sales and put it at the apostles' feet, and it was distributed to anyone as he had need. (Acts 4:32–5)

Soon church members were looking to sell their houses in order to buy larger properties suitable for community living. They called themselves New Creation Christian Community and, like hundreds of groups in earlier centuries, were in search of the utopian 'true way' to live together as Christians.

Not all members joined NCCC, and some opted to remain as fellowship members without living communally. Once people moved into community, they shared their income in a 'common purse', left in the hands of the house leader. They ate together, shared chores and took in 'needy people', often off the street or with addictions.

Currently the Jesus Army has over 60 community houses around the country (with a concentration in Northamptonshire), each functioning as a mini-community within the NCCC. About 800 people live in community, out of a church of nearly 3,000. According to John Campbell, it took time to work out the right mix of people to make up each community. There were (and are) struggles as people learned to let go of their possessions or individual preferences in favour of the good of the community. 'We are trying to abolish social injustice within the group, to banish *haves* and *have-nots* because we are all members of one body; all are one in Christ,' Campbell says.

Whilst restoring properties they had bought, they realized that working together was a good way to bring people together. So they decided to start community businesses, staffed by community members and owned by the church, but serving the local neighbourhood. There are building, decorating and plumbing firms, and a building supply service as well as a farm and a wholesaler called Goodness Foods. Goodness Foods started as a health-food shop based in Northampton and has grown into a company with 4,000 product lines and 90 staff from within the community. It is run along strict business lines, although all employees earn the same wage. 'It aims to mix ethical business principles with profit. It's a bit like a co-op, but based on Jesus' teaching,' Campbell says.

Despite all the worthy and unusual ventures I have heard about from Campbell, it is with a heavy heart that I visit my next Jesus Army meeting. Can something so brash, so dogmatic, so twee and so sexist really have anything to offer? The meeting, Alive 2000, is their annual jamboree, at which Jesus

Army members from around the country come together for a 'tent meeting'. The idea of sitting through a meeting full of noisy, turbo-charged charismatic Christians crammed into a marquee does not exactly fill me with enthusiasm. It is no accident that I arrive about an hour late at Cornhill Manor, one of their community houses in a tiny Northamptonshire village near Towcester.

I pull up in a field full of cars displaying brash stickers whose text is broadly along the lines of 'Get a Life! Get saved NOW!' I drive past about 30 pristine Ford Transit minibuses, garishly painted in primary colours with luminous crosses and the words 'JESUS PEOPLE: LOVING PEOPLE' scrawled thunderously across the paintwork. I can hear singing coming from the marquee hidden in a wood at the top of a slope.

By the time I enter the marquee, the singing has stopped and about 1,500 people are seated on chairs watching Noel Stanton talking on stage, flanked by a decidedly rough-looking bunch of young men. Pony-tails, crew cuts, skinheads, football shirts, leather jackets, tracksuit trousers and trainers: they could be at a football match or rock concert. To one side is a band made up of electric guitars, drums, synthesizers and a couple of computer monitors. I look for a seat where I can take notes unobtrusively. This proves difficult, because the tent is heaving and the people are feverish in their concentration, commitment and intensity. Taking notes in a dispassionate manner is bound to attract attention and, looking around me, I can feel that enquiries about the state of my soul are only seconds away.

Stanton explains his theme: our progress from disciples to servants to visionaries. He is an arresting speaker – one minute he is whispering, the next he is screaming or shouting commandingly at the top of his voice. The content is less arresting, and sounds like an overplayed record. It is the time-honoured exhortation to remain committed, to go the extra mile, to suffer as Christ did, etc., etc. 'Are you the slaves of God, the slaves of Christ?' he asks with what sounds like demented intensity. I nod off.

I am woken by a loud cheer as hundreds of people file forward, publicly to acknowledge their baptism during the past year. Most of them are men, young or middle-aged. There are several black people and a few Asians. What really strikes me is the breadth of people who are involved. These are not generally the typical, homogenous, middle-class Christians; they are rough-edged, youths with the latest street fashions, older 'anoraks', people off the streets, and a smattering of professionals. What is most remarkable is that they seem to like each other.

Next scores of 'covenant members' come to the front with their community leaders. They are introduced by their name and house. The house names remind me of John Bunyan's *Pilgrim's Progress*. (Bunyan also lived in a Christian community 350 years ago, just down the road in Bedford.) Bunyan's symbolism was crushingly blunt and zealous; these house names are similar: 'Living Faith', 'Cornerstone', 'Light House', 'Trumpet', 'Cool River', 'Spreading Flame', 'Well Spring', 'Vineyard', 'Battle Centre'. The members all wear the *Thunderbirds* camouflage jacket with epaulettes and slogans. They say a few words into the microphone, and this is followed by a cheer from their friends in the audience. I ask the middle-aged woman next to me to explain what is meant by 'covenant members', and within the space of four sentences she has asked me if I 'believe on the Lord Jesus'. I nod, a little lamely I fear, and she calls over Steve, a man in his early forties, to talk to me.

He is less earnest and tells me that covenant members are those who have vowed to belong to the Jesus Army for the rest of their lives. In exchange they get a *Thunderbirds* jacket. As Faustian pacts go, it's a rough one. He also tells me that about 200 church members have taken vows of celibacy. Why? 'Because they can give themselves fully to the Lord, to Christian service. People with kids just can't make the same commitment.' What if they change their minds? 'Occasionally they do, and they get married. That's OK,' he says, 'it's just a different path.'

Steve explains the different levels of involvement in the Jesus Army. Style 1 is basic church membership; Style 2 is people who belong to the common purse but do not live in community; Style 3 is full community membership, and Style 4 is people who want to be members but are in other countries or regions where there is no Jesus Army church. He tells me that Noel Stanton is 73 and has never missed a meeting. He lives in a simple room on the New Creation Farm, the biggest community dwelling. Steve says that Stanton has softened in his old age. 'Naturally he's autocratic, but he has definitely mellowed with age and now other community leaders are given more of a responsibility,' he says. 'We have learned as a church not to be so authoritarian. We have made mistakes,' he adds. He joined the Jesus Army with his wife some years ago. 'I was an atheist and socialist, but then I saw that these people were actually living it,' he says in his thick Midlands accent.

I join John Campbell for communal lunch at Festal Grange, the community house that he leads. It is a large converted rectory and stables which has about 30 people living in it. The large, robustly decorated rooms crowded with people remind me of a youth hostel. The back garden is idyllic, looking across a valley over trees, and buzzing with bees and birdsong in the sunlight. It must seem like paradise to people who have been living rough.

Over lunch (cooked and served by women) I meet James, a tall, thickset ex-soldier in his fifties. He is a Style 1 member, living in Norfolk but visiting Northampton when he can. Converted a few years ago after his wife's death, James came across the Jesus Army preaching on the street. He started reading the Bible and attending Jesus Army functions. Like all new converts, he was given a mentor to support and guide him in his Christian faith. He looks at me with his piercing blue eyes and describes his baptism: 'I've been through war zones and experienced quite a bit, but my baptism was the most amazing day of my life. It was like approaching a funeral as I thought about putting to death the old me and being born as a new creation.'

It strikes me that the sort of conversion and community that these people experience probably means cutting themselves off from their families or former friends. The symbolism of putting the old man to death and being born again in Christ makes this severance all too easy. After baptism James was even given a new name. His mentor gave him his virtue name, Resolute. It seems fitting. I ask him about the leadership structure and he speaks convincingly about the warmth of the community. What about authority? 'You can't lead unless you are led,' he says.

I go through to the lounge and chat to Neil. He is in his twenties and works for Goodness Foods. His conversion was similar to James's: he came out of prison and met the Jesus Army on the streets. He was impressed by their commitment and the simplicity and sincerity of their faith, and became a Christian. His parents joined too and they live together in the Birmingham community. He tells me that all community leaders are men, but things seem to be changing. Women can now baptize people.

After lunch I drive around various Jesus Army centres in the area. I visit the farm which employs about a dozen full-time workers, although at harvest time hundreds come out to help. There are acres of apple trees and gooseberry bushes, hundreds of free-range hens. The farm is a large Victorian manor house on a hill overlooking verdant fields, dotted with oak trees and thick old hedges. I stop off at Honeycomb Grange, another Jesus Army farm where asylum seekers are staying. As I drive through Nether Heyford, the tiny village which houses the Jesus Army headquarters, I keep seeing houses with the Army's small, luminous orange cross in the window or on a gatepost. It reminds me of the Jews daubing their doorposts with lambs' blood at the Passover.

The evening service starts with the traditional toneless and crushingly dull choruses. It strikes me that, however these charismatic choruses are played, they sound terrible. Perhaps the devil really does have all the good tunes. Even if Jimi Hendrix or André Previn played these choruses, by the end you would still feel like shoving their instruments somewhere painful. Singing such choruses might be appropriate as a form of last-ditch punishment before prison, but to come *out* of prison (as dozens in the congregation have) to sing them is surely to share unnecessarily in Christ's suffering.

After about 30 minutes, the choruses fade out to a lull which is filled by people 'singing in tongues', a harmonic fusion of disjointed syllables. Noel Stanton has been standing hesitantly on stage, arms folded and absorbed in his own world. He walks to the microphone and says, 'Wait. The Lord says, wait until you are clothed with clothes from on high.' I think he is prophesying. His eyes are closed as he shouts, 'I'm alive to God!' Without a pause, he screams the words again. Then he whispers, 'Are you hearing?' This seems to blend into his sermon as he continues, 'We are baptized in Christ in order to be freed from the old social barriers. A social dimension of unity, all divisions of class and race have gone: we are one family in Christ.' He continues, 'We reject all notions of white superiority; to go that way would be to go against God.' He pauses, as if for emphasis, but his delivery is so intense that I wonder if he is capable of such self-awareness. 'Rich and poor, we are one family in Christ. The social order has been revolutionized by baptism in water and in the Spirit. Age is no barrier,' he says.

I am reminded of a striking cameo from the morning service. A handsome, baseball-capped boy in his late teens sat down next to an old lady in front of me. She whispered something mischievous in his ear. He grinned and reciprocated. They both chuckled away. They were friends. Similar scenes happened throughout the day. The Jesus Army really have created a community with a real depth and breadth to their relationships. I am also struck, however, by the fact that there are no women on stage and no gay couples in the congregation of several thousand. Stanton finishes his sermon with the words, 'All competition has gone. We have love; living for one another is paramount.'

A few saccharine songs and an up-tempo rock number or two follow before what they call 'response time'. This is a period when they invite the Holy Spirit to work in them, and teams of helpers stand by ready to pray over people being affected. Stanton creeps up to the microphone, eyes closed tight, arms folded, slightly hunched over. 'You'll return to Jesus Christ with a full surrender, you'll know the cleansing power of Jesus, you'll know the spirit of joy again. Take up your bed and walk,' he whispers in prophetic mode. People start speaking in tongues, ethereal strings of syllables rising into the air.

Next Stanton addresses the demons that he believes are affecting members of his congregation. 'Some of your demons are determined to make people constantly ill. Your doctors may be right medically, but it is demonic powers within you. You will be able to jump out of the enchantments, out of un-holy magic,' he says. People raise their hands for prayer. Some lie on the ground while others lay hands on them. Vials of oil are passed around so that people can, as the good book says, be 'anointed with oil'. Some people are undergoing exorcisms, but it is low key. There is the odd groan, but no real histrion-ics. After about 20 minutes, people presumably believe that the demons and ailments have departed, because Stanton introduces the 'J Generation'.

It would be easy to say that scores of teen and twenties clones climb on stage and start dancing to techno music with very directive lyrics. But they are not really clones. Many are wearing purple T-shirts with 'Alive 2000' scrawled across them; others wear *Thunderbirds* jackets and army fatigues. But there are also skinheads, punks and 'long-hairs', all united in what they see as the common good. I notice a punk and a dis-abled youngster hugging. The music becomes more interest-ing and the service ends in a 'ritual' that sums up the Jesus Army. They make a chain of scarves all around the tent. It symbolizes their commitment and unity. Men and women, young and old, black and white, all hold scarves aloft as they sing their hearts out.

I walk into the night surprised that, contrary to my expecta-tions, I am not feeling angry and annoyed. I am impressed by the depth of community that I have seen. They really have created a sense of family and extended family. This may owe something to the simplicity of their fundamentalist purpose, but it is also a product of a strangely egalitarian, radical and progressive attitude. In many ways, the fellowship is quite liberal. They do work together for the greater good. Yet this is juxtaposed with a dogmatic form of personal piety, including demons, healing and speaking in tongues, and an extremely directive, reactionary sense of right and wrong.

I can understand why, in the early days, locals ran to newspapers with stories of a sinister cult taking over their area. I can see why hearing Stanton preach would confirm their suspicions. Yet that is not really how I see it. I am sure that the Jesus Army's attitude to women is restrictive and, for some, damaging. I am equally sure that their approach to homosexuals is deeply damaging. A church based on dogmatic 'truth' which demands this sort of commitment, despite its egalitarian approach, has to leave casualties in its wake. On the other hand, it has ex-addicts, ex-convicts and the reformed homeless in its favour. To suggest that they have brainwashed their members seems far fetched. The people I met have a clear sense of self and why they are doing what they are doing. They know the hardships of such a radical church and they know the benefits. As a church the Jesus Army is sensitive to the 'cult' accusation and has worked at improving links with other churches.

My last meeting with them, in fact, is at an event with other churches. They are with tens of thousands of Christians, mainly of an evangelical or charismatic persuasion, walking through central London on a March For Jesus. They stretch out for about a mile, but are never in any danger of being inspiring or imaginative. Yet there is more to March For Jesus than meets the eye. The leaders see it as a form of corporate exorcism on geographical areas. They think that the prayers and songs of believers on the streets will vanquish any evil spirits or 'principalities' located in the area. This means that the area should subsequently be easier to evangelize. In the early days, the corporate exorcism was included in the text for the different stages of the march. This was later toned down in order to attract non-charismatics to the march. It worked, but the predicted revival following the march's spread around the world never arrived.

It is a singularly dismal event. People walk the streets waving banners or placards, singing choruses of the sort that would make the population flee, never mind the demons. Naturally, the Jesus Army contingent are noisier and brasher than most. They all walk along the prepared route giving out newspapers to anyone who will take them. They remind me of the Hare Krishnas giving out sweets to embarrassed passers-by, except that every so often they stop for prayers. As I walk beside them, I feel just as embarrassed as I felt beside the shaved, robed, chanting neo-Hindus. The tenor of their prayers is combative. These Christians, as their name suggests, see themselves as being at war with the devil and the world.

I ask one young Jesus Army foot soldier how much contact she has with old friends. 'My old life was very different. It's difficult when you've changed from inside out – you just don't have the same interests,' she says. What about her role as a young woman in an organization run by men? 'The leaders are wise, they follow Jesus and things will probably change with time,' is all she says before asking me where I stand.

I leave the march early. It seems ridiculous that people really believe that the marches are making demons beat a hasty retreat. They are the ones beating a hasty retreat: from reality into a paranoid universe inhabited by angels and demons.

Jogging up by the Moon a few days later, several things become clear for me about the sort of God that the Jesus Army and other fundamentalist Christians worship. One of the most obvious revelations is that I do not believe in a miracle-working God – on principle. If God performs miracles to heal, or intervenes in weather systems very, very occasionally, then why not always? Do I want to rely on a capricious old chap running a wretched lottery for the terminally ill, whose fickle finger allegedly lands on a lucky person once in a blue moon? The stock answer to this objection is that 'God works in mysterious ways'. That's not good enough, I'm afraid. It's a cop-out. Also, if God did intervene, did break all the rules of nature or science and put a divine spanner in the works, it would seem silly and irrational – a stunt. Surely the real miracle is in nature or science itself? The wonder of creation seems a more likely source of the spiritual for me. If we are self-obsessed enough to demand an illness-free utopia or a push-button miracle-man, then more fool us.

I also reject a miracle-working God because miracles do not, in my experience, happen. They only happen to those who are willing to contort their story to fit, against all the evidence. Then they tell everyone about it, but become rather vague when it comes to detailed questioning. I am also aware that it says something rather worrying about our spirituality if it relies on the supernatural touch, the divine proof. Should it not rely on inspiring goodness, vulnerability and love? Does a preoccupation with personal divine intervention not betray a brittle, narcissistic faith? The really impressive thing about the Jesus Army is the sense of community which seems to cross some, though not all, barriers.

Nevertheless, I realize more clearly that I do not and will not believe in a dogma-peddling Pedant in the sky. I am not saying that all incarnations of the Christian God seem like pedants, or even that I do not accept (and even hope for) a tentative truth that is beyond me. I am happy, however, with core principles of the sort that are sometimes called 'natural law', or the sort that appear in the UN Declaration of Human Rights. Principles such as love, honesty, integrity, selflessness and a sense that all are of equal worth and have equal rights are more than fine with me – I am just not very good at fulfilling them. The sort of detailed pedantry that says that women *should* behave differently from men, or that same-sex, loving couples' love is inferior or tarnished, is unacceptable to me. If

God says that, then God is a sinner and I do not want to get involved.

I also realize that I do not have a problem with the concept of being fallen (I am as shoddy as the next person), but it still goads me that we should have a theology based round humankind being at fault because Adam ate an apple. I mean, that was not exactly *our* fault, was it? It also seems immoral to have a God who *needs* a sacrifice to forgive us for our shoddiness. Surely a deeper love would not need a sacrifice? I would feel a tad embarrassed, not to say pompous, if I went around demanding sacrifices from my subjects. The concept seems to say more about us as subjects than about any God or spiritual force. It seems to me to come from the mind of a sadistic PE teacher, not an awesome Divine Being. It also seems to me that the idea of sacrificing your son is just a little wobbly on the human rights front. I would not do that to my son. Perhaps 'son' is a metaphor, and it really means self-sacrifice, but still, the legalistic concept of measuring sin against sacrifice seems to me to miss the point. Is it really loving to need a sacrifice?

My visit to the Jesus Army was much more interesting than I had expected. Nonetheless, it crystallized my resistance to a judgemental, fundamentalist God. I know that there are other Christian interpretations of God, but this one is not for me.

13

The Sound of One Lobe Flapping

It is probably a bad idea to wander into the annual Mind Body Spirit festival at the Royal Horticultural Halls in Victoria nursing a slight hangover. I am a great one for damning people with a throwaway mental Post-it note. People I hardly know can be the subjects of quite lengthy, bilious internal dialogues. It may be unforgivable, but I cannot pretend that I do not enjoy pouring bile onto the disconsolates who walk, quite innocently, into my dyspeptic firing line. Very occasionally I vocalize my thoughts, but generally I am too cowardly. So you could say that, on entering this melee of spiritual entrepreneurship, I am in my element.

Naturally, the first thing I notice is New Age Promotions taking £8 a head off a queue of overwrought, middle-class ladies, spaced-out, overbangled hags and awkward, whey-faced men in flecked jumpers and John Lennon glasses. It is already three hours after the show's opening time, but the maroon-shirted women (with a whiff of henna and a scrub of aloe vera, no doubt) are still completely focused. They are making about £40 a minute, and that is without the stallholders' charges (£1,100 for the tiniest stalls over eight days). It seems a lot for a trade show, a lot to charge people to spend their money.

Inside the large, airy hall are hundreds of booths offering reflexology, massage, tarot, flower essences, colour healing and associated New Age paraphernalia. Many offer treatments (for a fee), and there are a few workshops (for a fee) and the odd free lecture or demonstration. I wander around and within moments realize that I am going to have to dodge a few stalls. There are my friends from the Aetherius Society, ISKCON and, most worrying of all, those demented followers of the portly Buddha Maitreya and his copper-and-crystal Meccano sets. I am also immediately struck by the queues of people paying for rather public therapies in chairs or on couches. On one stall some robed men do special massage while whistling and breathing in a particular way. Quaint, particularly as it sounds as if the people are being inflated, but a bit steep at £20 for a few minutes.

One queue is so long that there is a ticket machine to help the practitioners identify who comes next. This seems fair enough, until I see that the queue comes from a stall run by a team of clairvoyants! If they can't even tell *who comes next*, I am not likely to trust them with my future job prospects, news of my family, whether a terminal illness is winging its way to me, or a message from the dead (though that, admittedly, would be good value at £20).

Further on is Kirlian Aura Photography. For a tenner, I can put my hand on some photographic paper and have a woman in a purple shirt tell me about my body, mind and spirit. 'The print is a diagnostic tool,' the purple-shirted one tells me. 'The stronger the aura around the side of the hand, the more inner balance and energy you have.'

'This one's more or less expired,' I say, pointing to a very faint print.

'That's me,' she smiles. 'I'm feeling drained.'

'I hope you get better,' I say as I leave.

Just around the corner, I come across the wonderfully named Naomi Tickle, a Californian expert in Personology, the 'science' of reading the face. Her posters show different faces and how to interpret them. I learn that having a high forehead means that you are logical, but that a backward-sloping forehead means (wait for it) that you are a more streamlined decision-maker. An upturned button nose means that you enjoy helping others, but a thrusting great conk means that you are driven by ambition. A big mouth means, metaphorically speaking, that you have a big mouth. A small mouth means that you are concise and quite possibly tight with money. Based on your photograph, Ms Tickle will advise on suitability for different careers, or how to use your face to sell products, or will give tips on understanding your boss/lover/children.

The idea that this kind of nonsense might be dangerous is confirmed when I read that the theory was developed in the 1930s by a Californian judge. This judge confirmed his hunch about the faces of the guilty by researching the work of Italian criminologist Cesare Lombroso. Lombroso's work was roundly discredited, but nevertheless made life rather difficult for people with shifty, deep-set eyes and protruding jaws. There is a man at the stall having a facial reading. His face is no oil painting. I suspect that the almond-faced Naomi Tickle will not be using the popular euphemism 'nice personality' to describe that crooked smile and those cauliflower ears.

In the next aisle is a man claiming to be a Brahman priest. This elderly man with puckered face, yellowing, watery eyes, flagrantly dyed long hair and an awkward smile somehow interprets the minerals in his clients' fingers and palms and diagnoses physical and emotional problems. Then he heals by the laying on of hands. He is healing a young woman seated opposite him, rubbing her neck and shoulders with particular concentration. I ask him about his theory and how it differs from other hand-interpretation techniques. He looks up and explains, but I cannot pretend to be any the wiser.

'Massaging all day must be tiring as you get older,' I venture clumsily.

'You're only as old as you feel,' he says, feeling the young lady.

In one corner are a couple of stalls selling Native American products. This is of particular interest, because I recently heard a Native American on the radio claiming that the recent proliferation of New Age, pseudo-Native American spirituality has been wholly damaging. He claimed that an impossible number of Americans in recent censuses were claiming Indian origins, that New Age 'shamans' were completely transforming Native American spirituality into a narcissistic, self-indulgent, warm fuzz of feathers and fur. His final thought was that New Age imperialism was doing the same to Native American spirituality as the US cavalry and General Booth had done to Native American physicality.

There are rails of T-shirts with pictures of eagles, bears and wolves on them at £15 a shirt. Dream-catchers (wood and feather frames with netting for catching dreams from the wind) could be yours for anything between £6 and £35. A ceremonial dance arrow (it looks like any other arrow to me) is priced at just £35. A dead raccoon headdress is a snip at £95. Wooden flutes and small drums start at £115 and the ceremonial feathers at £7.50, displaying a 'Genuine North American Product' sticker, give a new meaning to feathering one's nest. Then I notice Chief Seattle's speech (the one I sang many months ago at the Rainbow Circle Healing Camp) for sale under the title *How Can One Sell The Air?* Looking around me, I feel I could answer him – but, assuming those were Chief Seattle's words (and they are much contested), it is sad that he has now become part of the process of selling the air.

Next I join a queue to find out about Clinical Iridology (health analysis based on studying one's irises). Someone from the Nutri Centre offers me a cup of green algae (cheers!) dredged up from the bottom of a lake ('not just any lake') and offering lots of protein, minerals, etc. I forget the details. After downing this verdant slime, I chat to the woman next to me. She tells me about a past life regression workshop that she did yesterday. It cost £12 for an hour, but she was disappointed about how vague it was. This was not helped because she was with about 50 others, all, one assumes, with different past lives. I imagine the leader lying them all down, getting them attuned and then saying, 'You lot on the left were Rasputin, you at the front were Cleopatra, at the back you were Henry VIII and on my right you were John the Baptist, with a smattering of headless cavaliers. Now give us your money and get out of here – I've got a workshop to take!'

I arrive in front of iridologist Dr Succar, who will take a photo of my irises and talk about them for 15 minutes for the small sum of £35. His young female assistant explains how the irises show the symptoms of the whole body. Feeling a little contrary, I say, 'But my eyes are fine.'

'But this isn't about your eyes,' she blurts out.

'My liver's fine, my kidneys are pukka, my bowels are functioning regularly, I'm healthy.'

Dr Succar looks up. 'He's healthy, he doesn't want to spend any money,' the doctor says, grinning.

'Very healthy, just a bit sick in the head,' I say and wander off. I am beginning to feel trapped and tetchy, crowded in by enticements and inducements on every side. It reminds me of my experience in Milton Keynes shopping centre.

To escape, I go upstairs and listen to the end of a performance of New Age music by the exquisitely named Bliss. Their three CDs have equally vivifying titles: *Flying Free*, *Through these Eyes* and *The Journey*. It is the most sickly, anodyne and saccharine music that could possibly stick to your ears. No doubt my irises are turning a brighter shade of jaundice, but while the rest of the audience are Blissed out, I am counting down the lachrymose harmonies until they Bliss off.

With slightly more enthusiasm, I attend a free demonstration of the ancient martial art of t'ai chi. The leader explains that 'chi' is inner energy created by balancing one's forces. The movements are all about creating a balance of yin and yang and focusing the energy. A selection of practitioners perform various exceedingly slow moves. I was hoping for a few throws and, perhaps, the odd scissor kick. They start doing slow-motion moves with swords, but WWF it is not. In fact, it is very graceful and their control is quite impressive. 'It is all about space, absence, potentiality, like the sound of one hand clapping,' the master explains. 'T'ai chi is about absence as much as presence. It is about the potential to heal as well as to defend oneself.' The inner peace that comes from a sense of space, of stillness, is something that, thus far, I have not explored. The Mind Body Spirit festival has not exactly filled me with stillness, so I resolve to explore this approach further. I rush out of the building to the sound of many cash registers ringing.

A week later, I am ready to start my oriental exploration into space and stillness. I have picked up a couple of books from the library on feng shui. This is an ancient Chinese technique which teaches people how to live in harmony with their surroundings by balancing the energy flows. The books both promise health, happiness and prosperity. I expect them to emphasize aesthetic balance and proportion, but soon find out that feng shui has more to do with five particular elements and 'magic' than any visual sense of equilibrium. One book tells of a Chinese family who built an extension without properly considering feng shui. Within a year, one was electrocuted, one killed in a car accident and another died of a terminal illness. It is all based on the cosmic balance between negative and positive, light and shade, joy and sadness, and ultimately between yin and yang. The family's extension unbalanced the energies and led to these tragedies. It is serious stuff.

I start off with an attempt to apply feng shui to my workspace, which is in our bedroom beside the bed. My wife's desk is on the opposite side of the room. As desks go, it is nothing special. It is big, but not beautiful (the top is Formica 'pine').With three deep drawers and deep shelves, it is well made and has sentimental value: my father made it for me before I sat my O levels. The real problem with it is the dusty, tea-stained surface. There is an in-tray containing piles of papers, newspaper cuttings, envelopes, receipts and books. There is no out-tray. A small bookshelf holds a thesaurus, dictionary, old notebooks and computer manuals, with an assortment of precariously balanced books and videos resting on top. Then there is a computer monitor, keyboard and speakers, piles of CDs, a phone, highlighter pens, pay slips, an index of addresses, ink cartridges, some headphones and the grotesquely named 'desk tidy' containing a yellow crayon, a rubber, a peg, three nails and a ticket to the Empire State Building. A six-shelf IKEA stack littered with books, bric-a-brac, camera and films overlooks the desk to the left.

One feng shui manual says, 'The more attention you pay to the positioning of your furniture in your bedroom, the greater your fortune.' Well, I have no fortune. I then learn that the head of my bed should not face west. It does, but there is no alternative option because of space restrictions. I then use the *pa che* compass (a circular protractor with Chinese hieroglyphs marking the points of the compass) to calculate my 'directional number' (men have to subtract their year of birth from 100, divide by 9, and work out the remainder), and discover that my desk position has a 'baleful influence'. If I put it on top of the bed, however, it should bring 'good fortune'. My front door is a 'disaster', but my wife's desk, buried under a morass of academic books and musty newspaper cuttings, should bring 'vitality'. Hmm. Terminal inertia might be closer to the mark.

The other book has a chapter on consecrating spaces. This clears space of 'psychic debris' and bad energy which can get into those nasty, malign, inconvenient corners. Objects can also hold bad energy, second-hand things in particular. This, the book explains, is why people always wanted to have relics of saints or holy men. This is also what is behind the practice of collecting autographs of football heroes and movie stars: people want the energy imprints on them. Photos or images can have a similar effect. Well, I have to admit to having a cork noticeboard (in the 'death' position according to the *pa che* compass) with Gary Lineker's autograph on it. I got it for my kids. As energy imprints go, that one should be pretty effective. While I would not expect to play up front for England, according to the feng shui book, some energy should be sprinkling its way down to me. Hmm.

My final exploration of feng shui is on an internet site (www.fengshui4free.com) which does feng shui readings on-line. I key in the dimensions of my workspace-cum-bedroom and discover the source of my misfortune. My computer and desk are located in an area that 'makes things difficult with finances, health and everything that is important to you'. No wonder I am still wearing polyester trousers and eating out of tins. All that time spent bashing out articles and books, wondering why I wasn't a tycoon. I thought it was down to having four children, no talent and no time. If only I had put my desk across the door, things could have been so different. That area promises a 'positive effect on knowledge and my working life'. I could always climb in through the window.

Next I find someone who can teach me falun gong (sometimes known as falan dafa), a system of movements a little like t'ai chi that is creating panic in the Chinese government as hundreds of thousands take to the streets to do it. It is a form of qigong, an ancient Chinese method of 'cultivating' oneself towards Buddhahood based on the cosmic principles of the universe. Master Li Hongzi started teaching falun gong in 1992 in a small Chinese province, and it now has over 100 million followers around the world, with several million in China. Drawing on Tao, Buddhist and other Chinese teachings, part of the appeal of Hongzi's teaching may be that he insists it is free to those who wish to learn.

The idea is to cultivate a falun, which is an intelligent entity and a small copy of the cosmos. It is a kind of spiritual wheel which whizzes around in your lower abdomen, transforming toxins and illness into pure energy. This cosmic alchemist in your bowels gives you 'supernormal energy' and moral wellbeing. Once one is sufficiently adept at it, the cosmic flywheel spins effortlessly 24 hours a day. As bad luck would have it, the falun/flywheel is swastika-shaped, but Master Li explains that this is nothing to do with Hitler, it is simply a symbol of perpetual motion and the energy of the universe. The Buddhist law wheels, the yin-yang of the Taoist school and everything in the universe are reflected in the falun.

It provides practitioners (or 'cultivators') with internal energy and the ability to possess truthfulness, benevolence and forbearance. It also allows them to shrug off bad karma from past lives by going back to them and 'cultivating' as a way of paying off the debt. This tiny little motor thing is basically God in your belly, the cosmos in your abdomen. All you have to do is to follow five exercises which enable cultivators to balance work and study – and everything else. I am a little bemused by this, because the instructor tells me that the exercises take nearly two hours. The most worrying thing she tells me, however, is that she teaches in the open air by a lake in the middle of a busy park in central Oxford.

I am quite relieved, therefore, that the day is overcast as I walk towards the lake in University Parks. I arrive at 10.30 in the morning and no one is there beyond a few ragged-looking ducks on the lake and a few joggers on the orange gravel paths. Graceful poplars, silver birches and exotic fir trees sway in the breeze over the River Isis. A few people go by in punts. *Perhaps the class has been called off because of the possibility of rain,* I think.

Then I notice two small oriental women with a small tape player and some bags on the other side of the lake. I walk round and introduce myself and, sure enough, it is Song, the instructor, and an advanced practitioner called Deniece Yip. Song's English is a little limited, so Deniece tells me some more about falun gong. 'Qigong' is the term for a number of spiritual disciplines that the Cultural Revolution outlawed as 'superstition'. Master Li learned various traditions before formulating falun gong. It allows much better 'cultivation' (the word, Deniece tells me, that they used to replace 'superstition') because it is based as much on principles and morals as the exercises themselves.

'The movements will help, but they are not enough alone,' she says. It is not a religion, she insists, but I assume that it is not exactly scientific materialism either. Doing the exercises, she tells me, creates a falun and a protective energy shield about 10 centimetres away from the body. I will not experience all this immediately, not until it is clear whether it is right for me. 'Master Li will see if you are compatible and if you are, he will put a falun in your lower abdomen,' Deniece says.

This is not a pretty thought, but I assume she is talking about *spiritually* inserting a falun into my lower abdomen. She tells me that the idea is to empty the mind while doing the exercises, to ignore thoughts that come and try to experience the emptiness.

Deniece starts to show me the movements. They look simple, but she makes it clear that details matter. 'Your knees must be slightly bent, to allow the energy to enter you. Your palms must not touch, just your fingers. Make your fists hollow.' Half a dozen more people arrive. Four are Chinese. Song puts the tape machine in the centre and we stand in a circle. I stand opposite Song. 'Men can stand opposite women,' Song explains, 'then the movement is all right.' She sets the tape going, and oriental string and flute music with instructions in both Chinese and English emerges from the machine. The rhythm is slow and peaceful. We stand with our legs apart, hands together, knees and hips bent, tongues touching the top of our palates, ready to start the Fozhan Qianshou Fa (or 'Buddha Showing Thousand Hands Exercise').

The movements are slow, but quite complicated. At first it seems easy to follow. We move into stretches and pushes and then relax. The relaxation is not just about letting everything flop: it is graceful, mannered, almost balletic, and not really relaxing at all for a beginner. The tape keeps saying, 'Action following the mechanism,' which means you should make your action follow the falun in your lower abdomen. The group moves as one, each person concentrating but looking serene. Gradually I grow attuned to the movements, which are repeated several times. It is not tiring, but it does become quite satisfying, moving in time, getting it right.

Then I feel a sharp, stinging pain on my left foot. Foolishly I have worn sandals and there, sucking my blood and inserting its poison, is a huge, greenish horsefly. I break the pattern to splat it with my other foot. Just as I start to relax, I am bitten again. *Do my companions believe in reincarnation?* I wonder, as I squash the second horsefly as surreptitiously as I can while doing synchronized Qianshou Fa opposite the instructor. *Do the* horseflies *believe in reincarnation?* The third and last horsefly dies (with a deft move of the ball of the palm onto my jeans) before he finds my flesh. For the next 10 minutes it is impossible to empty my mind. Horsefly bites take some transcending.

Then, strangely, I really start to enjoy an exercise called Falun Zhoutian Fa. This, they tell me, enables the heavenly circulation of energy in the human body to circulate over a large area. 'The energy circulates from the whole yin side of the body to the yang side many times,' Song says. It is intended to open up all the energy passages of the body so that energy will pass through the whole body gradually, from top to bottom. The falun is used to heal all illnesses and abnormalities via its mini-cosmos. Well, I enjoy it. The movement is flowing, balanced and peaceful. It starts to rain and I do not care. I can do this effortlessly. I can do it while watching people punting by on the river. Probably the most satisfying moment is when Song points to my pose and says, 'Roland is doing it perfectly.'

By this time it is raining hard. Ducks have swum to shelter, picnickers have left the park. The only people remaining are stranded in punts on the river. They stare at us as if we are insane. We move gracefully through the steady drizzle, water streaming through our hair, the tinny tape player sounding increasingly faint.

Then comes the trickiest movement: Shuangshou Tuidong Falun ('Turning Falun with Two Hands'). The instructions (all in a book with pictures of Master Li) read:

After completing Shuangshou Chongguan, move both hands downward along the head and chest until they reach the location of the lower abdomen. Now turn falun at the lower abdomen with the left hand inside for male, or the right hand inside for female. Keep a distance of 2–3cm between two hands as well as between the inner hand and the lower abdomen. Turn falun clockwise 4 rounds to spin the outside energy into the body. While turning the falun, keep the movements of the two hands within the area of the lower abdomen.

If you have ever tried patting your head while rubbing circles on your stomach, you will know the feeling. No doubt drummers and dancers can do it standing on their heads (whatever the energy consequences of that might be), but I struggle like a pig trying to dance. I get my left hand turning clockwise as smoothly as a finely tuned machine. Then I try the right hand, which has to turn clockwise in larger circles without touching the body and within that 10-centimetre energy shield. Of course, the inner hand goes haywire. After about eight attempts, suddenly I can do it. I am thrilled and find it hard to stop. It feels like quite an achievement. Still, I am pretty sure that my achievement does not quite amount to turning the cosmos around in my belly.

Perhaps, I think, *the secret of falun gong lies in Master Li's moral teachings*. The movements have a certain something, but I really cannot see how they could set 100 million people on fire and rock the might of communist China. After looking at the teachings, however, I can understand communist China's description of falun gong as 'superstition'. In eight chapters Master Li explains that we are in 'Havoc's Last Period' and that he is the only one who can bring about enlightenment. He is very possessive about the fact that he is the *Master* and that all practitioners are his disciples. He explains that human beings have been given an 'extra chance' via falun gong and that the higher powers should have destroyed us. Bad karma leads to illness, and people who are physically ill cannot 'cultivate' (which means develop oneself spiritually). This cultivation is a 'process of giving up human attachments' and attaining Zhen-Shan-Ren (truth, benevolence and forbearance). This can lead to 'supernormal' powers like clairvoyance and the ability to heal (which he does once we have reached an appropriate level of cultivation), but these should never be an end in themselves. I have a strong sense of having heard much of this before. Were it not for the fact that Master Li has over 100 million disciples, I would advise him not to give up the day job.

Perhaps Master Li's teaching has gained such phenomenal success in China because of the brutal and materialistic oppression that occurred during the Cultural Revolution. Enforced atheism is the perfect breeding ground for spirituality. It may have spread in non-communist countries for different reasons.

Falun gong, t'ai chi, feng shui and other oriental religions or spiritualities have certain aspects that seem to appeal to Westerners. The austerity, the emphasis on simplicity, emptiness and absence, seem a good antidote to the frenzy, the complexity, the clutter, of much of our life. In this context, the 'sound of one hand clapping', the resonance of space, of potentiality, is a potent idea. With such crowded and intrusive lifestyles, space itself becomes nirvana. The desire to escape worldly attachment is paramount. For me, managing and perhaps balancing worldly attachments is a better approach. I do not want to escape. I want to struggle, to criticize and to qualify my relationship with the complexity of modern life.

Balance is another factor. The yin and yang symbol has replaced the cross as the *de rigueur* spiritual icon to hang round one's neck or stick on a T-shirt. In many ways I can relate to this. Life seems so unbalanced, so linear, that the idea of balanced energies (or 'qi' as Master Li calls it) is a desirable one. To balance work and play, solitude and socializing, thought and action, is important – though I am not much good at it. Yet I find the yin and yang concept a tad problematical when attached to ethical issues. Is every ecological paradise to be cosmically balanced by an oil spill? Is every country at peace to be balanced by a war zone? Is every overweight European to be balanced by a hungry African? What can it possibly mean?

My next stop on the search for inner space and stillness takes me to Maharishi European Sidhaland in Skelmersdale. This may sound like a tacky Hindu theme park, but it is a community of meditators who believe that meditating for 20 minutes twice a day will change, well, just about everything. Meditators will experience better health, less stress, increased intelligence, creativity, memory and improved relationships. Society benefits too. If enough people meditate, then crime rates, drug abuse, pollution, congestion and all manner of social ills will decrease. School results will improve, people will live longer, conflicts will dissolve with the magical 'Maharishi Effect' – named after the guru and founder of transcendental meditation, Maharishi Mahesh Yogi. The grass grows greener in Skelmersdale.

Practitioners of transcendental meditation spent years telling the political establishment about the benefits of practising TM, as they call it, before they realized that their message was falling on deaf ears. They funded studies purporting to show the beneficial effects of 'yogic flying' (a kind of cross-legged bouncing practised by advanced meditators, called Sidhis), and still those flint-hearted politicians would only show polite interest behind firmly closed doors. So they decided to found the Natural Law Party, a political party fielding a candidate in every constituency, as a way of getting the message across. Despite its utopian claims and a national political party to carry these to the country at large, unlike falun gong, TM did not have politicians rocking back on their feet.

My first experience of TM was nearly 20 years ago when, as a chronic insomniac facing A levels, my mother suggested that I tried meditation. The local milkman does it, she said, and look how early *he* manages to get out of bed. Reluctantly, I traipsed along to a seminar room in Nottingham's Central Library. There I was told by a married couple, whose names I forget, that sleep would be mine again. They were friendly, if almost eerily calm. They also insisted that TM was not a religion and, no, Maharishi was not a guru, avatar, expression of godhead, or anything spiritual at all. Hey, he was just a regular guy who had decided to bring meditation from an ancient Indian tradition to the West.

I signed up and was invited to bring a flower, some fruit and a piece of white fabric to my initiation at the TM teachers' house. The flower, fruit and fabric were not worshipful offerings, they were just a way of honouring the tradition of meditation that Maharishi had brought to us. I would be given my mantra, a Sanskrit word that I was to repeat internally for 20 minutes each time I meditated. Distractions would enter my mind, but I was not to resist them. I was to let them go effortlessly as I sought 'transcendence', a completely thoughtless and blissful state of meditation. I was warned that I might twitch or experience strange sensations as I started meditating. This was usually stress relief, and it would happen because my body was not used to it. I must have asked what was special about the Sanskrit mantra and why *any* sound could not also do the job, but I cannot remember the answers.

I took an apple, some daffodils and a white handkerchief. The male teacher led me into a room, asked me to take my shoes off, and sat me before a picture of Maharishi and the Vedic teachers who had passed the techniques down to him. He started chanting in Sanskrit. Incense was burning and, possibly, a candle flickered. I placed my gifts before the picture. I think I was also asked to bow. But no, this was not spiritual. I then relaxed in a seat as my teacher told me my mantra. The word was *aing*, and I had to repeat it with him out loud before internalizing it. Then he left me for what I remember as a deeply peaceful 20 minutes. When the teacher returned, he quietly urged me to 'come out of' my meditation.

Over the weeks, my sleep improved slightly. I quite enjoyed the meditation. A few months later, I was invited to a posh hotel to witness the inauguration of the Nottingham City Parliament for World Government. I remember lots of unnaturally calm people, pictures of Maharishi, fruit, flowers, joss sticks and free cake. There was much grand talk of the Maharishi Effect and how it would transform the world and bring an end to conflict and manifold other ills. I got a lift home with our meditating milkman, who, it turned out, had been taught to meditate by Maharishi himself. He claimed that Maharishi's meditating powers were such that he could be in two places at once. He had seen it himself, he said. And of course, he said, it *was* a religion – it was the ultimate truth, the cosmic consciousness behind everything.

I approach Skelmersdale, therefore, as a lapsed meditator, grown up and wondering whether meditation might offer me anything now. I am also curious about the claims for the Maharishi Effect, and interested to see how the community works. Religion, spiritual path or science, does it offer the estimated 200,000 British practitioners another dimension, and can it transform society? What can it really offer Skelmersdale, a Merseyside new-town affectionately known as Skem?

I arrive in the early evening and my first impression is of a vast *Brookside* set where trim redbrick houses on culs-de-sac are outshone by gardens brimming with flowers and streets with a suspicious lack of litter. It is like a model village. Eighty houses surround a large golden dome resembling a low-lying flying saucer. The Maharishi Golden Dome of the Age of Enlightenment is where the community meet to practise yogic flying and meditating as well as to enjoy social and educational activities. Apart from this, there is a pristine business park, a spacious sports centre (under construction) and verges coated with blossoming border shrubs. It is a 20-year-old housing estate without a single smudge or flourish of graffiti. It looks like a scene from a promotional brochure.

I am met by Simon Cohen, the Dome's director, and his wife Dawn. They have offered me a bed for the night. He is a wiry, retired probation officer who radiates goodwill and vigour. Dawn ushers me solicitously into her home, proudly showing me pictures of her son and telling me that he works as communications officer for a bishop. She shows me her garden, a lovingly tended profusion of flowers and vegetables, before sitting me down for home-made pizza. Apart from the odd picture of Maharishi and a few of his wise words dotted around on noticeboards and mantelpieces, it is a typical, tidy house.

We are joined by a senior TM teacher and Natural Law Party candidate who, for reasons best known to himself, did not want to be named. Let's just call him Stephen. They seem very sensitive about how TM is represented. They keep emphasizing how the 200 or so people within the community are independent and have different interests. 'Some like walking, others like gardening, others like sport, some of us do educational courses in the Dome together. When we finish yogic flying, we're more likely to be talking about the football than anything abstract,' Stephen says.

'Don't worry, I don't think this is a sinister cult,' I respond, explaining that I am interested in how shared beliefs help to create a community.

'The community doesn't have a shared belief system. We just share the practice of yogic flying and meditating,' Stephen says.

'I don't mean religious beliefs, I mean values,' I say.

'Ah, yes, we share values,' Stephen agrees, in that *sotto voce*, unnervingly calm delivery favoured by so many meditators.

Then they unpack the wonders of the Maharishi Effect for me. 'Maharishi predicted that the beneficial effects of meditating would extend into the world once 1 per cent of the population meditated. Then he told us that only the square root of 1 per cent of the population was needed if the meditators were practising yogic flying in a group,' Simon explains. They point to academic studies that suggest that, since the meditators started bouncing in the Dome, the Merseyside crime rate has dropped. They hand me a sheet of paper on which various academics endorse the studies as if that settles the matter. But how does it work? 'When we meditate, we enter what physicists call the Unified Field, and by accessing this we personally grow in creative intelligence and we lose our collective stress. Everything improves,' Stephen says. The environment, pollution, congestion, the weather – you name it, it gets better. They send teams of meditators to trouble spots to bring peace. People can even fly and break the laws of nature once they reach 'cosmic consciousness' or 'coherence' in their meditation, Stephen explains.

'We're not much good at it. We're at the second stage of yogic flying, which is bouncing, but we will improve,' Simon chips in.

Maharishi has also opened their eyes to Ayurvedic medicine and Gandhava Veda, the scientific principles behind music, as well as the principles of Vedic architecture, education and prosperity. *Is there a Vedic approach to Scrabble?* I wonder. Sometimes this Vedic panacea is accessed by meditating; at other times there are practical changes that accord with the Unified Field. For instance, to use natural materials in buildings is good; to have the main door facing east is good; to eat naturally is good; to avoid GM foods is good (they were campaigning on this long before it became fashionable); to try natural Ayurvedic remedies for illness is good. Why? Because Maharishi says so. But meditation is the main route to the 'science of creative intelligence' and the Unified Field, which has made their school results the best in Merseyside and helped their child poets to win a series of national poetry competitions. Although Simon and Stephen admit that they do not fully understand Maharishi's science, to them these results prove that it is true.

I am reminded of the 'black box theory' of psychologist Christopher Evans, which he uses to describe the use of science by religious groups and spiritual movements. Just like George King's prayer batteries, the input is known (meditating and yogic flying) and the output is known (utopia), but only God (or Maharishi in this case) knows what happens in between, in the Unified Field.

Stephen says, 'Every part of creation comes from the Unified Field, and TM is simply a way to access it. The Vedic texts are a blueprint for natural law, they are the principles that undergird everything.' So the ancient Hindu Vedic texts just happen to encapsulate absolute scientific truth? 'Just look at the statistics,' Stephen keeps saying.

The Natural Law Party took this Vedic blueprint and turned it into a manifesto. 'One of the first things that we would do if elected would be to appoint 800 professional yogic fliers,' Stephen explains. What would that do to people's council tax? 'We'd need less police, less soldiers, less bureaucracy, tax would fall,' Stephen reassures me. The devil is in the detail, so I scour their manifesto pledges. On bureaucracy the Natural Law Party states, 'The size and cost of governmental bureaucracy can be reduced significantly by introducing administration through Natural Law – *automation in administration*. Natural Law administers the entire universe with perfect efficiency and without a problem.' Their defence policy is streamlined with similarly Vedic precision: 'The Natural Law Party's defence policy will be to promote the invincible, evolutionary power of Natural Law, which is characterized not by destruction but by happy evolution. No war or other harm could arise because the collective stress which causes enmity will be completely dissolved.' I do not foresee a Vedic landslide at the polling booths.

Before I go to bed, Simon says, 'Meditation is so simple; you don't have to change your lifestyle to do it, it doesn't make great demands. Maharishi always says, "Meditate, then get on with your life and live it to the full."' I decide to give it a go, sitting cross-legged and saying *'aing'* over and over. I am out of practice, and only manage a couple of minutes before lying down and falling asleep.

Simon wakes me early so that I can have a tour of the Dome before the meditators arrive for their Saturday morning yogic flying. I am not allowed to see them doing it, because it might distract them. Walking to the Dome, I cannot help but notice several burglar alarms on houses. Simon unlocks the Dome's door, checking that the alarms are switched off. *Why do they need all this security at the centre of the Unified Field and 'cosmic consciousness'?* I ask myself. The Dome is an elegant symmetrical structure, apart from a large satellite dish on one side. Inside is an entrance lobby and a shop selling healthy foods and Ayurvedic remedies. We take our shoes off. 'Not for sacred reasons, just because it's a nice, clean carpet,' Simon says.

We enter the yogic flying powerhouse, a large circular room with graceful pine ceiling arching towards a round window in the centre. There is foam matting on either side of a walkway and screen which separates men and women, 'to stop distractions'. Directly beneath the window is a perspex–covered futuristic model made up of strange symmetrical shapes and symbols. It is a Vedic observatory, Simon says, there to create stillness at the centre of the building according to Maharishi's Vedic architectural principles. At the front, above an 'altar', is a two-metre-high picture of the tradition of gurus from whom Maharishi learned. To one side is his own grinning, bearded, lank-haired mugshot, framed in gold. To the other side is a screen with a video projector. I ask what this is for. 'Maharishi broadcasts to us live from Holland where he is based,' Simon says. *So those are the 'educational courses' that TMers attend together*, I think. Around the room are posters with the words 'Heaven on Earth' across the top. In one of the anterooms which surround the yogic flying room is a plaque from a community in Holland. 'For Utopia in the UK,' it reads.

Meditators, all dressed in white, start to arrive and Simon ushers me out. At the door is a 'badge-checker', making sure that only bona fide meditators enter. *Surely 'collective stress' and enmity should be dissolved to the extent that such checkers are not needed?* I think.

I leave Sidhaland with mixed feelings. It seems a friendly, peaceful and positive community and people obviously feel that they benefit greatly from meditating. My impression is of a community of good people, having some success at creating 'utopia'. Meditators are not mind-controlled zombies: they appear to live fulfilled lives. Yet the idea of the Unified Field and the notion of Maharishi's science being coherent are in themselves acts of 'creative intelligence'. Studies have seriously questioned the Maharishi Effect and have pointed out that it is usually TMers who do the research, and they have not always been willing to offer their raw data for peer review. More damaging is the fact that a former dean of the Physics faculty at Maharishi International University in Maryland now claims that they cooked the books and calls it 'crackpot science'.

Part of the reason why I would not resurrect my practice of TM is that I do not have the patience for silent transcendence. The main reason, however, is the movement's coyness about it being 'spiritual'. The idea of it being a scientific rather than a spiritual movement is silly and appears to cause them much unnecessary 'collective stress'. Whether they see Maharishi as an avatar or messenger from God in the true Hindu tradition is difficult to say. Sitting in a room with the words 'How blessed we feel to be swimming in the ocean of bliss with you, together in alliance with Maharishi who is the greatest who know Brahman' displayed on the noticeboard, Stephen told me that 'flying is a completely normal human experience in the Unified Field' – then went on to say that there is nothing mystical, religious or spiritual about TM. As they say in Skelmersdale, 'And yogic fliers might fly.' I drive out of Merseyside hoping for something a little more honest with itself.

14

🛒

Which Witch Guide

About 10 years ago, I went for a walk in the woods at night. It is something that I do occasionally. I like the strange desolation, the slightly edgy mystery and, most of all, the profoundly different sense of place. A sunny glade is transformed into an intimate, sinister place whose dark intensity blasts its icy breath to the core of my being. It is invigorating and unnerving and, if you can still your nerves, profoundly peaceful.

At about midnight, I walked a few hundred yards along a muddy track overhung with trees on each side of a narrow valley. I came to a junction and headed up the path towards a grassy dip called Hidden Valley. As usual, I felt a strange mixture of nervousness and calm at the beginning of my walk. In my imagination every shadow, every distant rustle of leaves, hid a sinister person. Yet the stillness, the black emptiness, was inspiring. I cannot remember whether or not there was a moon, but probably not, because it was very dark. After I had gone a short way along the track, I noticed a small flame flickering about 200 yards into Hidden Valley.

I was shocked. These things are only supposed to happen in films or other people's overwrought imaginations. I steeled myself to creep closer and see what was happening. After a few more yards I heard loud voices orating to the sky. I stopped dead. I could not hear words, just several voices reciting. Then a grand, commanding voice spoke out. By this time I was imagining black-cowled lookouts behind every tree. I hid and listened for as long as I dared, then crept off to get a friend.

I called on my petrol-pump-collecting neighbour. He is a big, no-nonsense biker type – exactly the sort you can rely on in a tight corner. He was sceptical, but interested. 'Just a bunch of drunken herberts in the woods,' he said, as we picked up sticks. We approached through the beech woods along the ridge above Hidden Valley. We walked quietly, but heard nothing at all. It is quite a deep valley, so we started to creep down the side as silently as we could in the pitch black without torches. We stopped to listen again, and this time heard faint voices. We moved slowly down to within 50 yards of the valley floor. We could see nothing through the leaves, but the voices grew louder, and could have been chanting.

Then there was silence, followed by more grand oration. After another brief silence, a woman's voice half screamed, half sobbed, 'Oh f***ing hell!' I do not think that I am dramatizing if I say that her voice was full of despair. Something pretty nasty was happening, probably to her. She was not screaming for help, but she was either regretting what was happening or was struggling with it. I was terrified and ready to leave. My friend was braver. He wanted to stay, to investigate further. I said I would meet him at the top. In the end, he decided to come with me.

We did not phone the police. Perhaps we should have done, but I imagine all the people involved were willing participants. All we knew was that there was a ritual going on in the woods. I do not know whether it was witchcraft, some other form of paganism, or Satanism. It may have been none of those. With hindsight, I regret not creeping closer and taking a look. At the time, however, it had seemed impossible.

I imagine that not many people have experienced that sort of thing. It is exactly the sort of thing that fuels hysteria, however, and for some time I assumed that witchcraft and Satanism were interchangeable and that both were essentially 'evil'. My impression was of something malign and that, I assumed, was what all witches must be. This view was confirmed by the media and by evangelical Christians who embarked every so often on witch-hunts based on ignorance, prejudice and uncritical acceptance (encouragement, even) of stories told by converted witches. The truth is, however, that I do not know what it was I stumbled across that night. I simply have no evidence. I have since met local witches for coffee (as you do) and they have reassured me that what I describe was not witchcraft as they know it or would want to know it.

Nevertheless, 10 years later, I am feeling a little apprehensive as I push my vehicle through acres of water and wind on my way to the southwest corner of Britain. Outside the car, the wind is tearing across a blasted heath. Thick fog has been replaced by a vicious, stinging downpour which rattles against the windows. My wipers are frantically sweeping swathes of water off the windscreen. I am looking for Cassandra Latham, a famous witch who lives in the tiny village of St Buryan, a stone's throw from Land's End. I have given a lift to a local farm worker, hitch-hiking from Penzance, and strangely enough we arrive at his destination, which turns out to be miles from mine. He hops out with a wave and leaves me, completely lost, overlooking the wild, rocky coast. I follow a narrow lane across moorland. It really is like the scene in *Macbeth* before he meets the witches.

I arrive at the cottage half an hour late. Ms Latham calls herself a 'village witch' or 'cunning woman', and is going to initiate me into the basics of 'natural magic' in her home (half way between simple cottage and witch's hovel). As she makes up a witch's brew (PG Tips), I see – behind the candles, bottled potions, crystal balls and sprigs of mistletoe – a broomstick with a tax disk tied onto it. *Perhaps*, I reassure myself, *this witch has a sense of humour*.

Cassandra Latham, aged 50, started working as a professional witch after an accident forced her to give up nursing. While she was on a government Restart Scheme, her tutor, knowing of her unusual interest, suggested that she set up a business as a self-employed witch. She registered as a 'village witch' with the Inland Revenue and now offers tarot readings, spells, rituals and charms as well as psychic house-cleanings and a wart-removal service. She also teaches natural magic and performs handfastings (pagan weddings), baby blessings and last rites. The vast majority of her clients are non-pagans, she says, often in a crisis.

She returns with mugs of tea, a roll-up between her teeth, and sits me down at a low black table. 'Witchcraft is about magic, trying to change things or influence events,' she says. This may simply be changing the client's attitude, but it can also affect external reality. 'You have to be careful what you wish for,' she explains. 'To ask for money might bring about someone's death.' Much of the magic is crafted around the client. 'After reading tarot cards or counselling someone, I get an insight into the person which allows me to devise a ritual to free them of their problem, a spell to help them develop, or a charm to protect them,' she says.

Natural magic involves invoking the four elements: air, fire, earth and water. It often involves a creative or symbolic act. 'Sometimes people come to me who are finding it difficult to get over grieving. I tell them to write it all down, read it out to get in touch with their anger, then place it in a pot and burn it,' Latham explains. The client then smashes the pot, releasing the ashes to the open air, while Latham chants a spell. 'The four elements *literally* remove the grief,' she adds. Latham tries to involve clients directly in their healing or growth. 'I have told people to fly kites, to build sand castles; these are physical manifestations of the spiritual and psychological energies and it really helps people,' she says.

What about cursing? She hands me a leaflet entitled 'Personal Ethical Code of Practice' which says, 'Any requests for work which knowingly causes harm to others will be declined.' She has only cast a curse once, to work against some vandals who threatened to damage sacred sites. The curse was to come into effect if they carried out their threats. They did. 'I simply sent back their evil intent with a bit of welly,' Latham says. The vandals have since been taken into custody.

Some people come to her wanting to learn how to use magic themselves. Latham learned from a coven, but left them partly because they were too pedantic about rituals. Her shelves full of books of spells and rituals suggest that the knowledge is Byzantine and complex. 'I prefer a simple approach. I don't wear special clothes or have lots of para- phernalia,' she says. She explains that at the heart of natural magic is a reverence for nature.

The changing seasons are central to witches' key festivals and 'nature's way' is always seen as best. Most witches wor- ship the Goddess Diana, a matriarchal Mother Nature who controls the elements. The four elements relate to four princi- ples or attitudes. Air represents the intellect, fire represents the will, water represents our creative, imaginative energy and earth represents our ability to keep silent, to hold our- selves back.

Latham starts her work with me by reading my tarot cards. I have to shuffle them, then she lays them out and closes her eyes before turning them over. As she does so, she explains that I have been trying to achieve a balance, a compromise, recently, while cutting away from the past. Leaving the past can be difficult, she tells me. 'Better the devil you know,' she says, without a hint of irony. The central card is a man stabbed through by 10 swords. She tells me that this symbolizes the end of a nightmare, which is probably my mid-life crisis. I am not actually aware of having had a mid-life crisis, but I try to keep an open mind. She turns over a card showing a man carrying 10 sticks and tells me this suggests that I am too busy, trying to do too much.

We talk about the cards and Latham asks what has come out of them for me. I admit that the man with 10 sticks has a certain resonance. I *am* trying to do too many things; my life is too frenetic. I know that the next few months are going to be frantic. 'Find a single word for what you want,' she says, 'and we'll do some candle magic.' She lights a candle. I settle for 'peacefulness', and Latham brings out a white candle. 'It's the colour for tranquillity and lack of distraction,' she says, giving it to me with a knife and a book of rune signs. I am to carve the word in English and in runes onto the candle, from the top to the bottom. This is meant to draw the peacefulness to me as I burn the candle and stare at the flame.

While I am carving, Latham starts to prepare for her spell-casting. She places an African fetish at the edge of the table ('She likes to watch over,' she says with a grin), lights a candle, fetches a bottle of well water, some tongs and a large black tablet of incense. She lights the incense and places it in a crucible. 'That invokes the fire and air energy,' she explains. The well water cleanses the candle with earth and water energy. I give her my inscribed candle, she looks embarrassed for a moment, then closes her eyes and starts to chant,

This is the spell that I intone
Flesh to flesh and bone to bone
Sinew to sinew, vein to vein
And each one shall be whole again.

She washes the candle with well water, whispering, 'Cleanse and blessed be.' Then she passes it through the incense and hands it to me to light. She closes her eyes again and chants,

With this candle that I light
I will require of thee tonight
I pray that you will grant this boon
O lovely Goddess of the moon.

After a few minutes' silence, she tells me to spend five minutes every evening staring at the candle flame. Chanting the spell, she says, is optional. She encourages me to walk in the countryside. 'Try to make yourself aware of the changing seasons. Once we attune to nature, our stress levels fall because we see things in a deeper time frame than our petty man-made ones,' she says.

As I leave Latham's cottage, the sun shines onto a hawthorn tree festooned with ribbons (representing wishes), given to her on her fiftieth birthday by local well-wishers. I do not personally feel any more or less peaceful than before, but I am struck by how creative, natural and potentially therapeutic her craft is. It may be hocus-pocus, but it seems strangely good for the soul – as benign as druidism but with added magic. The closeness to nature appeals to me, and the earthiness, and, in some ways, the emphasis on the feminine. In a sense, that all seems natural. It is the magic and the spells that seem man-made and silly. Cassandra told me that this magic is an ancient religion passed down from pre-Christian days. I asked her about the evidence, and her knowledge was a little sketchy.

Further up the Cornish coast at Boscastle is the Museum of Witchcraft, where I hope to find some answers about the origins of the craft. The museum is in a long white building set above a narrow inlet-cum-harbour and below the steep-sided hills around the tiny fishing village. It claims to house the world's largest collection of witch 'artefacts and regalia' and was founded by Cecil Williamson, a witch active at the very dawn of the craft's modern renaissance in Britain.

On arriving at the museum, I am met by the new owner, curator and witch Graham King, who tells me that Williamson died just weeks ago. King is an ebullient, bearded chap with a thick woolly jumper. He tells me it is appropriate that the museum is in Cornwall, because the area has many witches and a long association with witchcraft. It is an ancient religion worldwide, but its origins are shrouded in mystery, he says. King talks generally about the prevalence of matriarchies in the ancient world, of goddesses rather than gods, and of links between witches' rituals and Egyptian beliefs. Witchcraft is older than Christianity, he says.

The museum does not shy away from the more controversial aspects of witchcraft. There is a section on cursing which includes poppets and pins, an eye with a splinter in it and some animal testicles punctured by thorns – a way of seeking revenge on someone in a farming community, apparently. King points out that most modern witches believe in the law of threefold return: what you wish on someone else will come back with interest. Most witches live by one rule: 'And it harm none, do what you will.'

Another section deals with the preoccupation of some witches with sex. There are photos of scantily clad or naked ('sky clad') witches performing various rituals, and several phallic candles, possibly not meant for lighting. The museum also includes a section on Satanism, making it clear that witchcraft and Satanism are different things. 'Witches don't believe in the existence of the devil,' King says, 'but we do believe in a horned God as a counterpart to the Goddess.' He explains that the Church in the sixteenth century decided that this horned god was the devil, although the Bible does not mention the devil in this form. This, he says, fuelled the witch-hunts of the sixteenth and seventeenth centuries which led to hundreds of thousands of deaths.

There is a display of shackles and a witch's bridle, as well as images of ducking stools and witches being burned or hanged. It is both interesting and shocking to see how people 'demonized' witches and saw them as sub-human. This allowed the authorities to treat them with brutality and injustice. In another room, however, is just the sort of thing that might have inspired such brutality. In a box is a dried-out (presumably pickled) human hand. 'We think that it is a "hand of glory", used by witches to bewitch people or put them to sleep for questionable purposes,' King explains. The museum faces up to the more dubious practices of some past witches (as well as their persecution), while stressing that modern witchcraft is a more benign phenomenon. I notice an old image of a bat drinking from a bloody cup with the caption, 'Come drink from the cup of forbidden knowledge.' Perversely, close by is a museum sign which reads, 'Parents, please ensure that your children are kept with you and under control.'

Before I leave, I tell King that I am keen to meet a modern coven. 'You'll be lucky,' he says. He tells me that most witches are wary of outsiders and will not give their names because they are frightened of the media. King tells me that witches are still persecuted: a drama teacher was recently sacked for going public about being a witch. The press, encouraged by some evangelical Christians, often fail to distinguish between witchcraft and Satanism, he confirms. In the 1980s, witches and Satanic cults were accused of sexually abusing children and many of these stories originated from evangelical church groups. Although sexual abuse had occurred which very occasionally involved rituals as a way of frightening and controlling the children, a government enquiry concluded that there was no evidence that ritual abuse (i.e. abuse of children as part of any religious practice) had ever taken place.

When I get home, I contact a man I first met at the druid gathering – Ronald Hutton, Professor of History at Bristol University and author of *The Triumph of the Moon: A History of Modern Pagan Witchcraft*, the first serious study of an area that is traditionally swathed in myth or drowned in hysteria. His view is markedly different from King's. Hutton's research has led him to demolish the concept of pagan witchcraft as an ancient religion. The pagan concept of the ancient Earth Goddess is linked with two scholars whose work in this area has been discredited, Sir James Frazer (of *The Golden Bough*) and Margaret Murray. They suggested that pagan witchcraft had survived from ancient origins until the seventeenth century, but their ideas were influenced by the German Romantics and they had no evidence on which to base their suppositions. 'In fact,' Hutton tells me, 'most gods in the ancient world were decidedly masculine and the goddesses were patronesses of cities, handicrafts, home fire, agriculture, love and learning; they weren't linked with the natural world.'

Hutton believes that the cultural forces which gave birth to witchcraft were the German and British Romantic movements, whose exaltation of the natural, wild and irrational (as opposed to the rationalistic Enlightenment or urban and civilized Christianity) became a potent countercultural force as industrialization swept through Britain in the eighteenth and nineteenth centuries. People *wanted* to believe in a matriarchal goddess who was mysterious, irrational and represented nature. Mother Earth was ripe for delivery – but she was conceived on the rebound, not as a child with a lineage or history.

According to Hutton, the same is true of witchcraft's arcane rituals. 'None of them goes back into antiquity; most of them are adaptations of rituals from other organizations like Freemasonry,' Hutton says. The notorious pentagram and certain other ritualistic elements of witchcraft can be traced to seventeenth-century Freemasonry, rather than, as is popularly believed, the other way round. Hutton's findings are shocking.

Who would have thought, for instance, that the first verifiable coven was formed in the 1950s near St Albans? Or that there is no secure evidence that the women who were persecuted in the Middle Ages were actually witches (most scholars believe they were women who did not conform – perhaps due to disabilities or psychic abilities)? These witch-hunts reflected Church hysteria (in a similar way to the Satanic abuse stories of the 1980s) rather than the existence of a witchcraft religion. Who would have suspected that the creator of pagan witchcraft was a retired tea plantation manager, or that most other figures in the early movement were politically Conservative?

Gerald Gardner, apparently, founded modern witchcraft in the 1950s. He was a typical ex-colonial type, except for his interest in religion and the occult. In his sixties he published *Witchcraft Today*, in which he claimed to have joined a coven led by 'Old Dorothy', a witch surviving from an ancient pagan tradition. Soon he attracted others and by the mid-fifties they had formed a coven and started rituals, including sky-clad dances and spells. These early witches were characterized by a desire to persuade people that they had gained their craft from a long line of witches stretching back to antiquity. While not quite calling them fraudulent, Hutton says that their rituals were generally based on modern sources. He paints a picture of mischievous eccentrics, with a penchant for drama, magic and taking their clothes off.

Hutton's academic research does dovetail with King's account when he describes the media panic caused by sensational journalism from the 1950s until the late 1980s, and the media's inability to distinguish between Satanism and witchcraft. 'This hysteria has lessened since feminism and environmentalism became dominant themes under the influence of Starhawk and other American witches,' he says. The birth of American witchcraft in the early 1980s shifted the political thrust of the movement to the left.

Hutton's research pulls the rug from under the notion of pagan witchcraft being anything other than a thoroughly modern religion. 'No one before the 1940s ever referred to *themselves* as a witch. It was a term used of others by people with suspicions,' he says. It is a religion whose roots and branches are a reaction against mechanistic industrialization and the separation from nature in contemporary life. He admits that many modern witches are ambivalent about whether magic is anything more than positive thinking. 'Most witches in my experience are a convivial bunch,' he adds. But, I persist, might it be possible to see a modern coven at work? He thinks it unlikely.

A few weeks later, I visit the site of the world's first coven. It is based in St Albans and, *en route*, I drop in on a High Priestess in Watford to see if I can persuade her to let me visit her coven. Gail, a single mum with two young boys, is a thoroughly convivial and modern witch. She runs the Neighbourhood Watch in her street and sometimes cooks the ingredients for spells in her microwave. 'All magic is one big placebo,' she says, adding without pause, 'and yet the forces are out there.'

She explains that there are different sorts of witch. Gardnerian witches work in covens with 'high magic' and tend to use robes, liturgy and rituals. Alexandrian witches also work in covens, but are less rigid in their rituals. Hedge witches work magic alone, but may work with others occasionally. Cunning women are usually healers, psychics or diviners and use less ritualistic 'low magic' for spells and charms. Can I meet her coven? They have only recently gained each other's trust and would not want an outsider to see them, she says.

I find the birthplace of modern witchcraft in Britain's oldest naturists' club, Brickets Wood. Gerald Gardner built the tiny chalet in the club because he hoped that it would give them the privacy they needed. It could not be less dramatic. The hut is 10 feet wide and 30 feet long, with narrow slits for windows. These are boarded up. It is covered in white and yellow plaster and mock Tudor wooden beams. There are beech trees overhead, and 50 years ago it may have been quite desolate, even frightening. Now the hut has rotting tyres and a compost pile leaning against it, and a trim chalet with plastic flowers and garden gnomes stands next door. It is within 15 yards of a shabby open-air swimming pool and several other naturists' weekend chalets. A hundred yards away I can hear the M25.

I search patiently for a coven that will say 'yes'. I am offered a cyber coven, chanting together on the internet. High Priestesses say they will ask their covens, but no one returns my calls. Imbolc passes (1 February), and Beltane (30 April), then, a few weeks before Lammas (1 August), I get an e-mail giving me a number to ring. I phone and High Priestess Kate Paine tells me that, so long as their confidentiality is guaranteed, I can meet her coven in Preston in a few days' time. They are arranging a conference for northern pagans and I can watch the opening ritual. They have no time for a proper coven meeting involving ceremonial magic, but I am welcome to talk to them about being in a coven.

The conference takes place in Preston's Grasshoppers Rugby Club. My first impression is of a tiny, more focused Mind Body Spirit festival. There are about a dozen stalls selling witches' paraphernalia. There are wands, broomsticks, ceremonial knives (athames), crystal balls for scrying, plastic pentagrams and pestles and mortars for mixing spell ingredients. There are tacky bits of pottery in the shape of naked witches, crystal penises, witches' rune stones, candles, flower essences and more crystals.

The opening ceremony is a disappointment. Five members of the coven call on the four elements, the Goddess and the

Lord of the Hunt, raise their hands and ask for 'mirth and merriment' to attend on the conference. They are not wearing ceremonial robes, preferring hippy gear with a gothic edge. It is reminiscent of the druids' ritual at Avebury, although this one takes place in the shadow of adverts for Braithwaites Bitter and a selection of framed rugby shirts rather than a stone circle. Afterwards Kate, dressed in purple patchwork overalls, tells me of the closeness of relationships within a coven. 'We have to have the right blend, otherwise witchcraft becomes bitchcraft,' she explains.

Debbie, another coven member, explains that she was drawn to witchcraft because of the balance it brought to her life. 'It helped me to settle my own beliefs, to develop and learn about myself,' she says. The solstices are usually celebrations of the stages of the year, and full moons are reserved for working magic. She likes the mixture of finding the divine in nature and doing magic for specific ends. 'Our work is mainly healing, but we also do spells for things like driving tests,' she adds. I am reminded of the push-button prayers of Peniel Pentecostal Church and the Jesus Army. Like them, the coven also offers support and a sense of community. 'The coven is like a family. We know each other really well and, like families, we do have arguments.' Debbie was drawn to the coven partly because she knew that she could learn a lot and partly because of the friendship.

Two seminars at the conference reinforce the impression that I gained from the druids about pagans (i.e. witches and druids) being more politically orientated than many new religious movements. Andy Norfolk, a witch and druid and the Pagan Federation's Press Officer, speaks about the importance of working with English Heritage, the National Trust and other bodies to protect 'sacred sites'. He attacks 'amateur pagans' for lighting fires and candles on or by standing stones, and urges pagans to get involved with archaeologists and official bodies via ASLAN (Ancient Sacred Landscapes Network) to help protect the sites. 'Don't change the sites, let the sites change you' is their motto.

A witch called Joany, representing Liferites, an organization committed to encouraging people to celebrate rites of passage, speaks passionately about empowering people in a society where faceless, bland institutions like registrars, hospitals, undertakers and the Church are forcing individuals out. 'We can regain control of our life stages and celebrate marriage, childbirth and death with dignity, but you will have to fight for it,' she says. Someone yells out, 'Crone power!' and is answered by a yell of 'Crones rock!' I realize that Ronald Hutton was right: witches are a convivial bunch.

I am not inclined to buy a broomstick or seek membership of a coven, but I am ready to see that these witches are very different from the baby-killing Satanists of popular imagination. There are several disabled witches and I note the care that is taken to make sure that their needs are met without patronizing them. These witches are friendly, down to earth and funny: no more out of place in a rugby club than in a quiet glade. As I leave, Kate Paine says, 'You must visit the coven at Samhain.' Samhain is Halloween. I am charmed (if not spellbound), but the ritual magic element seems less important now. After all, these are good, ordinary people enchanting themselves with their love of nature and mystery – and I am happy to go on seeing them as good, ordinary people.

15

Seeking the Damascus Turning on the Information Superhighway

It is good weather outside, and I am laid up with flu. Well, mild flu. The sort of flu that leaves you feeling pretty reasonable in bed and then, when you try to get up and do something, it hits you hard – liquid concrete in your limbs and glue in your mind. Normally, I can enjoy a good illness. Lots of pampering and nothing much to do is understandably most men's idea of heaven. But this has been going on for days and shows no sign of giving up. Each time I try to do something, my body gums up and my mind goes into slower-than-usual slow motion. Jogging is out of the question. Leaving the house in search of spiritual answers is equally impossible.

I prop myself up in bed, therefore, pull my computer keyboard over and decide to search for God, spirit or life force on the internet. In the end I opt for God, aware that in cyberspace, as elsewhere, the Christian path will take me resolutely away from concepts such as Mother Earth, life force, spirit or energy. I decide to concentrate on God for now, and leave those other spiritual paths for another day. The problem is that, facing my search engine's homepage, ready to surf, is a bit like standing before God, the universe and everything. It is all there, but where do I start? You might liken it to Adam taking the first, hard, cold crunch out of the apple. Knowledge, doubtless of both good and evil, is just a click away.

It is probably worth saying at this stage that I do not take the line that technology is neutral, it just depends what you use it for. I am sure the internet can be used for good or bad, but I am equally sure that it is not neutral. We have to look at the effects of the medium on our assumptions and attitudes. Just as the shift from a word-based culture to an image-based culture may nudge us towards intuition and away from analysis, so the shift from encyclopaedia, library, community, church or coven to cyberspace will affect us. We have to learn to see the web for the web pages.

Teetering on the edge of this virtual precipice, I decide to ask the medium the big questions. I start by typing in 'Find god'. I am immediately offered hundreds of relevant sites, but one in the first 20 catches my eye – 'Finding God in Cyberspace'. I visit and Lee Adams Young welcomes me to his 'cyberparish'. I e-mail him to ask what made him take on a global parish, but receive no answer. His website is a little dull, but includes links which act as a route-finder for the cyberpilgrim with a hankering for traditional religion. There are lots of click-boxes and scores of links for churches.

I put my mouse in the appropriate place and find myself in the First Church of Cyberspace (www.godweb.org), 'a church which exists only on the web', run by a New Jersey Presbyterian minister who says he is 'Building a Church for the New Millennium'. I very much doubt that it is the first (there are tens of thousands of churches on the web, and some must pride themselves on being strictly 'virtual'), but it is an intelligent and sophisticated website with scores of sermons, film reviews, even an art gallery subtitled 'Seeing is Believing' which tours the Sistine Chapel as well as showing more contemporary religious art. There are also some songs and radio interviews with Cyber Reverend Charles Henderson, in which he reassures an interviewer that surfers at his site 'do get a religious experience. They can come to church any time they want.' There is a prayer request line on e-mail.

The site also offers an Internet Relay Chat (IRC) discussion, fellowship and prayers every Sunday evening and more informal chat at any time. I enter the chat room and the topic for discussion is 'spiritual priorities'. Gimpy from Lake Michigan is chatting with Ray from Australia. They are talking about the weather in Lake Michigan. Perfect fishing weather, Gimpy says. They ask me about the weather in the UK. I tell them. The weather in Australia is not so good.

I ask about why they are in the chat room, and the question is ignored. I ask about their beliefs. Gimpy tells me he is 'a devout Christian'. Ray does not really know. Me neither, I say. Gimpy ought to be fishing in *real* reality, I suggest. He says he is fishing in virtual reality. Feeling a little spooked, I ask if he is fishing for souls. This is Gimpy's response: 'Yup :-)' The smiley face on its side is an 'emoticon', a symbol that reflects an emotion. *Do these make up for eye contact or body language?* I wonder. Gimpy, after all, cannot see me wince at his smug little smiley telling me he is trying to convert me. I don't fancy being on the end of his line, I tell him. Ray chips in with a 'hehe' (cyberspeak for 'I'm laughing'), and Gimpy goes offline in a huff without so much as a 'God be with you'.

Ray is, literally, too boring for words and I begin to feel as if I have been cornered at a party by some one-dimensional automaton who can only discuss the weather. At a party I could nip through to the kitchen to get a drink without causing Ray offence. Here I can tell him that he is a bore and click off – but, because a sense of character does come through on IRC, I cannot be that cruel. I ask him where he is going on holiday. He tells me. I try to make conversation. There are awkward, pregnant pauses when no text appears on the screen for seconds. No one else is entering the room either. Eventually I tell him that someone is knocking at my non-virtual door, and I leave the chat room. Perhaps wanting to escape from Ray, I go into the First Church of Cyberspace's sanctuary.

I am met by a pre-Renaissance triptych of flat images of Jesus flanked by gold-leaf paint and a halo. A fire burns in the darkness before the paintings and soothing organ music plays. I guess a sanctuary is supposed to be a retreat from real life, so a virtual sanctuary should be fine. To retreat from real life to virtual life does not work, however. A sanctuary has to be a *real* safe, sacred space. I would want a sanctuary to be long, dark corridors, monks' cells, an empty chapel with sun coming through. Mind you, that is only a mouse-move away. Here goes.

I arrive at St Michael's Abbey in Farnborough (www.farnboroughabbey.org) with a slow, steadily ringing bell drawing me in. I open a virtual leather and parchment book which gives a history of the abbey. The pages turn with a heavy vellum rustle. I learn that the abbey was founded in 1881 (nearly 1,400 years after St Benedict's death) by the Empress Eugenie in exile as a place to bury Napoleon III. I take the Virtual Reality Tour and find that I can walk around the abbey, the nave and the crypt. I can crane my head backwards and gaze at the vaulted ceiling, or stare monk-like at the Italian marble floor, simply at the move of my mouse. It looks beautiful. I e-mail the abbot immediately to see if they offer sanctuary or retreats – as St Benedict instructed his order to do. He does not reply.

Next I visit a site called 'Catholic Saints Online' (saints.catholic.org). I am interested to see that there is a virtual Catholic saint for nearly every conceivable job, predicament or situation. Mary of Loreto is busy sending prayers up for air crews. Bernadine of Siena is lobbying the Almighty on behalf of advertisers, St Vitus is tickling the Old Man's funny bone for comedians, St Eloi is rattling his tin before the throne of God on behalf of coin collectors. Meanwhile, St Ubald is keeping his watchful eyes on dog bites and the lovely St Adrian of Nicomedia is making sure that arms dealers slip through the Pearly Gates without crossing any moral minefields.

St Joseph must be taking it easy these days: he is in charge of keeping the Almighty's wrath focused on opposition to communism. And Sts Venantius and Dymphna have it pretty easy too. Overseeing the world's 'jumping' and 'sleepwalking' – what sort of job is that? But St Dominic must have his hands full, petitioning on behalf of all those juvenile delinquents. St Martin de Porres (public education), St Vincent de

Paul (hospitals), St Xavier (tourism) and St Sebastian (neigh-bourhood watch schemes) have their work cut out too. What would we do without them? But as for John the Baptist, how does he hold down the planet's highways and motorways portfolio? Unless, of course, all roads lead to where he is. If I were St Fiacre, however, I would not have taken the job: patron saint of haemorrhoids! I would have been sorely tempted to tell the Almighty (or whoever nominated me) where to go.

Which is exactly where I go next (via a strangely satirical religious site called 'ship-of-fools.com', which points me in the direction of several religious 'fruitcakes'). 'Welcome to Virtual Hell' is written across the lurid red and black page (www.virtualhell.org) with some tastefully dancing flames top-and-tailing the screen. A cigarette-smoking skull beckons me in to the accompaniment of Mike Oldfield's *Tubular Bells* while warning me that there is no easy way out. This skeleton takes on a satirical, worldly-wise persona as he ushers me through eternal torment. Pretty soon, however, it becomes evi-dent that beneath the skull is a fundamentalist Christian. 'So … you think being in hell is a real fun party time, eh? Well, let me give it to you straight. You don't have to do anything to come here … the only requirement is to believe that Jesus didn't die for your sins, or was buried or rose again from the dead.' He adds, with a nod and a grin, 'Come in and prepare to die.'

I do, but all I see is a man wobbling around, a spinning coffin, some lightning bolts and a syringe that squirts. I meet a demon in the form of a cyberscorpion. Next I see the 'serpent' – red, bulging head, mouth full of rapacious, canine teeth. Then I get a second look and the serpent has transformed into the Virgin Mary, accompanied by mocking, sentimental organ music. Other demons are New Age angels, I am told (Christian ones, I assume, are kosher, so to speak). Next I hear hell's 'theme tune', 'Imagine' by John Lennon, and realize (again) that the devil really does have all the good tunes. As the tour goes on, the satirical mask is dropped in favour of the usual poisonous hellfire preaching: 'Some day everyone will know your most evil thoughts, your every hidden perversity, everything that only you and the Almighty know.' Then the skeleton *really* goes below the belt. He beckons me to heaven rather than hell with one final temptation: 'There is no breakfast in hell.' Alongside these inspirational words are photographs of pancakes, toast, cereal, bacon and eggs. I run out of hell, screaming. Anyone with this set of attitudes already lives in hell – perhaps anyone who *believes* in hell does.

Full of theological dilemmas, I find my way to the 'Bible Answer Machine' (http://Bibleanswermachine.ww7.com), a religious vending machine made by a company of specialists in 'web-based artificial intelligence'. It is a grey box with a question chute into which I put my typed questions, and another chute which leads into the answer bin. Simple questions using key words are needed for it to work. It cannot process my query, 'Why should I trust the Bible?' (or shorter variations) which I would have thought was rather a fundamental question for a Bible Answer Machine.

'God alive?' I type, and it offers me, 'And it came to pass, when men began to multiply on the face of the earth, and daughters were born unto them, that the sons of God saw the daughters of men that they were fair: and they took them wives of all they chose. And the Lord said *My spirit shall not strive with man, for that he also is flesh: yet his days shall be an hundred and twenty years.*' Which does not exactly answer my question. I reassure myself that, if this is state-of-the-art 'web-based artificial intelligence', then the Transhumanists have some way to go before the post-humans can take over the world. The question it recommends is, 'When will Christ return?' which might seem a bit trickier. It gives me a passage (Matthew 24:36) which is a roundabout way of saying, 'No idea'.

My next website is surely the one to answer this question. 'Rapture Ready' (www.novia.net/~todd/rap2.html) is an index which attempts to predict the 'rapture' (the alleged period before the alleged second coming of Christ, when born again Christians are instantaneously whisked into heaven for some top-up lessons in being judgemental, while the rest of the population endures plagues, wars, famines, etc.) using the techniques of investment and futures analysis. There are 45 indices based on the webmaster's interpretation of prophecies in the Bible, which he measures against world events in the news. Indices include fairly straightforward categories like famines, droughts and floods. They also include more contentious ones: Antichrist (the Pope, naturally), the mark of the beast (credit cards or computer implants), beast government (the European Union, which is, of course, a papal conspiracy), liberalism (if Republicans do well, rapture recedes; if Democrats do well, it becomes imminent) and ecumenism (another popish conspiracy).

The factors are added up and given an overall rating, ranging from 'Slow prophetic activity' to 'Fasten your seatbelts' (a rating of 145 or over). The webmaster writes 'Nearing Midnight', a prophet-cum-stock analyst's evaluation of the week's events. It reads:

The drive towards the reformation of the Roman Empire is just about unstoppable at this point. It seems like everyday there's some new step being put forth to integrate the Western European nations into a global-reaching superpower. In recent months there has been a flood of news stories that highlight efforts in the region to consolidate things like Europe's military forces, financial exchanges, and corporate structures. The integration of Europe has become so advanced, I think many of us that follow Bible prophecy have lost sight of the significance of ongoing events. Right now we're down to looking for 10 key leaders to come out of what is now a 15 nation confederation. Once we have them, Mr AC is the next act. Not everything is smooth sailing. There still remains a host of problems: The EU currency has been savaged by the US dollar, England had cold feet on several issues, and poorer eastern countries like Poland are trying to crash the party. Despite these difficulties, the trends seem to be set on fulfilling scripture.

The Rapture Index on my visit stands at 162, against an annual high of 169 and an all-time high of 176. I undo my seatbelt before making another Lemsip.

Then things get pretty unpleasant. A few clicks later, I find myself at the intriguingly named 'Christian Identity' site. Based in Arkansas, the site is virulently anti-Semitic, racist and, I later learn, reflects a growing Christian movement in the USA. They attack liberals as stupid, guilt-riddled pawns of a sinister Jewish elite. They sell car stickers which say, 'Only white women date outside their race. Be proud of your heritage, don't be a race-mixing Slut.' An apparently innocuous advertisement speaks volumes:

WE NEED A QUALITY DEDICATED CHRISTIAN WHITE LADY to be part of this Christian Identity ministry. Varied responsibilities, preferably including secretarial skills. Desire a believer who is intelligent, reliable, competent, pleasant, neat, and careful in details. An important, interesting, fulfilling life on rural acreage located in the beautiful Ozark Mountains. Must be racially pure, honest and of high moral character. A compatible personality with genuine sweet, gentle, feminine mannerisms (not a pretense) is required. Government, Jewish, or other agents DO NOT qualify! Position should be regarded as a calling in Christian service, not just another job. Room, board, and spending money will be provided.

If you think this opportunity may be right for you, send your address, phone number, a recent photograph, and a description of yourself to this ministry. Girls under 18 need to have their parents' permission. Ladies of our race from Europe and other countries abroad, who qualify, are welcome to apply.

The mixture of cutesy, patronizing details with the sort of attitudes that appeared in the Third Reich is chilling. Holocaust deniers, the Aryan Nation militias and the American Nazi League are just a few clicks away from here.

Then, on one of the Christian Identity sites, I notice a link to a site for the British Israel World Federation (www.britishis-rael.co.uk). *Surely we don't have these paranoid redneck racists in Britain?* I think. I double-click and arrive in Putney at a refreshingly naive and unsophisticated site without any apparent racist content. The BIWF is a registered charity with a Lord, a General and a Squadron Leader as patrons. The site is designed in restrained red, white and blue with heraldic symbols vaguely reminiscent of the Union Jack and several heavily bound Bibles as icons. The only hint of nationalism is in an article called 'Britain's Unique Legal Heritage Threatened by EU Police State'.

Another article explains who the British Israelites are. Founded in 1919 out of various like-minded groups prevalent during the Victorian era, the British Israelites are Bible-believing Christians (in a variety of denominations) who believe that white Britons are in fact God's chosen people, the Israelites. This is why groups with these beliefs refer to 'the Identity' or 'Christian Identity': they are Christians who think that white people are the real descendants of the lost tribes of Israel. They claim that 72 marks of Israel in the Bible and archaeological research make this irrefutable. Apart from lists of books, video tapes and sermons with a patriotic and anti-European bent, the website says nothing more. At the bottom is a phone number.

A few days later, feeling better, I make a couple of phone calls and set out for Birmingham to meet the British Israelites' regional secretary and hear the national president speak. I am not expecting to be impressed, but if I am to write a book on spirituality in the UK, a group which argues that Britain has a special role to play ought to be included. I am curious and apprehensive, not quite sure what I will be walking into. Will it be shaven-headed hooligans, the religious arm of the National Front? I am aware there are some far-right pagans who worship Thor, Woden and the Nordic gods, so I half expect some young Christian thugs, led by 'educated' bigots. Michael Clarke, the regional secretary, sounded eminently respectable on the phone, if a bit oily. My only real misgivings stem from his directions into Birmingham's Sparkhill area, where the meeting is to be held. 'You'll know you're there when you begin to see Asians,' he told me. It is probably significant that his house is in a suburb that was once well-to-do but, these days, looks down-at-heel. Perhaps Clarke sees the area's decline as the fault of the Asians.

I note a 'Keep the Pound' sticker on the window of Clarke's pristine semi as he comes out to meet me in pink shirt, brown tie, slacks and polished brown shoes. He certainly does not look like the archetypal racist thug: in his late forties, with white hair neatly combed across his head, his face is eager, florid and friendly. In Clarke's living room are under a dozen people with an average age of about 60. The room is spotless, with pastel pink carpets, magnolia walls, a gas fire and water-colour scenes of churches and flowery fields on the walls. It is a quintessentially suburban English lounge, ordered, under-stated, polite. Despite the fact that it is a Tuesday evening, the people are dressed in their Sunday best: women wear flowery dresses and cardigans, men jackets and ties. Most attend evangelical churches which do not hold with British Israelite beliefs. They look more like members of the Women's Institute than a neo-Nazi militia. Then I notice a table with a lectern on top of it. Beneath that is draped a large Union Jack. It has a strangely chilling effect on me; I am just not sure what it signifies.

After a short prayer, Matthew J. Browning, the septuage-narian President of the British Israelites, starts his talk. It is called 'The Prize'. He reads out various quotes from Stalin, Attlee, Arnold Toynbee and others which suggest that the for-mation of a federal Europe is a part of a global hidden agenda that will lead to world government. This, he tells us, is against God's will. His talk is obtuse, detailed and incredibly boring. He has a Scottish accent and tends to use unnecessarily convo-luted sentences and lots of Old Testament language. He tells us that God will never desert the British, his chosen people, even if they desert God. This prophecy applies to all nations descended from the British (Australians, Canadians, South African whites, American whites and those of northern Europe). I notice some Asian men walking by on the street outside, oblivious to the cluster of members of the chosen white race inside this house.

Browning tells us that we have to be battlers in this iniquitous world. 'We must be overcomers in the Christian Identity movement. The identity of our people can no longer be in serious question ... we will win through,' he says. 'Our astonishing position in the world today compared with what it was a generation ago, when we were still worshipping the God of Abraham, Isaac and Jacob, simply adds another dimension to the marks of identity which we possess as a nation,' he adds. He seems to mean that we have lost our blessings as the chosen people because we have stopped believing. An elderly lady shakes her head and sighs, 'What is the world coming to?' It is such a small meeting that people do occasionally chip in. One man despairs at our nation because it is legislating to encourage sodomizing 16-year-old boys (I suspect this is a reference to the government's removal of Clause 28, which stops schools from informing pupils about homosexuality). In this pristine, ordered living room, there is a sense of civilization falling around our ears.

With a dour grimace and his tie tucked into his trousers, Browning tells us that we should be joyful. He also talks about the significance of various obscure numbers. Three is the number of completeness, apparently – and is it not spooky that we only entered the Common Market with Europe after our *third* application? I assume one is supposed to extrapolate from this that our entry into Europe was a *complete* mistake. I am beginning to feel that my entry into this meeting was an equally complete mistake. The president drones on in pompous, mock-Authorized-Version English for a long, long time. He sounds fluent and mild mannered, but the speech is rambling and incoherent.

At the end Michael Clarke shows me various publications and clarifies certain beliefs. He points out that significant events tend to happen to God's chosen people in multiples of seven, and suggests that we might be taken over by Rome (a.k.a. the European Union) in 2004. It is *de rigueur* for a certain type of Protestant to believe that Rome is Babylon and the Pope is the Antichrist, and Clarke confirms this. If we sign up to the euro, God will punish us, he says. He goes on to explain the route that he believes the Israelites took before their arrival in Britain in 500 BC. They became druids, he tells me, but Jesus came to Glastonbury, along with Joseph of Arimathea. (*Here we go again*, I say to myself.) The last Israelites were Anglo-Saxons and came in 1066. So all white Britons are, one way or another, the chosen race. At one point Clarke reveals his strangely selective logic. 'It sounds so far fetched that it has to be true,' he laughs. I am tempted to tell him that Rastafarians have similar far-fetched beliefs about being the lost tribe of Israel – Haile Selassie was their monarch, descended from the throne of David – but decide to let him keep talking instead.

'We have been protected in wars because we're the chosen race,' Clarke adds, handing me a booklet called *We Have a Guardian*. It argues that we have been miraculously protected by God whenever we have been under threat. From freak winds which scuppered the Spanish Armada, to mythical white angels on horseback at Mons in World War I, to Dunkirk and the Battle of Britain, God's divine hand was busy thwarting or slaying the enemy to rescue his chosen people. There is no sense that this might be morally objectionable, just a pre-Enlightenment attitude: if God said it, it must be right.

Our legal system, our heraldry, our constitution and parliament are all based on ancient Israel. That is partly why sovereignty is important, but nation states are also God's way, he tells me. Then he tells me that our royal family are the direct descendants of the throne of King David. They are drawing up an archaeologically reliable family tree stretching from Adam to Queen Elizabeth II. The Scone stone on which monarchs are crowned is the same stone on which King David was crowned. Clarke clearly believes in the divine right of kings.

We should obey our monarchs – it is our Christian duty because they are God's anointed rulers. When Christ returns, he will sit on the British throne. I nod lamely, then pluck up some courage.

'What about violent racist groups with similar beliefs?' I ask.

'Blacks would be welcome to join,' he says, and goes on to explain that British Israelites are not racist and distance themselves from some of the American groups which are. There is no sense of them being white supremacists, he says, because the British people have to serve, not dominate. 'We are a servant people, a light to the Gentiles. That is what Christian Identity is about.' Perversely, by 'Gentiles' he means Jews … and black and Asian people. They are serving the advancement of civilization which is God's purpose for the white people, he explains. This sounds a little bit like sophistry to me. Serving is not actually that different from dominating, if your service is telling people what to do. Look at what has happened in South Africa now that the black people have taken over, he says. Black Africans send letters to them, he adds, begging them to come back and show them how to do things. Presumably Clarke does not think this is racist – after all, he is not beating black people to the ground with a bullwhip, is he?

Several weeks later, I join the British Israelites at their annual convention at a conference centre in Swanwick, Derbyshire. I arrive just before Ernest Gage, a lay-preacher, is to speak. A hundred demurely dressed worshippers recite the Lord's Prayer before singing a full-throated rendition of the national anthem. In front of them is a six-foot Union Jack, flanked by the flags of South Africa, Rhodesia, Canada, the United States and other outposts of white civilization. In their floral prints and blazers and ties, they pray for Queen, nation and Commonwealth before a woman pleads with her God, 'You defended us against intruders, now Europe is about to invade – help deliver us.'

'The Anglo-Irish Agreement is treason,' says bow-tied, mild-mannered Ernest Gage. 'The European Court of Human

Rights is a Babylonian justice system.' He bemoans the fate of the Anglo-Saxon tradition within Britain. 'We flood the country with immigrants and so-called asylum seekers, and we all have European passports. What is there left?' he asks. 'We will never be free from the heart of Babylon until its heart stops beating,' he says. The 'outer layers of Babylon' are the European Union and the Catholic Church, but he does not explain what or who the *heart* of Babylon is. I ask him later over tea and scones. 'Money is at the heart of Babylon, and we have to use the word "anti-Semitic",' he says, pleased with what he sees as his oblique answer.

The movement sees the adoption of the euro as a defining moment. 'It is a crunch time. We will no longer be a nation if that happens,' explains Janice Dowse, the BIWF's administrator. She believes that, if we are 'allowed' to join, it will be God's way of punishing us for the nation's disobedience. 'We're being dragged into Babylon; what Hitler couldn't do overtly is happening covertly. Rome is the Antichrist and we're being lured towards it,' she adds. Still, relief is at hand: 'It is one of the signs of the end of the world.'

I decide to take the opportunity to ask President Matthew Browning some of the difficult questions. 'We are often accused of racism, but we don't dislike blacks,' he says. 'We distance ourselves from some of the extreme American groups.' Could a black person join? 'Yes, but I don't see why one should want to,' he responds. He claims that British Israelism is not white supremacist, but says, 'Israel is called to be a servant people by directing and leading the other races.' BIWF are opposed to Catholics or immigrants having the same rights as British citizens, because they believe that the British constitution and judicial system is the one true way, based on Old Testament law, and must not be corrupted by outsiders' influence. 'Other religions and nations shouldn't have the ability to change us, or have a foreign influence in our nation,' he says.

British Israelites oppose mixed marriage for similar reasons. 'We don't believe in mixed marriage because God is a jealous God and doesn't want his people to lose their religion,' says Janice, as we look over the rose garden at lunchtime. God has a special dispensation for half-caste children, however. 'Half-caste children are catered for by keeping them in the kingdom so that, over a few generations, the race will be purified.'

The conference, which has attracted white delegates from Australia, Holland and the United States, also includes lectures offering 'proof' of the identity of the British people. They find evidence of the white Britons' heritage in the most unlikely places. Alan Gibb, a retired accountant, says, 'The names of Israel are everywhere. Why is our coronation service based on the Old Testament? Why do we have sheep named "Jacob's sheep"?'

Janice Dowse adds, 'Of course, Jesus was white – why do most paintings show him as a Caucasian?' Echoing Glastonbury's Orthodox priest, they tell me that Jesus visited Glastonbury as a child.

Before I leave, Janice gives me a handful of leaflets and booklets. I am not particularly interested in flights of fancy about how the Jews are not really a race, or about the migrations of the Israelites. I am more interested in when this group originated and whether they influenced the Ku Klux Klan and the Christian Identity groups with Nazi sympathies in the United States. In my first meeting with him, Michael Clarke told me that there are hundreds of British Israelites in the UK and Ulster, and thousands more worldwide. But could this prim and polite Christian group, this remnant of a movement, have spawned virulent worldwide racism?

Over the next few days, I scour their pamphlets and confirm several things. They appear to be obsessed with the European Union. Matthew J. Browning writes in *Wake Up!*, British Israelism's magazine, 'Thus are the forces of Antichrist encouraged to strut the corridors of power, demanding rights they have ever forfeited by their denunciation and usurpation of promises made to Israel.' Their great hatred is the European Union (known as Babylon and synonymous with Rome), which is referred to as a 'dictatorship' and one of 'popery's' schemes to work towards the Antichrist's world government. The European Union's sinister, steady encroachment is a recurring motif of *Wake Up!* Lurid headlines abound: 'Britons Will Be Slaves Unless Britannia Rules Again', and 'Britain's Unique Heritage Threatened by an EU Police State'. They make me proud to be British. This kind of rabble-rousing rhetoric could gain serious support in a less sceptical and less tolerant country! (I accept that this has more to do with our history and economic prosperity than any innate or genetic sense of Englishness.)

They also have to battle on other fronts, however. Clarke talked to me about how they struggled to distance themselves from the racist Christian Identity militias. I asked if there were groups like that in the UK, and he said there were Identity believers in Northern Ireland and suggested that they could be pretty extreme. Not surprisingly, British Israelites are sympathetic to those Unionists opposed to the peace process. Indeed, Dr Clifford Smyth, Secretary to the Northern Ireland Unionist Party, is Consultant Editor of *Wake Up!* magazine. It seems that British Israelite doctrines fuel the Unionist paranoia about reconciliation and integration with Catholics. Matthew Browning, writing in *Wake Up!* about the 'betrayal' of Ulster, opposes any reconciliation, saying, 'There is Jerusalem and Babylon, God and Mammon, Christ and Satan.' He writes of the possibility of a united Ireland, 'Were this to be achieved it would secure the bridgehead for the conquest of Great Britain and the subjugation of its people to the whim and imperial ambitions of Rome and her globalist lovers.' His final words would not be out of place in a survivalist militia in backwoods America: 'There cannot be peace where righteousness does not prevail!'

The concept of 'chosen people' shows little sign of inspiring servanthood within the movement. Rather, they see themselves as under siege in an evil world under the sway of Babylon, Satan, Mammon – anything, in fact, that is not within the evangelical Protestant reformers' tradition. This causes a kind of religious racism in which they always side with the Christians. In Kosovo, they supported the Serbs. Another *Wake Up!* writer laments, 'Do you know that ordinary Russians and Ukrainians are asking why Western Christendom is helping Muslim terrorists (KLA) and fighting Orthodox Christian Serbs?' There is more anti-Semitism too. Clarke told me that Jews are not really a race, but a mixture of races. One article refers to 'the overlordship of a mercantile confederacy' and suggests that the Rothschilds and other 'super-rich families in Europe' want a world government. They will fall with Babylon.

The Jews are seen as a mixed race, and it is clear that British Israelites do not approve of any mixed-race marriages. I read in *Wake Up!* that

> discrimination is very proper when the reasons for it justly benefit all the subjects concerned ... we cannot forget that God created the nations, and the Most High set the bounds of the people according to the number of children of Israel (Deuteronomy 32:8). We ... are certain that the vast majority of people in all races have no desire to mix their seed with others. Only the reprobates among them seek to encourage confusion ... People are entitled to know who they are; to discover their roots. Indeed all are quite anxious in themselves to satisfy that deep sense of 'belonging' which is experienced most often and at best usually when we are with our own.

By now I am sure that this group do have the racist credentials to have inspired the US racist militias. Does history bear this out, however, or did the British Israelites import the racism from groups like the Ku Klux Klan? Their keenness to distance themselves from such groups suggests that perhaps they were the originators of these beliefs. I return to the internet, this time in search of empirical research rather than divine 'truth' or revelation. I find some excellent sites, including http://cti.itc.virginia.edu/~jkh8x/soc257/home.htm and http://wwwcesnur.org, both of which are academic centres. Some cult-watch groups have very informative websites too, although sometimes it is difficult to separate the cult-watchers' agenda from the raw information: http://www.trancenet.org, http://mindit.netmind.com and www.religioustolerance.org.

I discover that the concept of the British being the Israelites goes back to a mentally unstable sailor called Richard Brothers, who in 1794 declared himself 'Prince of the Hebrews' and said that he would lead the 10 tribes back to Jerusalem. He was committed to an asylum and, as often happens with founders of new religious movements, he died a pauper. It was 46 years later, however, that a scholar called John Wilson published *Our Israelitish Origin*, which explained the alleged route of the Israelites to Britain, as well as drawing parallels between ancient Hebrew institutions and language and English institutions and language. Wilson's views attracted support, perhaps because of a British sense of superiority as Britain 'improved' and colonized 'savages' far and wide in God's name.

By 1884, Edward Hine had exported these beliefs to the United States (after the formation of the Ku Klux Klan in 1869 by racist Confederate officers who could not accept the equality of blacks and whites after the Civil War). He had also become interested in pyramids, and it was at this stage that the British Israelite fascination for numerical significance started. The movement grew and, in the 1920s, a lawyer called Howard Rand joined. He added overtly anti-Semitic beliefs to the teachings and attracted racist members when he became National Commissioner of the Anglo-Saxon Federation of America. At this stage the movement had up to 100,000 followers in the USA alone.

In the 1940s Wesley Swift started a British Israelite church in Los Angeles while trying to revive the Ku Klux Klan. He went on to develop more extreme Christian Identity teachings, including the genocide of all Jews. According to the FBI's Megiddo Report on domestic terrorism in the USA, 'Wesley Swift was the single most significant figure in the early years of the Christian Identity movement in the United States. He popularized it by combining British Israelism, a demonic anti-Semitism and political extremism.' During this period, British Israelite beliefs also surfaced in Herbert Armstrong's Worldwide Church of God, which insisted on racial segregation in churches but was far less politically active.

Both groups spread throughout the English-speaking world, gaining hundreds of thousands of followers. The Christian Identity theology (in essence British Israelism) was a unifying factor within groups such as the Ku Klux Klan, Aryan Nation, the American Nazi League and other identity-based churches and organizations. These groups have developed race hatred beyond the tenets of British Israelism. Some refer to all non-whites as 'mud people' who have no souls or value to God; the Jews, however, were created by Satan to take over the world. All the American Identity Christians see Jews as the enemy and black people as inferior, created to be slaves for the chosen people. Mixed marriages create offspring who are mentally, morally, biologically and spiritually degenerate. Just as the British Israelites based in Britain see Rome and Europe as conspiring against all that is good and wholesome, so their American counterparts see the US government and a Jewish elite in the media as attacking all that is good there. The more extreme groups are survivalist bands who train for an all-out war with the government to create a breakaway nation of whites in Canada and the northern part of the USA. Timothy McVeigh, the Oklahoma bomber, was a member of a Christian Identity group.

British Israelism has therefore supplied white supremacists with the theology they needed to develop their hatred. Their silly, almost wilfully ignorant, lineage tracing the links between Adam and Queen Elizabeth II is a lot less convincing and sinister than the lineage that comes from their movement. This is a lineage that has fuelled bigotry and suffering. It is the source of a poisonous stream which started among some Victorians with a 'polite', stifling sense of Britain's superiority. On a deeper level, perhaps the source of the stream goes back further still. In my view, any God who endorses the notion of a 'chosen people' or even tribalism is a racist. But then again, perhaps each generation's priests and shamans simply project their own prejudices onto their god or gods. That is why, for me, God is going to have to be an internationalist who likes all people equally. If the internet is really to be global (rather than Western), then as a medium it might lead to such a god or virtual-god. Right now, I think I would prefer the cyberspirit to the real thing.

16

Chaotic Bytes and the Virtual Vortex

Later in the same week, anxious to leave the murky world of the British Israelites behind, I take the virtual pathway away from Christendom. My immediate problem is that there are so many pathways, so many 'key words' to power my search engine. In a sense, a good search engine can act as an extremely unscientific gauge of what or who our gods are. An initial search on an obscure group like the Aetherius Society or the British Israelites will probably only call up five or six site matches. Try typing in 'scientology', and you get scores of matches. 'God' will net you tens of thousands. Try 'shopping', and you will find hundreds of thousands. 'Sex' gives you enough site matches to glue up your computer for a fortnight. So, we worship sex and shopping. Who needs market research and focus groups? My search engine is not omniscient, but it really is the next best thing: it is good at reflecting market forces. God comes way down the pecking order, but perhaps we underestimate him/her, because he/she comes in all shapes and sizes.

I start off with 'goddess' and find wiccans, pagans, non-pagan goddess worshippers (whatever they may be) and lots of film stars. I also find a 'Goddess of the Internet' who is hard to fathom. Perhaps 'inscrutable' is a more accurate description. The site invites me to 'come and worship at the Net Goddess'. I arrive and there are a few mediocre stunts (lightning, a shooting star, music, a fireball) and an invitation to make a donation (credit cards accepted) to the goddess. There is a prayer written by Appalachian Man, 'Servant of the Net Goddess':

> Oh most wonderful, splendid, all powerful Net Goddess, please give us thy favor. May you grant us good connections, continuous connections, fast loading pages, fast loading pictures and graphics.

Does *she* do this? No. What else does she do? Well, she … er … takes your money. What for? For being the Net Goddess. I kind of like her. That kind of brazenness makes me feel good about being alive. I find it refreshing that humans can act with such guileless avarice. That sort of innocence belongs in Eden.

After having my stars read in a rather predictable way, the word 'magic' leads me into a dangerous, edgy nether region – 'chaos magick'. According to web chaos magician Mark Chao,

> Chaos is not in itself a system or philosophy. It is rather an attitude that one applies to one's magick and philosophy. It is the basis for all magick, as it is the primal creative force … There is no set of specific spells that are considered to be 'Chaos Magick spells'. A Chaos Magician will use the same spells as those of other paths, or those of his/her own making. Any and all methods and information are valid, the only requirement is that it works. Mastering the role of the subconscious mind in magical operations is the crux of it, and the state called 'vacuity' … is the road to that end.

He continues his web essay by explaining that 'chaos' is the creative principle behind all 'magick'. He describes aspects of new science in which randomness and the absence of causality seem to be central as showing 'science mimicking magick'. By working with the 'subconscious', things can be brought into being and this is chaotic, dangerous, 'the essence of magick'.

Other online chaos magicians emphasize that chaos magick is not suitable for those with an 'internalized' moral code: many consider it black magic because it is beyond good and evil. It is all about achieving the state of mind (somewhat vaguely described, but called 'gnosis' or 'vacuity') in which magical power is generated. Gnosis is achieved through pain, sex, confusion, or any other method that works. It aims to be destabilizing, to push boundaries, to unsettle. As online chaos magician Mark Defrates says, 'Since it is designed to deconstruct belief, dearly held opinions, the stories we tell ourselves to lull ourselves into a sense of security will tend to fray and unravel. Unless the magician is willing to forsake these old ideas, to allow the boundaries of personal identity to be disrupted the result of magickal action may be chaotic indeed.'

The first order was started in 1976 by a German and an English magician in a disused ammunition dump deep in a Rhineland mountain. According to chaos magician Phil Hine (http://www.phhine.ndirect.co.uk), it grew massively in the following decades because of the internet. They now have hundreds of orders around the world. 'Many early chaotes [chaos magicians] were computer programmers, gamesters and essentially they decided to make up a religion and putting it in virtual reality made perfect sense,' he says. Fantasy literature has been an inspiration for some chaotes and is as relevant as anything else in a world where the central principle is that nothing is true. Spells and initiations are unapologetically drawn from fiction or anywhere else. The groups have wonderfully camp names like 'the Illuminatos of Thanateros' and 'Esoteric Order of Dagon'. 'As an occult strand, we have no interest in trying to prove our ancient heritage; we make it up as we go along and if spells work, we use them,' says Hine. 'Nothing is true, everything is permitted' is a key phrase.

Some see the internet as a magical force in itself, but Hine does not approve of this (still, as they say, 'nothing is true, everything is permitted') because it leads to power trips and individuals trying to control groups. Hine sees the internet as a tool to keep in touch with other magicians. Many do online rituals, but he prefers to work offline. There are scores of spells on the internet and several obscure chat rooms devoted to online rituals. I find a sado-masochistic online ritual which seems both strange and pathetic. It reminds me of children playing with spells and candles, but I am struck by how desta-bilizing it could be for some:

Pain Capacitance/Discharge Working
Purpose:
The purpose of this working is an attempt to transmit a physical/tactile sensation over the Internet. One individual will serve as a focal point for a group of participants, acting as a capacitator to store and then discharge a surplus of en-ergy. A give-and-take is, of course, quite implicitly implied here, and for this reason it is of some importance that par-ticipants to do not 'hold back' out of fear. The pain-causing actions chosen herein are meant to cause intense sensation without permanent disfigurement. The more smoothly the transaction of energy can be allowed to occur, the more likely that any results may be gauged by the participants.

Participants should also have in their possession a com-mon linking object, which is the same as the tool used by the 'capacitator' to perform the body modification on hirself. In this particular instance of this working, the 'capacitator' will be using a knife to make a 1/8" deep cut into hir arm as the initial stage of scarification. The cut will be colored with ashes, and participants should also have some of these.

Materials:
Toothbrush, Baking Soda, Dental Floss
Salt & Water
Rubber Bands
Knife
Atomic Warheads
Computer access

The rubber bands mentioned above should be of the wider type, and about the participants' wrists before the working proper begins.

The Working:

-1. An opening/banishing is performed. In this instance, the opening will consist of a ritual purification of the working area by the 'capacitator', via the sprinkling of salt water prepared using the knife as a stirrer.

0. Participants abandon their keyboards for a few minutes to very harshly brush their teeth, in such a manner that the gums bleed a little. Each should take no more than 5 minutes to do this, and acknowledge their return to their terminal. In our working, the 'capacitator' will undertake the role of shepherd; as he is the only one not leaving his terminal to achieve 'hygienosis', it's fitting that he keep track of when everyone has come back.

1. The 'capacitator' mentioned above cries out 'HUT!' (start). Participants put the salt in their mouths and hold it there for as long as they can bear it (i.e., until the sensation reaches a plateau and no longer becomes more intense).

2. During this time, the 'capacitator' is chanting (as one would a mantra) or screaming: FACH LOHIXOZ JAFRIX JAWENGOJ (I invoke pain into myself).

3. When the pain has become overwhelming (i.e., gnosis is achieved), participants will shout out: FETH HAVAWANG OXO JAWENGOJ (We evoke our pain).

Note that because individual pain threshholds vary greatly, it would be very difficult for a group of people who can't actually see one another to synchronize their arrivals at gnosis via this method.

4. Without pause, hair should now be forcefully removed from some sensitive part of the body. Suggested means include the use of an Epilady-type device, wax, or simply pulling a few hairs out.

5. Repeat 2 & 3.

6. A small amount of a very powerful pepper or hot sauce should now be ingested. If desired, the participants can do this repeatedly, as this can heighten the effect of the pepper into successive increases in sensation. Certain very hot chili peppers will do.

7. Repeat 2 & 3.

8. A sharp object (a knife, pin, syringe, etc.) should now be used to break the skin in some sensitive place (NOTE: please strive for maximum sterility in doing this).

9. Repeat 2 & 3.

10. Participants regroup, and those who feel that they have achieved as much pain as they can tolerate should bail out now. The remaining participants begin snapping their rubber bands and chanting 'OHM'.

11. The 'capacitator' now performs the body modification on hirself. Participants are intentionally sending the effects of their gnosis to the 'capacitator', who discharges the energy back to the participants with this action.

Capacitator (at the moment of making the cut): FACH HAVAWANG JAWENGOJ (I evoke pain). All: BICOW JAWENGOJ! (In pain).

NOTE: Participants should be aware of any increase in painful sensation when the body modification is performed by the 'capacitator'.

12. Participants fully experience the pain. Move into next room (assuming MUD). Banish physical space as desired. Discuss, banter, explain, etc.

Next to this spell is a document which logs what actually happened when the ritual was conducted online. Because the ritual took place in a closed 'newsgroup', it is recorded from beginning to end. One magician designed a series of rooms for the participants to go through once the stages of the ritual had been completed and the 'capacitator' told them to. There were also virtual magicians or creatures who would add special effects to the room or the dialogue at different points. (These are computer programmes which chip in at apposite moments.) One called Cynobyte would stagger into the room and scream, 'PAIN!' at various points. One called Abyss simply howled through walls.

About six people from Britain and the United States took part. It is a little different from the written rite, because the 'capacitator' needs reminding of some bits and the pain gets too much for some people. The capacitator forgets to 'open' the ritual and, in true chaos-magician form, instead of invoking the four elements he invokes Marvel comics, Spam, Fruitopia and Barney. Some bits are improvised for maximum pain:

> Marik says, 'Don rubs hot sauce and salt in the cut'
> Marik says, 'Marik wusses out'
> Avacado exclaims, 'FETH HAVAWANG OXO JAWENGOJ!'
> KiloKhan yells, 'FETH HAVAWANG OXO JAWENGOJ'
> Ain says, 'feth HAWAWANG OXO JAWENGOJ'
> Marik says, 'FETH HAVAWANG OXO JWENGOJ"

At one point they opt for drinking chilli:

> Avacado exclaims, 'F***ING FETH HAVAWANG OXO JAWENGOJ!!!!'

By the end, one person has vomited, one is bleeding onto his keyboard, they have all wounded themselves with a knife, and one has pierced his nipple. The next day, they add an evaluation to the log. One girl reflects,

> I brushed my teeth (nice bleeding) I held the salt, OUCHIE I pulled hair (no pain, even tho the hairs were from my 'area') I did the sauce, that got me flying, 3 swigs
>   Cutting was interesting, rubbing in salt and hotsauce heightened the sensation
>   When the capacitator capacitated and threw energy back at us I didn't get it instantly. My calf started to dully stab about 5 minutes afterwards and continued off and on for a while, then my left elbow (all this was on my left side, did s/he pierce their left nipple?) really hurt for a while. The multiple slashes on my hand stung like crazy giving me extra pain for an hour or 2.

An equally revealing contribution comes from a man making his excuses for leaving the ritual early.

> Sorry, I had to drop out ... but just as I grabbed the sauce a car sped by our house and hit and killed our Golden Retriever. I was up all weekend doing grief-work and heal-ings on the wife and kids. I am exhausted! This is the last time I ask for pain and don't get specific about it – physical PLEASE! Anguish and suffering I've seen too much of – explored them plenty – mine and others.

Not only do I find it odd that a man with a wife and kids (rather than a lonely cybernerd) should be doing this ritual, but the fact that he sees no irony or self-indulgence in going out of his way to seek pain and then doing 'grief-work and healings on the wife and kids' is bizarre.

It seems as if these chaotes have been sucked into a magical virtual vortex that has dislodged their sense of reality. Of course, in some senses, chaos magick is a game. And just as nothing is true, so the identities of the magicians could be 'vir-tual'. The powerful magicians could be teenagers or aspects of people's personalities. The rituals are sometimes light-hearted or ironic, while at the same time being a genuine attempt to touch the supernatural. It seems a playful, if sinister, form of spirituality. These games, however, could take on a worrying significance. They could send someone over the edge.

In a silly, self-indulgent world where right and wrong does not matter, this may be irrelevant, but it is not a world in which I am interested. Like ceremonial magicians throughout history, these chaotes are fundamentally interested in power. The spirituality that I am seeking will be more interested in giving power away. Another, less important criticism is that there is no evidence that chaos magick works, or that there is anything more substantial to their beliefs than the vistas painted by crude, gothic imaginations. These are people who are, for whatever reason, in search of grandeur, telling them-selves that they are embracing the void.

After browsing through a couple of New Age sites, I come across David Icke, the former Coventry City goalkeeper, *Grandstand* presenter and spokesman for the Green Party who metamorphosed into the Son of God during an interview with Terry Wogan. That is, after many messianic mumblings, he said that he was the Son of God when asked by Wogan, playing the part of Pilate. Not surprisingly, the media crucified him. Ten years later, his website addresses this ridicule. Beneath his smiling face is the phrase, 'Mad, bad or just prepared to go where others fear to tread?' Underneath this it says, 'Today's mighty oak is just yesterday's nut that held its ground.'

The website is layered and complex. It is a treasure-trove of exotic conspiracy theories and opportunities to buy Icke's self-published books. According to a letter from his website host server, the site (www.davidicke.com/icke/index.html) attracts so many visitors that they cannot keep counting them. On average it attracts 3,000 per hour or 500,000 per week. Is this the New Messiah's way of unmasking a global Satanic plot, or is he 'yesterday's nut'? I am fascinated by how a rational and articulate man can go so spectacularly off the rails. What is it about his beliefs that is so compelling? I e-mail him, and a couple of days later he invites me to visit him on the Isle of Wight.

It is a bright July day as I climb aboard the hovercraft which takes me from Portsmouth to Ryde. The Solent is buzzing with dinghies, speedboats, cruise liners, pilot boats and old sailing ships. The seafront at Ryde is crowded with visitors wandering in and out of amusement arcades, fish-and-chip shops and cafés. As I wait for David to pick me up, I imagine that he will take me to a spacious bungalow with a pool on an isolated stretch of coastline. I cannot imagine him living in such a crowded resort. I envisage him in a turquoise shellsuit, glistening in the colour that he told us attracted positive cosmic vibrations. He is to pick me up in a blue Volvo, and I imagine an advertising campaign for a gleaming estate with the catchline, 'Driven by the Son of God'.

When he arrives, however, it is in the normal, dirty, litter-strewn car of mere mortals. He is wearing unpolished black shoes and a slightly tired, black Calvin Klein T-shirt supporting a paunch. His trademark grey messiah-with-a-mullet hairstyle is intact, but it looks a little yellowy at the edges. We drive to some Victorian flats. As we climb the dingy stairs, I am reminded of a rented student bedsit. Inside, the flat is spacious but sparsely furnished. There are piles of books and magazines along one wall and someone else's mail is beside the door. He introduces me to Pammy, his blonde, 40-going-on-20 American partner, who tells me that they have only recently moved in. Pammy apart, it is not what I expected. We sit down for the interview and David asks if I mind if he keeps the golf on while we talk.

We start by discussing the sorry state of English football. 'We won't develop good players until we stop putting foreigners in all the key positions: strikers, sweepers, midfield creators and keepers,' he says. He is friendly and articulate, but there are no earth-shattering revelations – although he says that he has just resigned from writing an online column for a football website because they refused to print his allegations about a high-level conspiracy behind England's failure to get the 2002 World Cup. Pammy brings in some tea.

Conspiracy theories can be incredibly complicated, so I ask him if he can explain what the big picture is before moving in on particular confederations, countries or institutions. 'You need an open mind and not to give a sh*t what others think to accept this. People aren't willing to break out of their eggshells; they are afraid of ridicule or condemnation,' he says. I nod. 'There is a massive web of corruption and control made up of pyramids within pyramids, headed by about 13 families who are reptiles from another planet and who practise child sacrifice, drink their blood and rape them, probably to keep their mammalian skin.' I sip my tea. 'They are called the Illuminati and want to create a globally central society, world government, a world army to suppress opposition, and a microchip people,' he continues. 'They have control of the media, military, transnational corporations, key educational establishments, banks, the government and Church.'

How? 'The Illuminati have created the institutions, like Hollywood and media corporations, that make meaning. After the blunt approaches of fascism and communism, they have created the illusion of choice and freedom by creating our desires and society's norms so that people do what they are told is acceptable without needing to be coerced,' he says. They are not by any chance Jewish, are they? 'No, whites are the predominant race of the Illuminati,' he says. He is unstoppable. 'All religion is about mind control; rigid dogmas were created to stop people asking questions and different religions were created to encourage arguments between them, to stop people seeing the real deception.' All religions, he says, including New Age beliefs, are 'prison religions'.

David explains that the Anunnaki (from whom the Illuminati are descended) are a reptile race from another planet. Hundreds of thousands of years ago, they brought their advanced technologies here and created the pyramids, Stonehenge, the Aztec and Mayan temples of central and South America and others. There was a global culture which he calls the 'Golden Age'. This hi-tech culture explains how Stonehenge was built with rocks which had been transported hundreds of miles. Then, between 11000 and 5000 BC, there was a great cataclysm, probably a massive tidal wave caused when Venus hit Mars, which destroyed civilization. Some people escaped by climbing mountains, others by burying themselves underground, but the Anunnaki simply took off in their flying saucers.

They returned to Sumeria in the Middle East in about 4000 BC and started to re-establish civilization. From this point on, they started to breed with humans. Archaeologists accept that this area was the cradle of civilization. What they do not know (or pretend not to know) is that the Anunnaki spread into the key positions in all civilizations via their offspring, the Illuminati. The Knights Templar, the Freemasons, the Church hierarchy, the royal families, aristocracy and political elites were generally (give or take the odd good egg) Illuminati. It is no coincidence that reptiles feature in religious symbols around the world. The Illuminati worship them. That is what gargoyles are there for. 'They also mock us with their symbols: torches signifying illuminated ones are in statues around the world as a way of mocking people's ignorance of the truth,' David says. When I ask *why* the Anunnaki would engage in this elaborate subterfuge, he falters. 'I suspect that the Anunnaki are involved in a struggle for supremacy with other aliens for this part of the galaxy,' he says.

He has encyclopaedic knowledge of his alternative universe. 'George Bush, Al Gore, the House of Windsor – they're all reptiles. They sacrifice children and drink their blood in secret rituals,' he says without blinking. I am quite sympathetic to the idea that the royals might be reptiles, but what evidence does he have? 'Princess Diana's friend claims that Diana called the royals "lizards" and "reptiles" and said that they were inhuman,' he explains. David does not appear to have considered the possibility that 'reptile' could be a derogatory term rather than a literal one. Several people have seen George Bush shapeshift from a human to a reptile, he tells me. 'And if it isn't true, why don't they sue?' he asks. 'I called Edward Heath a Satanist, torturer and murderer of children. When journalists asked him, the only reaction he gave was to say, "I think David Icke must be ill." Why is that?' I decide not to answer.

What *real* evidence does he have, though? 'I only assume that something is true after it comes independently from different sources. I am very careful. The last thing I want to do is to accuse people without hard evidence. You also feel it intuitively, and this confirms the evidence,' David explains. 'Why else would all the royal families and aristocracy be interbred? It's not just snobbery, it couldn't be,' he adds. Did I know, he asks, that all 42 presidents of the United States are related in the same bloodline? When I ask about archaeological evidence, he says, 'Academics dare not go public if they want preferment. So they engage in cover-ups.' The top academics at Oxford University, he says, are blood-sucking reptiles and they control the naive and ignorant academics beneath them.

He looks up to see Tiger Woods extending his lead at the St Andrews Open and calls Pammy in to see. I ask him about his beliefs. 'We are all tiny droplets swimming around in an ocean of consciousness. Once we start to open ourselves to the ocean, we start to see with different eyes, to access our intuition,' he says. He is not the Son of God, then? 'That was a mistake. I thought Wogan asked me if I was *a* Son of God,' he says. 'But that mistake set me free. The ridicule I received was good for me, it stopped me from caring what people think of me and set me on my path of uncovering the story and revealing it to people.' David reminds me of an Old Testament prophet in the wilderness, shouting into the wind.

David's key belief, however, reminds me of The Forum. 'We create our own reality, we are the imagination of ourselves,' he says. Most people quivering within their eggshells might agree that David creates his own reality, but I see a problem with this line of thought. 'So, did the Jews in the Holocaust create their own reality? Did they want to be destroyed?' I ask. It is not that simple, he says. Some managed to avoid it by their positivity, and maybe others needed it because they had lessons to learn in this life so that they could progress in the next one. Being positive, he explains, stops anything negative happening. Is he not borrowing some pretty unacceptable bits from Hinduism? 'There is *some* truth hidden away in the major religions, despite how they're used as prisons,' he answers.

Before I leave, David warns me that minute mind-controlling microchips are being put into people via hypodermic needles. Cars also have chips that can stop them at a signal from a satellite. *Surely this can only happen,* I think, *if I'm open to the possibility of my mind being controlled or my car stopping at the dictates of Illuminated chips?*

As David drives me down to the seafront, I ask if he ever has doubts. 'I have no doubts about the theme, but I do about the detail,' he says. Did he not predict that the Isle of Wight would sink into the sea before too long? 'When people say that I've changed my mind, I say that they used to put their dinner on top of their heads, but now they use a knife and fork,' he replies. Does he miss the life of a sports presenter? 'I saw Des Lynam and others doing the same thing year in, year out, and thought, no, I don't want to be doing this when I'm 50.'

It strikes me that his idea about viewing everything positively means that he can never be wrong and, therefore, he is, as he says, creating his own reality. If anyone's beliefs are a prison, then David's are. Although he appears completely rational, I cannot see a key to unlock the door of that prison. Perhaps, when he went through the ridicule threshold on *Wogan*, there was no way back. It is not for me to say whether he suffers from pride or madness or neither, but there is something of King Lear about him. After such humiliation, perhaps facing the unreality of his position became more difficult than ploughing the same paranoid furrow into obscurity.

As I leave the island, I realize that obscurity is exactly where he is headed. He may or may not get millions visiting his website, but that is virtual reality. In the real world he is literally and metaphorically on an island. He does not attend conferences of conspiracists because they become slanging matches. He self-publishes his books with the help of two other people, and he does virtually all his research on the internet. The media are no longer interested in him. What can you do to attract attention when your last media splash was the news that the House of Windsor were a bunch of child-killing, blood-drinking reptiles? It is sad when you are considered so unhinged that no one can be bothered to sue you. David, of course, sees this as proof of the allegations rather than the ultimate humiliation. Sadly, I think he believes it. He does not, in my view, speak with a forked tongue. It would be better for him if he did.

Driving home, I realize that the internet has probably not helped David, his fellow conspiracists, chaos magicians, British Israelites, Identity Christians or the myriad others who, to greater or lesser degrees, have slipped off the real world and into virtual reality. The internet is like some vast, primordial soup, pregnant with uncensored, limitless potentiality, waiting for the Big Bang. Drawing like-minded streams and extremes of belief together, whole universes of belief are created. However extreme or silly these beliefs are, searching the internet will allow people to find others with similarly extreme or silly beliefs. Microcultures will develop and grow, attracting self-selecting people who confirm and contribute to these virtual universes. These converts, conspiracists and devotees use web pages, chat rooms and e-mail to nurture their deeply held spiritual needs and ideas.

The problem is that, by 'connecting' to these communities of belief or suspicion, people will be disconnecting from any real interface – the sort that challenges their beliefs and keeps them in *real* reality. The possibility of connecting with people holding unreal extremes on the internet may well lead to a sort of rarefied hyper-reality as people find the meanings they seek being confirmed and amplified. This technology is not neutral. It takes us away from each other and from diversity and takes us towards the possibility of an alienated paranoia. Of course, the internet does not *have* to do this, but it allows the possibility. David, the chaotes and others seem to me to be cloistered, imprisoned even, by the internet. David sees all religion as control without seeing the controlling effect of being surrounded by a community of flatterers. It allows him to escape his critics and to confirm his conspiracies. If anything is conspiring against him and his kind, it is probably the internet itself.

This is no place for me. The internet is not going to bring spirituality into my life. There is no sense of belonging, no real meaning, and a diminishing sense of reality. I prefer the way the druids and witches are rooted in something you can hold onto: the landscape. With this in mind, I head back up to my favourite landscape in search of a radically different form of Christianity.

17

🛒

Soulfood and a Place to Eat

It seems ironic that I have to cross the Isle of Mull *en route* to
Iona. The contrast between the two islands is greater than the
contrast of both with the mainland. Travelling around Mull on
single-track roads, I see huge moors sweeping up to sheer volcanic plugs, and cliffs falling away to thick pine forest. It is
refreshing after a week in cyberspace. The open countryside
testifies to more than dramatic and uncompromising geology.
It is also due to the existence of huge country estates owned
by aristocratic families and clan chiefs who were responsible
for depopulating Mull during the Highland Clearances.
Because of this there is little arable land. Highland cattle graze
the sparse heather, gorse and bracken moorland. Deer roam
wild across the mountains in the evening, hiding in thick
forests and desolate valleys during the day. Dotted amid the
wide, deserted vistas are game lodges, castles and stately
homes.

Strangely, the sombre and striking Mull landscape only
begins to make sense on visiting such homes. On entering
Torosay Castle, I am met by dozens of stag's heads and
antlers. Inside the manicured Victorian rooms are other
stuffed 'trophies', oil paintings of sportsmen and hounds and
an estate book with details of each day's stalking. I note a picture of a fleet of warships moored in the Sound of Mull (just
outside the window). A caption explains that the admiral
popped up for a bit of shooting with his friends at Torosay.
The ambience of genteel, privileged decadence is pervasive,

indoors and out. Mull is a land of men who were officers, sportsmen (i.e. hunting and fishing) and MPs, in that order. It is a bit like visiting a set in a period drama or a Walter Scott novel. Of course, the majority of the population are ordinary hard-working people, but for a visitor, at least, travelling across Mull is like glimpsing an imperious, elegant, yet stifling past.

Iona, a tiny island at the tip of Mull, is completely different. The landscape is less bleak: lush grasslands stretch up to craggy, contorted, grey and rose-pink outcrops, reminiscent of the Outer Hebrides. Large parts of the island are fringed by white sandy beaches. It is also dotted with small crofts, gardens, vegetable plots and a couple of shops – cars are not allowed. The most imposing building is the restored Benedictine abbey which was founded by St Columba, the sixth-century Irish monk reputed to have brought Christianity to Scotland. The squat, grey abbey sits above the shore, with side chapels, living quarters and a cloistered garden. Its muted grandeur testifies to a great deal of hard work in inhospitable conditions. To have created such an ordered environment in this wilderness seems awesome. It is a peaceful, wild place, but, unlike on Mull, there are people wandering between the abbey, the ruins and the beach.

Many of these people are a consequence of a more recent piece of history. In 1938 a Church of Scotland minister, Reverend George Macleod, founded the Iona Community, an ecumenical community committed to seeking new ways of living as Christians. In the middle of the Depression, Macleod started bringing unemployed workers from his Glasgow parish out to the island, to reconstruct the ruined buildings. Tradesmen did the skilled work, while theology graduates, ministers and curates did the donkey-work. Macleod believed that ministers should stay close to ordinary people and was convinced that worship and work were part of the same thing. By 1967 the abbey was restored and had become a place of pilgrimage and an ecumenical centre.

The abbey is not a watering hole for the aristocracy: it is a retreat for ordinary people. In contrast to the genteel decadence of Mull's country houses, the abbey reflects an earthy open-ness and creativity. In the north transept is a big 'peace and justice' display, with Debt Relief posters, children's artwork and red Aids Awareness ribbons. The community now has 240 full members (along with thousands of associate members and friends), mostly based around Britain, who agree to pray, read the Bible and account to one another for how they use their time and money while working for peace and justice. That may sound twee, but they also have a reputation for strapping themselves to the rails of Ministry of Defence prop-erties, canoeing into the path of nuclear submarines and going to jail.

Walking across sandy grassland to the beach at the northern tip of Iona, Kathy Galloway, a casually-dressed, 40-something community theologian and writer with nose stud and brown hair, explains how their faith has led to law-breaking. 'Outside Faslane, where submarines with Trident missiles dock, we formed a barrier to block the workers from entering. We took Communion and sang "We Shall Overcome", the anthem of the Civil Rights Movement. We can't separate worship from action for justice, they're symbiotic. We believe those weapons are illegal and evil and it is an act of worship to oppose them,' she says. Ninety people were arrested. She shows me some of the liturgy used on the day. It is a psalm, and part of their daily office:

The World belongs to God
The earth and all its people
How good and how lovely it is
To live together in unity
Love and truth come together
Justice and peace join hands.

It reminds me of the pagans' use of Chief Seattle's speech as a rallying cry for people to protect the planet.

Kathy, who is normally based in Glasgow, says that the Iona Community identify with the justice-orientated liberation theology of Latin America. 'Liberation theology is based on practical involvement in which Christians see from the position of the powerless or those fighting injustice and pray and think about what they should do in the situation,' she explains. Then they do it. 'We have campaigned to change British immigration laws in which black Britons are treated unfairly. This is an issue of justice and we also see this concern in the Bible,' she says with feeling.

The community accept that the Bible was written with a variety of different interests, but nevertheless think that God's voice comes through. In a move that seems eminently sensible, they have rejected the Bible's sexism and homophobia in favour of deeper values of justice and peace. 'Not to take a fundamentalist view of the Bible doesn't mean having a lukewarm faith. We take faith very seriously, not as a set of prepositions, but as a way of life,' Kathy explains. These values must always lead to action as well as belief. 'In Glasgow we have started urban regeneration schemes, co-ops, and we do a lot of youth work. The work in community centres or hospices is just as valuable as the more radical nonviolent resistance, it's just a different calling,' she says.

Kathy was 'born into' the community, but realized that she wanted to stay involved in her teens. 'It represented values and vision that I found acceptable, credible and authentic,' she says. But is God more than our positive aspirations? 'I believe that God is transcendent and immanent, out there and in us, but God is active in human history first of all through Jesus Christ and in us as human beings. We are his hands on earth.'

Kathy tells me about a tradition of radical Christianity that is worth exploring. 'They don't get the headlines, they get on with quietly campaigning for debt relief, helping asylum seekers or the unemployed in a way which is rooted in prayer and worship,' she says. She points out that the Jubilee 2000 campaign to free the world's poorest from debt was started by Christians inspired by passages in Leviticus, an obscure Old Testament book. I feel ashamed of having ignored these groups earlier. She recommends the Quakers as a good place to start.

On my way back from Scotland, I come off the motorway soon after crossing the border into England. I am heading for the birthplace of Quakerism, at the foot of the Yorkshire Dales near the small town of Sedbergh. It was in this area that, in 1652, George Fox came across a group of people called the Seekers. He had been 'moved by God' on Pendle Hill and directed to the Seekers in the Dales. They were disillusioned Nonconformists who felt unable to belong to the Anglican, Catholic or Puritan Churches in time of civil war and religious conflict. Fox was a shoemaker who left his Leicestershire home on a religious quest when he was 19. He felt that God had told him to go to the Dales and he stayed with a farmer who was a Seeker. Together they climbed Firbank Fell where there was a small Seeker chapel, and after the service Fox preached to about 1,000 people. From this outdoor meeting, Fox's message spread throughout the country. The new group called themselves Friends.

One thing that perplexes me as I approach Brigflatts Meeting House, one of the first to be built, is this: What was so original about George Fox's message? Was he not just another dogma-peddling hothead in the mould of St Paul, Cromwell and countless others? What was it that enabled Quakerism to metamorphose into a movement that became synonymous with pacifism? Inside the whitewashed stone meeting house are simple oak benches, a wooden balcony with more benches and a small library leading off it. The walls are white and it reminds me of the simplicity of the Free Church of Scotland on Berneray. It is austere, or simple and natural, depending on one's view.

In the tiny wood-panelled library, I find out that George Fox was in fact a bit of a hothead, but he was an egalitarian firebrand rather than a fundamentalist one. From the beginning he told people that authority came from the 'inner light', then the Meeting House, and lastly the Bible. It was probably this democratic approach that was so attractive to the Seekers, fed up with dogma and the judgemental Church authorities. This approach led to women having the same right to speak in meetings as men. The meetings had no leaders and were silent until someone felt moved to speak. Fox resisted the pressure to write a creed or set of rules. He was not interested in sin: he was interested in finding a divine spark of goodness in those he met. He accepted the existence of evil, but said that, if we kept the light in view, we would win through. The political outworking of the Friends' movement started early in their history. Fox set the precedent of pacifism by turning down the offer of a captaincy in Cromwell's army, and Friends were frequently put in prison for refusing to pay taxes to Church authorities and the military. In 1661 the Quakers declared to King Charles II their opposition to all war.

As I leave Brigflatts library for the blazing July sunshine and wander off along a narrow lane, I feel that I am beginning to see what it was that made Fox different. For an uneducated shoemaker to have such views 350 years ago seems quite remarkable. I head for Firbank Fell, where Fox addressed the Seekers in what is thought of as the Friends' first meeting. All that is left of the Seekers' chapel on the fell is a walled enclosure with a couple of windblown larch trees and a few gravestones that are probably more recent. It is a strangely desolate and high setting for a chapel. Beyond it, on a rocky ledge, a plaque marks the place where Fox said his piece. I walk around it to the top of Firbank Fell, where I sit and take in the view.

Behind are the steep scree slopes of the fells above Sedbergh. The bright sky seems vast and empty, except for the odd hooded crow drifting on the breeze. Black-faced sheep are baaing their plaintive whinges across the valley in front of me. Uneven dry-stone walls divide the khaki and green fellside that would normally reflect a bleak, moody beauty but today seems exhilarating and gentle. What is it about mountain tops? Moses, Jesus, George King, Rael, King Arthur Pendragon and George Fox all claim to have had mystical experiences on mountains (or Tors). Nature certainly seems to rock us in such places. I can just hear the distant M6 beyond the rocky outcrops and grassy hummocks of the fell opposite, and I have a sense of people rushing past the ordinary, the unsensational, and missing out on quiet faith with integrity. I nod off among the thin, swaying grass stems, heavy with seed.

A few days later, on a bright Sunday morning, I visit Jordans Meeting House in Buckinghamshire, hoping to meet some Friends. It is set in the meandering lanes and thick beech woods of the Chilterns and, like Brigflatts, it is easy to drive past. William Penn, the founder of Pennsylvania, worshipped here after he joined the Friends. He was famous for being one of the only early settlers to treat the Native Americans as equals and to pay them what was considered a fair price for tracts of their land. He welcomed those of all religions to his state.

Walking from the car park down through an orchard, I half expect the meeting to be filled with a handful of octogenarians. There is nothing wrong with that in itself, but, perhaps because the Friends are rooted in the seventeenth century, it is hard to imagine them as relevant to modern times. And how will I manage an hour's silence? I pass a few small gravestones and arrive, a few minutes late, at the elegant, 300-year-old red-brick building. I creep through an ancient-beamed vestibule and into the large, white and wood-panelled meeting room.

Inside, on plain wooden benches, are about 60 people sitting in rows around a table with some flowers on it. Most have their eyes closed, others stare up and out of the high latticed windows or at the white walls. It is not an oppressive or self-conscious silence. Benches creak, distant birdsong drifts in, people occasionally clear their throats or shuffle. I even hear a sweet being unwrapped. Some people are dressed casually; others are wearing blazers or tweed jackets. There are slightly more women than men and, it has to be said, most (but not all) must be teetering on the edge of retirement. Although it is a full meeting, I cannot imagine that it will be the same in 20 years' time. I settle down for some quiet.

The interesting thing about sitting in silence with others is that it forces you into a reflective mood. There is something peaceful about this communion of people gathered for a single purpose. Sitting in silence by myself, I would be too easily distracted. Here thoughts flow in and out of my mind (as they do when I am jogging) and I begin to realize that silence need not be boring. It could be a way into the stillness that Simon Cohen found in transcendental meditation and Deniece and Song found through Master Li's falun gong movements. There is one difference that matters for me, however: this Quaker version of stillness encompasses the intellect. The others are a means to bypass it. This stillness has a moral or ethical dimension. It does not see good and bad as equal and in equilibrium; rather, it seeks goodness, peace and fairness in a tolerant way. It strikes me that this silence draws people towards what Fox called the 'light within', or the 'inner light', and that is why Quakers call this worship. It makes me reflect on my own intolerance. I do not feel condemned by this confrontation with my shortcomings, just reminded that it is something on which I should work.

After about 15 minutes, an elderly lady stands to speak. She expresses concern over a child in the news who has left his family to join a Christian sect. Then she sits down. Ten minutes later, a lady in a wheelchair says, 'Spirit of Christ which we hope is in us, breathe it out in our living.' Someone reads a verse from the New Testament, adding, 'Not to be taken literally.' In terms of content, that is it. The silence continues until the hour's worship is over, when a couple on the benches by the table turn towards each other and shake hands. Everyone else follows suit and people start to chat. The Clerk of the Meeting invites visitors to introduce themselves, before people go into the kitchen for coffee. The offering is to be donated to Alternatives to Violence, a Quaker mediation and reconciliation project in Northern Ireland.

Afterwards I talk to Steve, the warden, and his wife Mary, a teacher. They were drawn towards Quakerism, they tell me, because of its liberal but ethical attitudes. 'I like it because it is so creative and open. The boundaries are all self-imposed; it is something about the silent meeting that people respect.' Do some people not hold forth each week? I ask. 'Not really. Some people I find less helpful than others, but we're all different,' Steve says. Mary stresses that it is everybody's responsibility to make the meeting work. Steve likes the fact that there is no leadership structure and their way of arriving at decisions is very democratic. 'If we have a decision to make,' he says, 'we have silent worship between each speaker and then at the end the Clerk records what he feels the consensus is. He consults us before it's passed. Basically it refuses to take people's power away.'

Steve tells me of an example of this mutual respect and principled tolerance which is said to have occurred with Fox and Penn in the early days of the movement. William Penn, a wealthy gentleman convert, asked Fox whether he should stop wearing his sword when he was with pacifist Friends. Fox's reply was, 'I advise thee to wear thy sword as long as thou canst.' At a subsequent meeting, Fox noted that Penn was not wearing his sword and asked where it was. Penn replied, 'I took thy advice. I wore it just as long as I could.'

Despite their pacifist credentials, it is an ongoing area of debate within the Friends movement. 'It was interesting during NATO's attacks on Yugoslavia – it was barely mentioned in meetings because people didn't know what they felt about it,' Mary says.

On my way up through the orchard and back to my car, I notice William Penn's grave. The tradition of religious tolerance that he exported to the United States seems like an antidote to the poisonous stream spawned by the British Israelites. Strangely, perhaps, the benign stream was rooted in an earthy radicalism, while the malign stream grew out of a respectable, 'polite' sense of Britain's superiority.

I follow the benign stream as far as Harvey Gillman, the Society of Friends' Outreach Secretary at Friends House opposite Euston Station in London. A small man in his late forties, wearing cords, a white cotton shirt and a tiny earring, Harvey radiates friendliness. He comes from an academic background and a Jewish family, and I wonder what brought him to

Quakerism. 'I had been an atheist and also extremely interested in Buddhism,' he tells me, 'but I gradually I yielded to the sense that there was something greater than me that was within me. Walking in the Lake District one day, I had a real revelation of God in everything around me – the cosmic glue, holding all things together.' The radically egalitarian values also appealed to him. 'There weren't many religious organizations that treated all as equal and looked for the light within each person. As a gay man, that meant a lot to me,' Harvey says.

To me, the movement's pacifism seems like a stumbling block. I would only reluctantly be willing to fight, but my father risked his life by joining the Dutch Resistance in opposition to Hitler and I like to think that I would do the same. The only justification for violence that I can think of is a pretty good one: to alleviate suffering and/or save others. I accept that pacifism is not the easiest thing to stand up and fight for, of course. Harvey tells me that Quakers do not have a rule on violence, but tend towards peace-making, mediation and addressing the causes of violence. Some Quakers fought in the American Civil War to bring about the emancipation of black slaves; some fought Hitler, while others worked in the Quaker Ambulance Service. The Society of Friends has a long record of opposing nuclear weapons, working with asylum seekers and mediating in conflicts.

Harvey explains that, although Quakerism is within the Christian tradition, there are Quakers of other faiths or no faith. 'It is universalist in spirit. Most Friends think that Jesus is the Son of God; others think that he was a great teacher,' he says. The Bible has a special place in Quakerism, but they treat it critically, with an awareness of the context in which it was written. He insists that Quakerism is not humanism, because the thrust of the movement is to do with seeing the divine within. 'We're not human beings having a spiritual time: we're spiritual beings having a human time,' he says with a twinkle in his eye.

So, do they believe in a miracle-working God? 'As a movement we don't. I like to think of prayer as getting in touch with that which *is* rather than trying to persuade God to do what we want.' That is why, Harvey explains, they use the word 'convinced' rather than 'converted'. 'People are convinced from within. Conversion suggests something outside taking you over,' he says. I have to admit, it sounds pretty convincing.

Later that afternoon, I head up the road to a shambling Victorian vicarage in Holloway. The prospect of visiting a vicar is not quite as scary as it sounds. I have known this one for years and he does not appear to have taken the obligatory Bible College courses in Social Ineptitude and Pastoral Blind Spots. Reverend Dave Tomlinson was, in a previous incarnation, a charismatic miracle-merchant who gradually realized that it was all just wishful thinking. He was also deeply unhappy about the narrowness and judgementalism of evangelical and charismatic Christianity, but felt that he had experienced something in the faith that had integrity and depth.

He gave up leading a network of churches and started meeting like-minded people in a pub in Brixton. The meeting was called 'Holy Joes' and it addressed the needs of people who felt that they had a faith but could not relate to church, church attitudes or church authority. I went to a meeting several years ago and was impressed by the variety of members and the honesty of their quest. Dave was more a facilitator than a leader and there was a real sense of everybody having an equal right to contribute. It was also clear that, although the membership was fluid, people supported each other. Language was colourful and debate was combative: a sort of Christian anarchy with belly laughs.

Well, five years on, this pastor-made-good has reverted to type and become a vicar. Seeing him with his leather jacket, short-cropped hair, pugnacious face and dog collar is a shock. If Alexei Sayle were to come back as a vicar, he would be Dave Tomlinson. Knowing that he is big enough and ugly enough to take it, I have decided to save up all my theological objections to the Christian tradition for him.

I get down to business straight away. Is a God who intervenes not a bit sick in the head? What about all those he ignores? 'I believe in an immanent God, that is, a God who is present in the human struggle,' Dave says in his thick Scouse accent. He believes that is what the cross was about. So it was not about the rather dubious concept of God sacrificing his son so that we could be sinless? 'The idea of atonement through blood sacrifices is one rooted in the mindset of the ancients,' Dave replies. 'But other models of interpretation can be applied to the death of Christ. For me, it is showing God revealed in weakness and vulnerability, it is a way of showing us that God can't go any further in demonstrating his acceptance of us.' He believes that God forgives us regardless of the cross, but that it both demonstrates and mediates God's love and forgiveness. Is this not just an example of the Church using shame to get us in line? 'Human nature is, in my view, ambivalent and being offered forgiveness in a deliberate act is, for many of us, profoundly liberating,' he says.

Is the Bible God's word? 'If you mean, is it without error, then no, it's not. It was written within a certain worldview. We need to approach it critically, but try to see the big story which is about the dignity of humankind and God's selfless and just nature,' he says. Dave believes in the virgin birth and the resurrection, but does not see any evidence of supernatural miracles in modern times.

I ask him to sell Christianity to me, and this is what he says: 'What I like about Christianity is its balance; the way that Christians are free to use their rationality without going to the extremes of some mechanistic scientific thinkers; the way that it points strongly towards social justice in the here and now, whilst accepting a spiritual dimension; the way that it stresses endeavour without avoiding social responsibility; the balance between using and protecting nature. It speaks of a creative and compassionate God who is reflected in our human nature.'

In the evening I head further east, towards the Clapton neighbourhood in Hackney. I arrive at the Round Chapel, an

enormous United Reformed Church built in 1871 as a presti-
gious monument to the Nonconformist tradition. 'It's the
opposite of what radical Christianity should be about. It holds
1,000 people, but it lost members every year since its opening
until it dwindled to 16,' says community worker Chris
Lawrence. It is a sort of symbol of the death of conventional
Christianity: a misplaced sense of its own importance, and
a beautiful exterior which opens to reveal emptiness and
irrelevance.

Chris, a 35-year-old theology graduate in jeans and T-shirt,
takes me inside the Clapton Park United Reformed Church,
an annexe of the Round Chapel, which is itself bigger than
most churches. Inside, in the early evening light of the airy
hall, about 100 people appear to be having what can best
be described as an indoor street party. It is extraordinary and
deeply ordinary at the same time. Children are tearing
around, a bewildering array of adults sit at tables, eating and
chatting. There are professionals, single mums, unemployed,
black people and white people, a lesbian couple, and some
families. Pop music is playing from a ghettoblaster. What
brings such a disparate bunch out on a Thursday night?

I queue for vegetarian pasta, sauce and salad, then sit down
beside Chris. So, what is it all in aid of? 'It's a community
meal for the neighbourhood of Clapton. We've been doing
them for a couple of years,' he says. Why? 'We want people to
rediscover what it means to be neighbours; there's so much in
the consumerism and busyness of modern life that alienates
people from their neighbours, and we want to resist that and
say that people are the most important thing, and community
matters,' he explains. Most have nothing to do with the
church. A business consultant beams across the plastic table-
top. 'It's good to feel a part of a place and to meet new people,' he says, almost apologetically. A tin is sent down the
table and we all put a pound in it before passing it along.

I wander over to a couple with a child. Merle, a teacher, has
been coming for about a year. 'It's really easy-going, there's no
agenda, we get together because we enjoy it,' she says. But

what is it that pulls them away from the television on a Thursday evening? 'It's nice to get out and meet people,' her partner chips in, opening a can of lager. It is that simple and that profound. Jon, a gay man, says it is one of the few churches in which he feels relaxed. Victoria, an 80-year-old Jamaican mother of 10, says, 'It's good to bring new people together, you get to know different people.' She is also a member of the church. 'It has all happened since Chris and Doug, the minister, arrived. They think the neighbourhood matters. They're putting some heart into this place,' she adds.

On a table to one side is a woman running a credit union that the church helped to start. People bring pay-slips and money, which is placed in a cash box. 'It's a way of helping people who couldn't normally get credit to have access to it,' Chris says. Six hundred people pay into it and borrow, once repayments have been arranged. 'In this sort of area, some families can be put under immense pressure by loan sharks or unsympathetic banks. We wanted to use local money to work to help local people,' he says. The union, which has been going for two years now, has well over £150,000 in funds, of which £90,000 is out on loan.

Until the 1940s, there was a mutual insurance society which helped the poor to have access to capital. 'I don't want to idealize life in Clapton 60 years ago,' says Chris, 'but there were extended families living in the neighbourhood offering support and friendship, shops were locally owned and were meeting points for people, the neighbourhood went off to the beach together in a charabanc.' Then, he says, people's access to cars, televisions and technology led to the neighbourhood breaking up. 'People didn't need each other and our creature comforts and gizmos separated us from each other.' The whole culture moved away from relationships and interdependence to isolation. 'Most people in London don't seem to know who their neighbours are; we're trying to rediscover what it means to live together,' he adds.

I am reminded of the sense of community in the Outer Hebrides. 'Aren't you, um, pissing in the wind?' I ask.

'No, we're sailing across the wind, we're making a compromise with consumerism which allows community.'

The church has organized three coaches for a trip to Margate and other activities for the summer holidays. They also run a crèche and nursery for local mums. Chris takes me to see E-Five, a small co-op selling wholefoods and fairly traded household products ('fairly traded' means producers in developing countries are paid a fair price for the goods), as well as offering customers cheap internet access. 'We started this because we wanted to encourage people to keep money in the local area. Normally businesses come in and they don't give anything back to the community; we want this shop to serve the community; it's the community's shop,' he says. For a £15 membership fee, customers get a 20 per cent discount. It has 30 co-ordinators and 230 members who do a shift per month. Bula Anderson, the shop's Rastafarian manager, says, 'What I really like about the shop is that it's our shop. We decide what to sell, we run it. The bloke running the till one day is the customer the next.' Sam, a single mum who is new to Clapton, works as a co-ordinator because it allows her to meet people. 'It gives me some time when I can talk with adults, which is good when you've got a young child,' she says.

Later, over a beer, I ask Chris where spirituality fits into all of this. 'My faith is holistic – you can't separate it from other aspects of life,' he tells me. 'Christianity has a bias towards empowering the powerless and supporting the poor. I believe in an inclusive God.' Relationships and working for justice are at the heart of Christianity, he says. So is Chris doing it because God tells him to? 'When we pray, we tune in to God. I'm not doing it out of guilt, but I do gain inspiration in worship.' The church has two services on a Sunday, a conventional one in the morning and a more creative and contemplative one in the evening.

Chris was converted to Christianity as a teenager, but found himself unhappy with the personal piety of the evangelical tradition, and with the pointless theological debates which he experienced as a Cambridge undergraduate. 'For me, a turning point came whilst working for a group of churches about 10 years ago,' he says. 'Nearly 4,000 Kurdish asylum seekers arrived over a six-week period. The Home Office sent them to a tiny Kurdish centre and I got involved trying to find them accommodation. I realized how irrelevant my faith was and decided it had to change.' Chris has also been inspired by liberation theology and its bottom-up perspective. 'Seeing things from the perspective of homeless, frightened asylum seekers forced me to change,' he adds.

As I drive home, it seems appropriate to me that a spiritual movement is offering resistance to the pressures of capital in Clapton. Global capitalism might have conquered most aspects of modern life (and, indeed, spirituality), but it is heartening to see the 'soul' fighting back. I am sure that the Round Chapel would make someone a very nice carpet warehouse, but the people of Clapton would be the losers.

I am impressed with this radical faith but I struggle with the virgin birth, walking on water and other miracles, and the resurrection. If that happened then, why not now? If, as I concluded after visiting the Jesus Army, such exhibitions of power are unethical and distasteful now, would they have been any more acceptable in ancient Palestine?

Yet I am clear that the faith of Dave Tomlinson, Kathy Galloway and Chris Lawrence adds something unique to their work. They have a commitment to social justice, but they have an equal commitment to self-sacrifice and to refusing to exert power over others. This really is not the way of the world; it is irrational but inspiring.

I think about Chris. He is earnest, but not naive. He is not in any way showy, pushy or proud. He is ordinary, except for his extraordinary commitment and integrity. As Kathy Galloway suggested, the radical Christian tradition is obscured by quiet diligence. This is humbling. I think of one of Jesus' parables that Chris mentioned in relation to the church's work in Clapton: 'The kingdom of heaven is like a mustard seed, which a man took and planted in his field. Though it is the smallest of all your seeds, yet when it grows, it is the largest of garden plants and becomes a tree, so that the birds of the air come and perch in its branches' (Matthew 13:31–2).

18

🛒

Spirituality for Cynics?

So, the next time I go for a jog, I am wearing sandals and the fields are full of wheat ripe for harvesting, right? Well, yes, kind of. My trainers are worn out, it is early August, and the crops are hanging heavy, waiting for the sower to return with his combine harvester. I follow my special two-mile route and the symbolism builds up around me as I run. Purtle Springs has a trickle of water and the sun blazes down. Personally, however, I am not quite ready for harvesting.

I was impressed with Chris and his work in Clapton. It was the antithesis of the experience in Milton Keynes that set me off on my pilgrimage. Visiting Clapton was a completely unemotional experience for me, and yet, as I look back on it, it begins to affect me. The church's emphasis on the importance of relationships reminds me of thoughts that I had as a child. It is so obvious that relationships are really what matter, and yet we live our lives as if they are something that we can switch on and off or manipulate into certain 'windows' for our gratification. Are we not likely to be missing out? I am pretty sure that Chris's relationships are as varied and vibrant, as intrusive and rewarding, as possible. All I do is see a few good friends for drinks, give a bit to charity and pick up the odd hitch-hiker.

I have heard that Alcoholics Anonymous unearth similar truisms buried beneath layers of members' busy routines as part of the rehabilitation process. Things like the equality and value of all people and the importance of the integrity of the group. I have heard that hospices are places where, faced by the reality of dwindling days, people often work on a deeper, truer level. To try to visit such places as a spiritual tourist would be decadent, but Chris's church seems to be working on that sort of level as a matter of course. Although it is hard work, they enjoy it. It is the only way that they want to be.

I sit at the top of a distant field that I rarely reach on my normal runs, looking down on my usual route. I am not in search of a 'mountain-top experience', but I want to try to make sense of my travels over the last year. To start with examining the context of my quest will allow me to consider my position in it. Once I have some idea of the lie of the land, I will be able to trace the route that I have taken and establish where I have got to. In a sense, we all bring more than ourselves on pilgrimage: we also bring our reactions to the society around us.

My pilgrimage has certainly taught me that we design our divinity to match our values. Just as dogs resemble their owners, so we get the gods that we deserve. The conservative-minded Conservatives at Peniel Pentecostal Church revere an authoritarian, all-powerful, conservative God. Druidism and witchcraft tend to attract those who are reacting against the calibrated confines of modernity. Spiritualities involving science seem to attract men more than women. It strikes me as probably no accident that the pain-free, sometimes narcissistic New Age beliefs and practices are often Californian exports. Those who feel that white people are superior manage to create a God with a special place in his heart for whiteness. Of course, they would all say that they are simply responding to the way God, the Elohim, or Mother Earth actually is – but I just cannot see Matthew Browning, President of the British Israelites, dressing up in the green robes and medallions of the Aetherius Society. Neither do I see Chris Lawrence exchanging his undemonstrative jeans and T-shirt for a King Arthur suit and waving Excalibur around his head.

Our view of the soul (by which I mean those aspects of our personality that relate to the spiritual or ethical) also seems quite revealing. Transhumanists would call the soul chemical; some Christians seem to see it as an ethereal leash by which God can pull us up; some witches and some New Agers would see it as vital but morally inert energy. Other New Agers seem to see it as a commodity in need of embellishment. The devotees of Krishna see it as something to be painfully extinguished in universal bliss. Our souls and our gods seem to tell us more about us than about whatever or whoever is out there.

Is God, therefore, merely a great vending machine in the sky, responding to our culturally based aspirations? I am not sure, but I do know that the cultural backdrop is highly significant. For me, the sense of frustration and impotence I felt in Milton Keynes shopping centre was partly frustration with what I saw as empty materialistic consumerism. Even the physiological effects of jogging are not neutral: some would see jogging as part of a cultural fitness obsession, and without jogging I might never have gone on the road in search of spirituality. My choice of colourful, lively or extreme groups to visit also gives away a media-influenced desire for sensation.

The media as a meaning-making machine which idealizes wealth, romance, excitement and immediate gratification and which shows life as a series of intense experiences seems to be having an effect on virtually all forms of spirituality. These values could be said to have affected Reverend Moon's love affair with syrupy American family values just as much as sci-fi films appear to have affected UFO-based spiritualities. The druids' romantic view of a golden age is based in values and customs created in Hollywood. The British Israelites' sense of white people's superiority and black people's inability to lead is not hard to find in media representations. In the absence of spirituality, the media and its values can make a good substitute, and you do not have to be David Icke to work out that the media has a hidden agenda which skews things: the desire, above all else, to make money.

The media is just one aspect of global capitalism and the rise and rise of consumer culture. There are multitudinous aspects of this, but a rather large one is the effect of globalization on the planet, which some would compare to the effect of a plague of locusts. The reaction against science by some spiritual groups seems to me to be a consequence of this. Many people no longer trust modernity. The linear path that has brought us this far is seen as bulldozing its way through the environment, through romance and mystery. It is being replaced by unruly, wild, curvaceous tracks because people do not trust modernity's authority figures (be they institutions, politicians, scientists or priests). In search of 're-enchantment' and 'remythologizing', people 'discover' ancient labyrinths. The chaos magicians do this with added irony by admitting that they are making it up, but not caring.

Sociologist Grace Davie has noted that people still have belief, but no longer want to belong to institutions like churches. In my view, people have a real yearning to belong. The reason that they do not is that they do not trust authority and they will not generally accept a judgemental god. They are more wary and possibly wiser, but they do want community. The desire to believe is undiminished, but people want to believe less traditional things. Except in tiny enclaves whose beliefs are likely to become increasingly estranged and exotic, people will not accept a dogmatic god (or authority) who tells them that he knows what they need. It is interesting to note in this context that the number of alternative, New-Age-style healers is now greater than the number of doctors (though admittedly they will only work a fraction of the hours). Is this, I wonder, an example of people rejecting authority and scientific 'dogma' in favour of a more personalized, intuitive approach?

I jog downhill, enjoying the wind across my face, pleased with the terrains I have mapped in my mind, but aware that my quest is not over.

I return to Milton Keynes to buy some new trainers and to see if I can fathom the depths of my soul. I find some nice, sturdy trainers at a good price and with a near absence of hieroglyphs. Then I *just do it*.

Sitting with a black tea in a café in the plaza, the heart of the linear labyrinth, I start to consider what I liked and disliked from the various traditions I visited. I liked the pagans because of their desire to open their souls to nature. I am not sure I believe, as druids and witches seem to, that all of nature is 'spirit'. Are the burnished marble tiles in the plaza really buzzing with the energy of the universe? Do faeries really flit about the compost and bark that house the artificial palms in the walkways? I am happier with the idea of god or spirit speaking through creation. I felt nature tugging at me on the Hebridean shoreline, but could not actually believe that the sand and the seaweed were 'god'. Nevertheless, the honesty and goodness of the pagans was refreshing.

What I found so objectionable about the Christian tradition was its arrogance, judgementalism and use of shame. The legalistic use of sacrifice to balance our 'sins' and the belief in a capricious man in the sky whose whims it is not our business to question hardly warmed me to it. Its use of power over people was a sin. These difficulties, however, did not seem to apply to the Quakers, the Iona Community, Chris in Clapton and the radical Christian tradition. Their more measured faith was something I found both morally and intellectually coherent. They believe in working towards the kingdom of God in this life, they believe in protecting the weak, in sacrificing themselves in the fight for justice. This commitment is the stuff of the abolitionists and Martin Luther King: it is humbling. Such commitment could bring an end to Third World debt. I liked what I saw there, but the sad thing was that I saw it so little. Most Christians I observed seemed more concerned with building themselves mansions in heaven built of dogma and stony righteousness. Ultimately, these are mansions made of sand.

The Eastern paths seemed to address this judgementalism with the concept of 'karma'. What goes around comes around. We simply have to accept our situation and find peace in it. This is so unjudgemental, however, that they do not intervene to help improve *this* life. They chant, meditate or do cosmic exercises to improve themselves and transcend this reality. The best bit of my time with the Hare Krishna devotees was spent in the mobile curry kitchen, and yet they could only justify this intervention by telling themselves that it was spiritual food that they gave to the homeless, which would help their karma. And they thought the homeless were on the street because they deserved it, based on their past lives. Perhaps it is no surprise that Hinduism is the world's oldest religion: this sort of thinking is hardly going to bring about a revolution. There is much about inner peace and accepting what *is* (and much more, no doubt, to learn) that appeals to Westerners, but this fatalism is not the answer to my quest. Is pollution or famine really no more than bad karma?

The strength of the New Age tradition seemed to be the power it gives to individuals. People are their own priests, deciding what works (or does not work) for themselves. If it does not fit with their intuition, they reject it. They seem less open to abuse by dogma or dogmatic leaders than fundamentalist Christians are. Yet this individualistic approach seems to me to restrict the possibility of growth: I want to be open to the possibility of challenge from others and the possibility of community. Without this, my growth will be monochrome and quite possibly a little unreal. The New Agers did seem incredibly gullible, and I suspect some of the 'therapies' or practices I saw were cynically made up. Ultimately these beliefs seem narcissistic. The power they offer to people is too often the power of the consumer. It may be a reaction to a soulless society, but New Age spirituality seems the ultimate religion of privatized global capitalism.

Interestingly, I think to myself as I sip my tea, *the strengths of these different paths so often turn out to be their weaknesses too.* The balance that I seek, however, is not the morally inert yin and yang, spinning off into an undiscriminating infinity. In the end I decide to design my own god, to create a sort of psychological profile of whatever or whoever is responsible for putting me here. I scribble down a list of the sort of characteristics that I would hope to find at the heart of my spirituality.

This is it:

- I would want it to give power away and refuse to take it back.
- I would want it to marry the heart and the head.
- I would want it to be generally nonjudgemental and accepting of weakness.
- I would want relationships to be vital.
- I would want it to revere nature.
- I would want it to be creative and outward-looking.
- I would want it to fight for the equality of all people and to empower the powerless.
- I would want it to challenge me *and* to inspire me.

Then I write a list of things that I do not want:

- No dressing up in silly clothes.
- No prayer batteries or sacred mountains, please.
- No necessity to practise 1,000-mile stares in public.
- No pointless rules.
- No relentless diet of vegetarian curries.
- No five-hour sermons.
- No CDs of Tulka Buddha's excruciating invocations to angels.
- No miracles involving dead people.
- No reptiles beneath the skin.
- God must *not* have taken the three-day course at The Forum or been trained by Werner Erhard or associates.

So, is anyone there? Do the scales fall from my eyes in the plaza in Milton Keynes shopping centre? On the plus side in my reckoning is creation, which even Nick the Transhumanist admitted was 'fine-tuned'. The wonder of creation could have been hard-wired into our psyches during evolution, but it is a miracle that we are here at all (although, in an infinite universe, San Miguel bottles float around space and everything is probable). Yet, if a transcendent force created the planet, one has to wonder about the mental state of that transcendent force. Was it, in fact, such a good idea to start the ball rolling? It could be seen as an act of cruelty, or a cavalier cosmic gamble at the very least. Perhaps that is unfair, however: we are responsible for what we have done while we have been here. We cannot lumber the transcendent force with that problem. I suppose one has to hand it to the transcendent force: he/she/it is creative.

The transcendent force also has something else working in his/her/its favour. Once again it relates to Nick the Transhumanist. Not many of us believe that we live in an amoral universe. In such a place, the only thing left would be power. Talking to Nick, it struck me that what it means to be human needs basing in something *beyond* the human. If we are our only reference points, then we cannot argue with any sort of behaviour. Who says that might cannot be right? Why do we have questions or misgivings about uploading, cloning or completely reinventing human nature? Why is life, so to speak, sacred? Why, in fact, was Nick so helpful and friendly? He would say this was rational self-interest, but I think he would be being both ungenerous towards himself and a little disingenuous.

It all comes back, then, to George Fox's 'light within'. This is meant to be a reflection of the transcendent force. We have a conscience which can inspire and challenge us, and this seems to me rather helpful. Not only does it mean that, if I treat someone unfairly, then I know that I really ought to make things good, but it also stops me from disappearing down some ever-deepening hole of my own digging. Morality and ethics are not always seen as popular, but this may be in reaction to the rigidity of some of the Church's stupid, spirit-crushing rules.

Certainly, moral absolutes seem best tempered according to the situation. Generally they should come from within, then be tested by our friends. We can only ever have partial knowledge of good and evil, but few would see genocide, paedophilia, environmental destruction or greed as good. The light within as an echo of the transcendent force is, in my view, something we need. I *could* operate with this light without rooting it beyond human experience, but it does not seem quite honest to do so.

It seems suspiciously like a religionist's sleight of hand to reduce joy and sorrow, creativity and shame, friendship and sacrifice, to chemicals or a self-interested social construct. To my mind, the complex ethical landscapes that reverberate through our beings point beyond.

Equally, however, I know that I could not cope with the sort of cloying personal relationship with the transcendent force that characterizes the faith of some Christians. The sort of God that guides one into work every day, tells one which washing machine to buy, or offers an intimate directive on the 'rightness' or otherwise of pursuing a relationship, is always going to have us as prepubescent 'saints' unwilling or unable to grow up. I do not mind an omniscient God, but, if he/she/it is busily counting the hairs on my head, then he/she/it probably has obsessive compulsive disorder. Echoes of him/her/it in creation and obscure, tentative inklings in our hearts seem much healthier.

So, what do I have left to believe in? A few days before my trip to Milton Keynes, I told a friend how remarkable it was that George Fox was such an egalitarian 350 years ago. My friend is not religious, but his response made me think. 'Not quite as remarkable as Jesus 2,000 years ago,' he said. He was right, and George Fox would have agreed with him.

I am not sure if I can believe at this point. I find some of the stories hard to swallow. That is not the heart of it for me, though. To paraphrase George Fox, I am waiting to be convinced.

I put on my new running shoes, leave the shopping centre and head back home. They might be wondering where I've got to.